Learning OpenShift

Leverage the power of cloud computing using OpenShift Online to design, build, and deploy scalable applications

Grant Shipley

BIRMINGHAM - MUMBAI

Learning OpenShift

Copyright © 2014 Packt Publishing

All rights reserved. No part of this book may be reproduced, stored in a retrieval system, or transmitted in any form or by any means, without the prior written permission of the publisher, except in the case of brief quotations embedded in critical articles or reviews.

Every effort has been made in the preparation of this book to ensure the accuracy of the information presented. However, the information contained in this book is sold without warranty, either express or implied. Neither the author, nor Packt Publishing, and its dealers and distributors will be held liable for any damages caused or alleged to be caused directly or indirectly by this book.

Packt Publishing has endeavored to provide trademark information about all of the companies and products mentioned in this book by the appropriate use of capitals. However, Packt Publishing cannot guarantee the accuracy of this information.

First published: October 2014

Production reference: 1221014

Published by Packt Publishing Ltd.
Livery Place
35 Livery Street
Birmingham B3 2PB, UK.

ISBN 978-1-78398-096-3

www.packtpub.com

Credits

Author
Grant Shipley

Reviewers
Somsubhra Bairi
Isaac Christoffersen
Michal Fojtik
Ian Dexter D. Marquez

Acquisition Editor
Rebecca Youé

Content Development Editor
Susmita Sabat

Technical Editors
Anand Singh
Ankita Thakur

Copy Editors
Roshni Banerjee
Stuti Srivastava
Laxmi Subramanian

Project Coordinator
Kartik Vedam

Proofreaders
Simran Bhogal
Maria Gould
Ameesha Green
Paul Hindle

Indexers
Hemangini Bari
Monica Ajmera Mehta
Rekha Nair

Graphics
Disha Haria

Production Coordinator
Kyle Albuquerque

Cover Work
Kyle Albuquerque

About the Author

Grant Shipley is a senior manager at Red Hat who is focused on cloud technologies. Prior to this, Grant was a software development manager and was responsible for the `www.redhat.com` website and the supporting infrastructure. He has over 15 years of software development experience, focusing on Java and PHP. In his free time, he contributes to several open source projects as well as developing mobile applications. He has been using Linux on a daily basis since 1994 and is active in the FOSS community.

> First of all, I would like to thank my wonderful wife, Leah, who is the love of my life. She has continued to encourage me when I have felt like giving up and is the best mother and wife that a man could ask for. I would also like to thank our children, who have sacrificed time playing video games with me to ensure that I was able to complete this project on time. I also wish to thank my parents, William and Luster, who purchased a computer (TI-99/4A) for me when I was 8 years old, which sparked my interest in developing software. Lastly, I would like to thank the entire OpenShift team, including Ashesh Badani and Matt Hicks. Without their leadership and focus, this project would not be where it is today.

About the Reviewers

Somsubhra Bairi is a software/web developer, an active contributor for KDE (an open source software community), and is currently an undergraduate student at DA-IICT, India. He is an advocate of anything that is free and open source.

Somsubhra wrote his first program at the age of 15 in C. In his university, he learned C++ and started hacking on KDE software. He started full-stack web application development for various projects in his university and other developer challenges that he competed in. In his free time, he likes to tinker with software and new programming languages.

Isaac Christoffersen is a technology generalist, community steward, and open source advocate. He has more than 15 years of experience in IT and has a proven track record for delivering cloud-centric solutions for innovative, pragmatic technology. He has clients across a broad range of business domains, including retail, government, logistics, nonprofit, and finance.

Isaac is passionate about the acceleration of application delivery through disciplines such as DevOps, Agile engineering, and IT infrastructure automation. He currently works with clients to harness cloud services that roll out business applications to public, private, and hybrid PaaS and IaaS environments.

In addition to being a chief architect with Vizuri, Isaac has been actively involved with many professional organizations and technology-focused user groups including Open Source for America, the DC chapter of Association of Computing Machinery (DC ACM), and the DC JBoss Users Group.

Michal Fojtik is 27 years old and is working as a senior software engineer at Red Hat, located at Brno, Czech Republic. He has more than 8 years of experience with different cloud services, and he is an active contributor to projects such as OpenStack, Apache Deltacloud, and OpenShift. He also contributes to the Fedora Linux distribution and various other open source projects.

His native programming language is Ruby; however, he also performs programming in Go, JavaScript, Python, and many other programming languages. Recently, he has been involved in projects such as Docker or GearD. He is also a frequent speaker at local meetups and various conferences.

Ian Dexter D. Marquez is a Linux systems administrator at a large multinational financial institution in the Philippines. As a Red Hat certified engineer, he has more than 10 years of experience in managing Linux for financial services, information security, and government. In his spare time, he teaches himself programming and application deployment on PaaS platforms such as OpenShift.

www.PacktPub.com

Support files, eBooks, discount offers, and more

You might want to visit `www.PacktPub.com` for support files and downloads related to your book.

Did you know that Packt offers eBook versions of every book published, with PDF and ePub files available? You can upgrade to the eBook version at `www.PacktPub.com` and as a print book customer, you are entitled to a discount on the eBook copy. Get in touch with us at `service@packtpub.com` for more details.

At `www.PacktPub.com`, you can also read a collection of free technical articles, sign up for a range of free newsletters and receive exclusive discounts and offers on Packt books and eBooks.

`http://PacktLib.PacktPub.com`

Do you need instant solutions to your IT questions? PacktLib is Packt's online digital book library. Here, you can access, read and search across Packt's entire library of books.

Why subscribe?

- Fully searchable across every book published by Packt
- Copy and paste, print and bookmark content
- On demand and accessible via web browser

Free access for Packt account holders

If you have an account with Packt at `www.PacktPub.com`, you can use this to access PacktLib today and view nine entirely free books. Simply use your login credentials for immediate access.

Table of Contents

Preface 1
Chapter 1: Creating Your First OpenShift Application 7
  Creating your OpenShift Online account 7
  Installing and configuring the Red Hat Cloud command-line tools 9
    Installing the RHC command-line tools for Microsoft Windows 10
    Installing the RHC command-line tools for OS X 13
    Installing the RHC command-line tools for Linux 14
    Configuring the RHC command-line tools 15
  Creating your first OpenShift Online application 16
    What just happened? 19
      Placement of your gear 19
      Creating your application account 19
      Configuring your application 20
      Cloning the remote Git repository 20
    Adding the source code to your application 21
  Using the web console 23
  Summary 28
Chapter 2: Creating and Managing Applications 29
  Learning the essential RHC commands 29
    Displaying information about an application 30
    Deleting applications 32
  Understanding cartridges 33
    Web cartridges 33
    Add-on cartridges 34
  Using cartridges 35
    Adding cartridges 36
  Using databases with your application 38
    Adding the phpMyAdmin add-on cartridge 38

Developing the application	42
Understanding the code	44
The cron cartridge	**46**
Adding the cron cartridge	46
Adding a cron job	47
Summary	**48**

Chapter 3: Application Maintenance — 49

Stopping and starting applications	**49**
Viewing application logfiles	**50**
Creating your own logfiles	51
Viewing a single logfile	53
Backing up and restoring applications	**53**
Creating a snapshot	54
Restoring a snapshot	55
Secure shell and your application	**56**
Understanding and viewing the /etc/passwd file	58
Understanding and viewing cgroup information	59
Setting the timeout parameter and viewing logfiles	60
Understanding environment variables	**61**
Setting your own environment variables	64
Summary	**66**

Chapter 4: Using an Integrated Development Environment — 67

To use an IDE or not to use an IDE is the question	**67**
Installing and configuring Eclipse	**68**
Downloading and installing Eclipse	68
Downloading and installing the OpenShift plugin	72
Importing an existing OpenShift application	**74**
Creating and managing a new OpenShift application	**77**
Deploying changes	80
Viewing your application's logfiles	85
Embedding add-on cartridges	86
Viewing your application's environment variables	88
Viewing the details of an application	89
Deleting an application	**90**
Integrating OpenShift with other IDEs	**91**
Summary	**91**

Chapter 5: Creating and Deploying Java EE Applications — 93

The evolution of Java EE	**93**
Introducing the sample application	**95**

Creating a JBoss EAP application	**96**
Adding database support to the application	98
Importing the MLB stadiums into the database	99
Adding database support to our Java application	102
Creating the database access class	**103**
Creating the beans.xml file	104
Creating the domain model	**105**
Creating the REST services	**106**
Verifying the REST web services	110
Creating the user interface	**111**
Creating the map using Leaflet and OpenStreetMap	112
Verifying that the map was deployed and is responsive	117
Getting the stadiums from our REST services	119
Adding the stadiums to the map	119
Automatically updating the map	120
Testing the application	120
Taking the easy way out	**121**
Summary	**121**
Chapter 6: Creating and Deploying Spring Framework Java Applications	**123**
An overview of the Spring Framework	**123**
Creating a Spring application	**125**
Taking the easy way out	126
Creating a Tomcat gear on OpenShift	127
Adding the MongoDB NoSQL database to our application	128
Adding Spring support to the application	130
Adding a configuration to the application	131
Adding the domain model to the application	134
Adding the REST endpoint to the application	136
Deploying the application	**137**
Adding the web frontend	**138**
Having fun with the web UI	143
Summary	**145**
Chapter 7: Adding a Continuous Integration Environment to Applications	**147**
What is continuous integration?	**147**
Adding support for a Jenkins server	**149**
Verifying that the Jenkins server is up and running	151
Embedding Jenkins into an existing application	**152**
Using the Jenkins web console	**154**

Building code with Jenkins	**158**
Troubleshooting the build	160
Manually triggering a build	**161**
Summary	**163**
Chapter 8: Using OpenShift for Team Development	**165**
Setting up multiple domains	**166**
Adding a new domain with the command line	166
Adding a new domain with the web console	167
Adding members to a domain	**169**
Managing members with the command line	170
Modifying a member's role in a domain	171
Deleting a member from a domain	172
Managing members with the web console	172
Modifying a member's role and deleting a member	176
Promoting code between environments	**176**
Promoting the code	178
Adding access using SSH keys	**180**
Summary	**182**
Chapter 9: Using the OpenShift Web Console	**183**
Creating applications	**183**
Using instant applications	187
Modifying the source code	191
Managing applications	**193**
Adding cartridges	194
Restarting an application	196
Adding a custom domain name and SSL certificate	197
Creating a URL for application cloning	200
Deleting an application	201
Summary	**202**
Chapter 10: Debugging Applications	**203**
Using port forwarding	**203**
Connecting to MongoDB	205
Using Eclipse for Java debugging	**208**
Using IntelliJ for Java debugging	**214**
Using logfiles for debugging	**219**
Summary	**224**
Chapter 11: Using the Marker and Action Hook System	**225**
An overview of the marker system	**225**
The hot_deploy marker	225
JBoss-specific markers	226

Creating and using markers	**227**
Using the hot_deploy marker	228
Using the force_clean_build marker	229
An overview of the action hook system	**229**
Creating and using action hooks	**231**
Creating the deploy action hook	232
Testing the deploy action hook	236
Summary	**239**
Chapter 12: Scaling Applications	**241**
Why scaling matters	**241**
Vertical and horizontal scaling	**242**
Using automatic scaling	**243**
Creating a scaled application with the command line	244
Creating a scaled application with the web console	246
Using manual scaling	**249**
Setting scaling limits	**252**
Viewing the load-balancer information	**255**
Customizing the scaling algorithm	**256**
Summary	**258**
Chapter 13: Using the Do-It-Yourself Cartridge	**259**
Understanding the DIY cartridge	**259**
Creating an application with the DIY cartridge	**260**
Stopping the default web server	**263**
Creating a Tomcat 8 server	**265**
Summary	**270**
Appendix A: The RHC Command-line Reference	**271**
Top-level commands	**271**
Getting started	271
Working with applications	272
Management commands	273
Appendix B: Getting Involved with the Open Source Project	**275**
Contributing to the project	**276**
Index	**279**

Preface

Cloud computing and OpenShift particularly, is rapidly changing the way software engineers approach software development. OpenShift allows you to focus on what you love—writing software. This is accomplished by creating an environment where most of the system administration tasks are handled for you by the platform. This allows you to focus on your code instead of mundane tasks such as patching application servers with the latest security errata updates.

This might be your first exposure to OpenShift and Platform as a Service. To understand how OpenShift fits into the overall cloud computing landscape, it's important to understand the three most common types of cloud computing:

- Infrastructure as a Service (IaaS)
- Software as a Service (SaaS)
- Platform as a Service (PaaS)

IaaS provides IT organizations with the ability to quickly spin up machines in an on-demand fashion. This greatly increases the speed with which they are able to deliver servers to their customers. However, once the server has been created, they still need to perform all of the typical system administration tasks just as if the hardware were physical machines racked in their data center. This includes things such as installing the operating system, installing application servers and databases, performance tuning and monitoring of the services, and applying security errata. The dominant player in the IaaS market is Amazon and their EC2 offering.

With IaaS, the only thing provided is the hardware. You are typically responsible for bringing everything else that is required to deploy applications on the environment to the table.

Preface

At the complete other end of the spectrum is SaaS. In a SaaS environment, everything is provided for you, but you have little or no control over the software. A couple of common examples of SaaS type applications are Facebook or Salesforce.com for a companies' sales organization. Typically, in a SaaS model, the things you have to bring to the table are the users and their data.

OpenShift sits right in the middle of these two extremes. This type of environment is called a PaaS. With PaaS, everything is provided for you except the application code, the users, and their data.

In this book, we will learn how to the use the popular OpenShift Platform as a Service.

What this book covers

Chapter 1, *Creating Your First OpenShift Application*, explores how easy it is to get started with the OpenShift platform. We will create an OpenShift account, install the client tools, and then create and edit a PHP application.

Chapter 2, *Creating and Managing Applications*, introduces the basic techniques to manage applications that have been created in the OpenShift platform. You will learn the basics of cartridge management and use the mysql, cron, and metrics cartridges.

Chapter 3, *Application Maintenance*, covers administration tasks for your applications. You will learn how to stop and start applications, how to view logfiles, how to create custom logfiles, and how to SSH to the server your application is running on.

Chapter 4, *Using an Integrated Development Environment*, introduces the ability to use plugins provided for the Eclipse IDE to interact with the OpenShift platform.

Chapter 5, *Creating and Deploying Java EE Applications*, shows you how to develop and deploy Java EE-based applications to the OpenShift platform using the JBoss EAP application server. We will create a geospatial mapping application using LeafletJS and OpenStreetMap while also using MongoDB for our spatial queries.

Chapter 6, *Creating and Deploying Spring Framework Java Applications*, explores how to develop and deploy Spring-based applications using the Apache Tomcat servlet container. This chapter will focus on porting the Java EE code from the chapter to the Spring Framework, complete with MongoDB and REST services.

Chapter 7, *Adding a Continuous Integration Environment to Applications*, details how to use the Jenkins environment for applications deployed to the OpenShift platform.

Chapter 8, Using OpenShift for Team Development, introduces how to add and manage a team of developers who are all working on the same project that is deployed on OpenShift.

Chapter 9, Using the OpenShift Web Console, explores how to perform tasks, such as the application creation and deletion, using the web console. This chapter also explains how to use instant applications on the platform.

Chapter 10, Debugging Applications, shows you how to enable the remote debugging of Java applications as well as how to use port forwarding.

Chapter 11, Using the Marker and Action Hook System, explains how to plug in to the application deployment life cycle of applications. You will also learn how to enable things such as the hot deployment of applications and which version of the Java SDK to use.

Chapter 12, Scaling Applications, introduces the types of scaling that are available in the OpenShift platform and when it makes sense to use each one.

Chapter 13, Using the Do-It-Yourself Cartridge, explores how to extend the OpenShift environment to run binaries compatible with Red Hat Enterprise Linux in the platform. As an example, we cover how to install and run a newer version of the Tomcat servlet container than what is provided out of the box by the platform.

Appendix A, The RHC Command-line Reference, is a quick guide that shows you the available commands that we can use from the command line to interact with the OpenShift platform.

Appendix B, Getting Involved with the Open Source Project, explains the different ways in which we can get contribute to the upstream open source project that powers the OpenShift platform.

What you need for this book

In order to be successful with the examples in this book, some familiarity with software development is required. You will also need to run Linux, Microsoft Windows, or OS X and have the Ruby programming language installed.

Who this book is for

If you are a developer who wants to get up to speed with OpenShift, this book is ideal for you. A basic understand of how to use the command line is recommended in order to follow along the examples in the book.

Conventions

In this book, you will find a number of styles of text that distinguish between different kinds of information. Here are some examples of these styles and an explanation of their meaning.

Code words in text, database table names, folder names, filenames, file extensions, pathnames, dummy URLs, user input, and Twitter handles are shown as follows: "The app command will allow us to create and manage applications on the platform, while the cartridge command will allow us to add and manage embeddable cartridges."

A block of code is set as follows:

```
@Bean
public MappingJackson2JsonView jsonView() {
        MappingJackson2JsonView jsonView = new MappingJackson2JsonView();
        jsonView.setPrefixJson(true);
        return jsonView;
}
```

Any command-line input or output is written as follows:

```
$ rhc app create springmlb tomcat7
```

New terms and **important words** are shown in bold. Words that you see on the screen, in menus or dialog boxes for example, appear in the text like this: "At the top of the web page, you will see a **Download** button, which will allow you to download the installation program for the language."

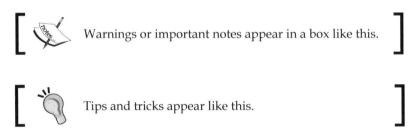

Warnings or important notes appear in a box like this.

Tips and tricks appear like this.

Reader feedback

Feedback from our readers is always welcome. Let us know what you think about this book—what you liked or may have disliked. Reader feedback is important for us to develop titles that you really get the most out of.

To send us general feedback, simply send an e-mail to feedback@packtpub.com, and mention the book title via the subject of your message.

If there is a topic that you have expertise in and you are interested in either writing or contributing to a book, see our author guide on www.packtpub.com/authors.

Customer support

Now that you are the proud owner of a Packt book, we have a number of things to help you to get the most from your purchase.

Downloading the example code

You can download the example code files for all Packt books you have purchased from your account at http://www.packtpub.com. If you purchased this book elsewhere, you can visit http://www.packtpub.com/support and register to have the files e-mailed directly to you.

Downloading the color images of this book

We also provide you a PDF file that has color images of the screenshots/diagrams used in this book. The color images will help you better understand the changes in the output. You can download this file from https://www.packtpub.com/sites/default/files/downloads/0963OS_ColoredImages.pdf.

Errata

Although we have taken every care to ensure the accuracy of our content, mistakes do happen. If you find a mistake in one of our books—maybe a mistake in the text or the code—we would be grateful if you would report this to us. By doing so, you can save other readers from frustration and help us improve subsequent versions of this book. If you find any errata, please report them by visiting `http://www.packtpub.com/submit-errata`, selecting your book, clicking on the **errata submission form** link, and entering the details of your errata. Once your errata are verified, your submission will be accepted and the errata will be uploaded on our website, or added to any list of existing errata, under the Errata section of that title. Any existing errata can be viewed by selecting your title from `http://www.packtpub.com/support`.

Piracy

Piracy of copyright material on the Internet is an ongoing problem across all media. At Packt, we take the protection of our copyright and licenses very seriously. If you come across any illegal copies of our works, in any form, on the Internet, please provide us with the location address or website name immediately so that we can pursue a remedy.

Please contact us at `copyright@packtpub.com` with a link to the suspected pirated material.

We appreciate your help in protecting our authors, and our ability to bring you valuable content.

Questions

You can contact us at `questions@packtpub.com` if you are having a problem with any aspect of the book, and we will do our best to address it.

1
Creating Your First OpenShift Application

OpenShift Online was released to the general public in June 2012, and has rapidly grown in popularity with developers because of the speed with which they can quickly spin up a new development stack and do what they love: develop software. In this chapter, we will learn how to sign up for the OpenShift Online service and then create our first application, which will be available on the public cloud. To become familiar with the platform, we will initially create a basic PHP application and then later create a WordPress-based blog that is deployed on the cloud. Don't worry if you are not a PHP developer as OpenShift supports other languages, such as Java, Python, Ruby, Perl, and Node.js. So sit back, grab your cup of coffee, and prepare to get your first application deployed to the cloud.

Creating your OpenShift Online account

To get started with using the OpenShift Online platform, the first thing a developer needs is an account that will provide access to create and deploy applications. Fortunately, the OpenShift Online service is free to use for both development and production applications. However, in order to create an account, you will need a few basic pieces of information that OpenShift Online requires in order to begin using the service:

- A valid e-mail address
- A password

Wait, what? You are probably asking yourself at this point whether these really are the only two pieces of information that the OpenShift Online service requires in order to create an account that will enable you to start deploying applications. The answer to this question is: yes. You will not be asked for your first name, last name, dog's name, or any other information about yourself or the types of applications that you want to deploy to the public cloud.

In order to begin the signup process, open up your favorite browser and type in the following URL:

```
http://www.openshift.com
```

Once the page has loaded, you will see a **SIGN UP** button in the top-right corner of the page. After clicking on this button, you will be presented with a web form to create your OpenShift Online account:

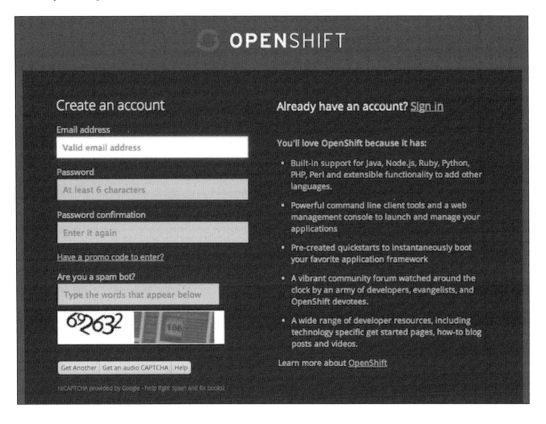

Enter in your e-mail address, select a password, provide the CAPTCHA answer, and then click on the **SIGN UP** button at the bottom of the screen.

When selecting a password, it is suggested that you choose to create one that is considered a strong password. Using strong passwords lowers the risk of your account getting compromised by a brute-force attack.

A Completely Automated Public Turing Test to tell Computers and Humans Apart (CAPTCHA) is a system that OpenShift Online uses to determine whether the entity that is signing up for an account is a physical human or a programmatic bot. The OpenShift Online implementation uses the popular reCAPTCHA system provided by Google and helps to digitize books, newspapers, and old-time radio shows.

After you have clicked on the **SIGN UP** button, the OpenShift Online platform will send a verification e-mail to the address that you provided. You cannot access the OpenShift Online system until you have verified your account by clicking on the link in the e-mail.

If you don't see the verification e-mail right away, check your Spam folders and/or filters. If you still don't find it, try searching your e-mail with the subject `Confirm your OpenShift account and get in the cloud now`.

Once you have clicked on the link provided in the verification e-mail, you will be redirected to a page that lists the legal terms associated with your account. If you agree to the legal terms, click on the **I Accept** button at the bottom of the screen.

Congratulations! You now have an OpenShift Online account with all the permissions required to create and deploy applications.

Installing and configuring the Red Hat Cloud command-line tools

In order to create, manage, and deploy applications from the command line, it is required that you install the Red Hat Cloud command-line tools and the Git revision control system. The RHC command-line tools are written in the popular programming language, Ruby. In this section, we will cover how to install the tools on the three most popular operating systems today: Windows, Mac OS X, and Linux. Once you have installed the command-line tools and Git for your operating system, you can skip to the next section in this chapter.

Installing the RHC command-line tools for Microsoft Windows

Unfortunately, Windows does not include the Ruby language runtime by default, so the first thing you need to do is install the latest version of the runtime.

For this book, I will be using version 1.9.3 of the Ruby language and version 8.1 of Microsoft Windows.

In order to install the Ruby language runtime on your operating system, open up your favorite browser and go to the following URL:

http://rubyinstaller.org

At the top of the web page, you will see a **Download** button, which will allow you to download the installation program for the language:

The next page will list the various versions of the programming language that you can install. Select to download the latest version of Ruby and save the installation program to your local computer.

After the installation program has downloaded, start the program by double-clicking on the executable in the folder where you saved the file. Once the installation program has started, accept the license agreement and click on the **Next** button.

During the installation, you can accept all of the defaults, but it is mandatory that you select the **Add Ruby executables to your PATH** checkbox in order to run Ruby from the command line.

The first screen of the installation wizard will allow you to specify the installation directory where you want the runtime installed. On this screen, it is critical that you select the checkbox to add the Ruby executable to your PATH variable, as shown in the following screenshot:

Adding an executable to your PATH variable will allow you to run the command while at a terminal prompt, regardless of the location of the executable or directory that you are currently in. You can think of adding this command as a global variable that is available anywhere on the filesystem.

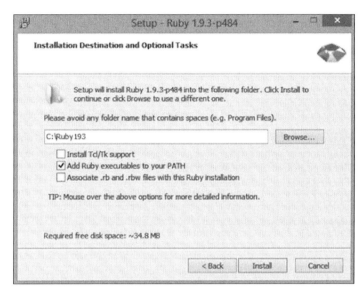

Ruby installation wizard

After the installation is complete, you can verify whether the installation was successful by opening a command prompt on your machine and typing the following command to display the version information:

`C:\> ruby -v`

Once you have executed the previous command, you will see the version number displayed as shown in the following example:

`ruby 1.9.3p484 (2013-11-22) [i386-mingw32]`

You may have a slightly different Ruby version than the one listed in the preceding example. This is fine as long as the version number is greater than 1.9.

Creating Your First OpenShift Application

The next step is to install the Git revision control system on your operating system to ensure that you are able to clone your application repository to your local machine. You can download the latest version of Git for Windows from `http://msysgit.github.io/`. Once you have entered the URL into your web browser, click on the **Download** link to list all of the versions available for your operating system. Click on the link for the latest version, and save the installation file on your computer.

Just as you did when installing Ruby, ensure that the Git executable is added to your `PATH` variable by selecting the **Run Git from the Windows Command Prompt** checkbox from the installation wizard:

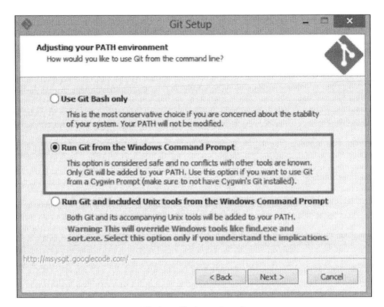

Git installation wizard

Now that you have both Ruby and Git installed, you can use the `ruby gem` command to install the RHC tools.

> Ruby gem is a package manager for the programming language, which allows users to easily install Ruby programs and libraries.

Open up a new command prompt and issue the following command to install the
Ruby gem that contains the RHC command-line tools:

`C:\> gem install rhc`

Depending on the speed of your Internet connection, the installation may take a
few minutes while it downloads and installs all of the dependencies for the tools.
During the installation process, you will see an update with the current progress
of the command.

Installing the RHC command-line tools for OS X

Modern versions of the OS X operating system include Ruby by default, so all you
need to install is the Git revision control system. You can install Git by either installing
the full Xcode Suite or using Git for the OS X installation program. For this book,
we will be using Git for the OS X installation program. Open up your web browser
and go to the following URL:

`https://code.google.com/p/git-osx-installer/`

Click on the **Download the installers here** link in order to view a list of all of the
available installation disk images for your operating system. Download and mount
the disk image, and follow the onscreen instructions to install the program.

> If you get an error message stating that the package can't be opened
> because it is from an unidentified developer, you will need to modify
> your security and privacy settings. To do this, open up system
> preferences, click on **Security and Privacy**, and under the **General**
> tab, select to allow the installation of apps that have been downloaded
> from anywhere. Remember to change this back after the installation
> is complete.

Now that you have both Ruby and Git installed, you can use the gem command
to download and install the RHC command-line tools. Open up a new terminal
window and type the following command:

`$ sudo gem install rhc`

Depending on the speed of your Internet connection, the installation may take a
few minutes while it downloads and installs all of the dependencies for the tools.
During the installation process, you will see an update with the current progress
of the command.

Installing the RHC command-line tools for Linux

There are many different distributions of the Linux operating system, and covering the installation procedure for each variant is beyond the scope of this book. Given that Ubuntu is considered to be one of the most popular desktop distributions available, we will be using version 13.10 of this distribution for the instructions in this section. If you are using Fedora or any other distribution, you will need to modify the commands as appropriate for your distribution.

The first thing you need to do is install the Ruby runtime, since Ubuntu 13.10 does not include this by default for a new installation of the operating system. In order to install Ruby, open up a terminal prompt and use the apt-get command by typing the following command:

```
$ sudo apt-get install ruby
```

> The **Advanced Packaging Tool** (**APT**) is the default package management tool for Debian-based Linux distributions. The apt command will resolve all dependencies and then perform the installation or removal of software packages on the operating system. If you are using an RPM-based distribution such as Fedora or Red Hat, the equivalent command is yum (Yellowdog Updater, Modified).

After the installation is complete, type ruby -v on the command line to verify that the installation was successful. If all went well, you should see the version number printed on your terminal screen.

Now that you have Ruby installed, you also need to install the Git revision control system. In order to install the Git package, use the apt-get command like you did to install Ruby:

```
$ sudo apt-get install git
```

Lastly, you can install the RHC command-line tools using the gem command that was installed as part of the Ruby package:

```
$ gem install rhc
```

Depending on the speed of your Internet connection, the installation may take a few minutes while it downloads and installs all of the dependencies for the tools. During the installation process, you will see an update with the current progress of the command.

Configuring the RHC command-line tools

If you have followed the information presented so far in this chapter, you should have an OpenShift Online account created as well as the RHC command-line tools installed on your operating system. We will now configure the RHC tools to communicate with the OpenShift Online platform. This setup procedure will allow us to create our OpenShift namespace domain as well as create and upload the necessary SSH keys to authenticate us to the service.

Open up a new terminal prompt and begin the setup procedure by typing the following command in the prompt:

```
$ rhc setup
```

Upon executing the preceding command, the first thing you will be asked for is the username that you created earlier in this chapter. Enter in the username and password that you used to authenticate the OpenShift Online platform and press the *Enter* key.

After you enter in your credentials to authenticate the service, the setup program will ask if you want to generate an authentication token. Generating a token will allow you to run RHC tools without having to authenticate with a password each time you issue a command. It is recommended that you generate a token to speed up the time it takes to perform management commands for your application. If you want to generate a token, type in `yes` and hit the *Enter* key.

The next step of the configuration process is to generate and upload an SSH key-pair for your account. The SSH key is used by the platform for authentication when cloning the source code repository for your applications that you create. The SSH key is also used if you want to secure shell into your remote application. In order to upload your SSH key, type in `yes` and press the *Enter* key.

> We will discuss SSH in more detail in *Chapter 3, Application Maintenance*, of this book.

Next, you will be prompted to create a namespace for your account on the OpenShift platform. A namespace is a unique identifier for your account, which will be used as the basis for all URLs for the applications that you create. Keep this in mind when selecting your namespace as it will be included in the URL for any application that you create on the platform.

> A common practice is to use your username as your namespace.

Once you create a namespace for your account, it means that the RHC command-line tools have been configured and you are now ready to begin creating applications.

 All of the information related to your OpenShift Online account is stored in a configuration file named `express.conf` located in the `.openshift` directory that resides within your user's home directory.

Creating your first OpenShift Online application

The time we have been waiting for is finally here! We get to create our first application that is deployed on the OpenShift Online cloud. I hope that when you see how simple and fast it is to create and deploy applications, you will be amazed at the possibilities this new technology (PaaS) can provide for your software projects. Let's dip our toes in the water by creating a simple PHP application and then modify the source code to practice the development workflow.

Let's start by creating a directory where we will organize all of our OpenShift projects. I prefer to use a directory named `code` that is located in my home directory, but feel free to use the standard directory convention that you have been using throughout your software development history. Create the `code` directory if you don't already have one, and change to that directory from your command prompt. For example, if you are using Linux or OS X, the command will be the following:

```
$ mkdir -p ~/code
$ cd ~/code
```

Once you are inside of the directory where you want to organize your source files, you can create a new OpenShift Online application by leveraging the RHC command-line tools that you installed previously in this chapter. The RHC command is actually an umbrella command that will allow you to perform many different operations on the OpenShift platform. To create an application, use the `app create` subcommand. The syntax to create a new application is as follows:

```
$ rhc app create application_name application_type
```

For instance, create a new PHP application and name it `myphpapp`, and specify that you want to use the PHP-5.4 language. In order to create this application, enter in the following command on your terminal, ensuring that you are in the directory where you want to organize your source files:

```
$ rhc app create myphpapp php-5.4
```

After you enter in the previous command, you will see the following output that indicates the progress of the application creation:

```
Application Options
-------------------
Domain:     packt
Cartridges: php-5.4
Gear Size:  default
Scaling:    no


Creating application 'myphpapp' ... done


Waiting for your DNS name to be available ... done

Cloning into 'myphpapp'...
The authenticity of host 'myphpapp-packt.rhcloud.com (184.73.118.31)' can't be established.
RSA key fingerprint is cf:ee:77:cb:0e:fc:02:d7:72:7e:ae:80:c0:90:88:a7.
Are you sure you want to continue connecting (yes/no)? yes
Warning: Permanently added 'myphpapp-packt.rhcloud.com,184.73.118.31' (RSA) to the list of known hosts.
Checking connectivity... done


Your application 'myphpapp' is now available.

   URL:        http://myphpapp-packt.rhcloud.com/
   SSH to:     52bf4758e0b8cd189d0000d9@myphpapp-packt.rhcloud.com
   Git remote: ssh://52bf4758e0b8cd189d0000d9@myphpapp-packt.rhcloud.com/~/git/myphpapp.git/
   Cloned to:  /home/gshipley/myphpapp

Run 'rhc show-app myphpapp' for more details about your app.
```

> Once you enter in the `rhc app create` command, you may be prompted to accept the authenticity of the application hosts. Type yes and hit the *Enter* key.

Congratulations! You have just created your first application that is running in the cloud. Don't believe me? Take a quick look at your application to verify that it was deployed correctly. Open up a web browser and enter in the URL for your application that was provided by the `rhc app create` command. The application URL always looks like `applicationName-namespace.rhcloud.com`

For example, I used the unique namespace of `packt` for my account, and I named my application `myphpapp`. Given these two bits of information, the URL for my application would be `http://myphpapp-packt.rhcloud.com`

If everything went smoothly, you should see the following screen in your web browser:

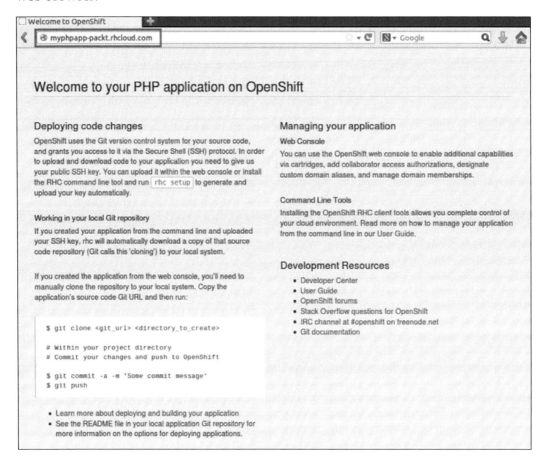

I know you are anxious to dig in and start modifying the source code, but stick with me just a little bit longer. To truly appreciate the benefits of using a PaaS, such as OpenShift Online, we need to understand all of the glue that just happened at the backend.

What just happened?

Once you understand what just happened behind the scenes, you might start to think of the `rhc app create` command as some type of magic. Let's take a closer look at everything that happened to enable your application.

Placement of your gear

When issuing the previous command, the first thing the OpenShift Online platform did, after authentication of course, is determine which server to place your application gear on. The algorithm used to determine the best location for your gear takes many factors into account, including (but not limited to) the current load on each server, the application runtime, and the amount of memory the application is configured to consume.

> OpenShift uses the term "gear" to define a set of resources allocated to provide your application with the environment that it needs to run effectively. A gear contains resources such as memory, CPU, and disk space. You can think of a gear as an application container on the operating system that segments your resources from other users on the system.

Creating your application account

After the platform has determined the optimal server for your gear to reside on, the system creates a Linux user ID for your account. This is an actual Linux user on the system that your gear will run under. Having this account created will allow you to SSH to the gear in a later chapter.

After the account is created, OpenShift then applies the **Security Enhanced Linux** (**SELinux**) contexts and **Control Groups** (**cgroups**) for your gear. In a nutshell, cgroups allows the kernel to allocate resources such as memory, CPU time, and network bandwidth to processes on the system. SELinux allows the system to set contexts to determine access control for files and processes. Both of these technologies are implemented by OpenShift Online to secure your application gear as well as provide multitenancy of the platform.

Creating Your First OpenShift Application

Don't worry if you don't understand these technologies in depth, as this is where one of the true benefits of deploying applications to OpenShift Online comes into play. You get all of the benefits of using these kernel features to provide a secure environment for your application without having to know the ins and outs of configuring and maintaining complex security policies.

Given that this is a book for using the OpenShift Online platform for development, we will end the discussion of these technologies here. However, if you have an interest in security and system administration, reading up on these two Linux technologies will prove to be a fun exercise. A great resource to learn more information about these technologies is Wikipedia. You can find in-depth information on SELinux and cgroups at the following URLs:

- `http://en.wikipedia.org/wiki/Selinux`
- `http://en.wikipedia.org/wiki/Cgroups`

Configuring your application

Once the gear has been placed on a server, and the access controls for your gear have been enabled, OpenShift Online then begins the process of configuring all of the necessary components to run your application code. In this example, we decided to create and deploy a PHP application, so OpenShift Online enabled the Apache and `mod_php` module for our gear.

After the web server process was configured, the platform then created a private Git repository for us on our application gear and added a PHP application template to the repository. The application source code was then deployed to the web server, and DNS for our application was propagated worldwide. This means our application will immediately be available on the public Internet once the `rhc app create` command is complete.

Cloning the remote Git repository

The last step of the application creation process is when the RHC command-line tool clones your Git repository from your OpenShift Online gear to your local machine. This part of the process will create a directory with the same name as your application in the filesystem location from which you issued the `rhc app create` command.

> A common error that users encounter when creating an application is the failure of the system to clone the Git repository. This normally means that your local machine could not authenticate to the OpenShift platform using the SSH key for your account. If you see this error message, ensure that you upload the generated SSH key while running the `rhc setup` command.

Adding the source code to your application

The application creation process created a new directory on your filesystem that is named after your application. This directory is created in the location that you issued the `rhc app create` command in. If you have followed the conventions laid out in this chapter, you should be able to change to your application directory with the following command:

```
$ cd ~/code/myphpapp
```

Once inside of the `myphpapp` directory, if you issue the `ls -al` command, you should see the following items:

```
gshipley@author-workstation ~/code/myphpapp $ ls -al
total 56
drwxr-xr-x   4 gshipley gshipley  4096 Jun 11 21:23 .
drwxr-xr-x  17 gshipley gshipley  4096 Jun 11 21:23 ..
drwxr-xr-x   8 gshipley gshipley  4096 Jun 11 21:23 .git
-rw-r--r--   1 gshipley gshipley 39627 Jun 11 21:23 index.php
drwxr-xr-x   5 gshipley gshipley  4096 Jun 11 21:23 .openshift
gshipley@author-workstation ~/code/myphpapp $
```

> The `ls` command is a command for the Linux and OS X operating systems that will display all of the files and directories at the current location. If you are using the Microsoft Windows operating system, the equivalent command is `dir`.

We will discuss all of these items in more detail in a later chapter, but for right now, the only directory you want to concentrate on is the `root` directory. This is the location where all of your source code files will need to be placed if you want them available to the web server.

After listing the files inside of the `root` directory, you will notice that only one entry exists:

- `index.php`

This is the main HTML page that you saw when you verified that your application was created and deployed correctly, earlier in this chapter. This file is standard HTML and provides instructions on how to get started with the OpenShift Online platform.

To understand the application deployment workflow, create a new PHP source file and name it `hello.php`. Open up your favorite text editor and add the following code to the `hello.php` file:

```
<?php

echo "Hello, Cloud!";
```

The next step after saving the new file is to add it to your Git repository on your local machine. Since you created a new source file that your revision control system doesn't know about, you need to first add the file:

```
$ git add hello.php
```

Once the file has been added, you need to commit the changes that you made and provide a comment message that describes the change:

```
$ git commit -am "Added hello.php"
1 file changed, 3 insertions(+)
 create mode 100644 php/hello.php
```

If you are not familiar with Git, you may have expected that once you have committed your source code change to your local repository that the OpenShift Online repository would have also been updated. It is important to understand that when you commit changes to your local Git repository, they have not been pushed to the remote repository that resides on your OpenShift Online gear. In order to take all of the changes that you committed to your local repository to your upstream OpenShift Online repository, you need to push these changes using the `git push` command:

```
$ git push
Counting objects: 6, done.
Compressing objects: 100% (3/3), done.
Writing objects: 100% (4/4), 401 bytes | 0 bytes/s, done.
Total 4 (delta 1), reused 0 (delta 0)
remote: Stopping PHP cartridge
remote: Waiting for stop to finish
remote: Building git ref 'master', commit 9dfe837
remote: Building PHP cartridge
remote: Preparing build for deployment
remote: Deployment id is 9fb0c7ee
remote: Activating deployment
remote: Starting PHP cartridge
```

```
remote: Result: success

remote: Activation status: success

remote: Deployment completed with status: success

To ssh://52bf4758e0b8cd189d0000d9@myphpapp-packt.rhcloud.com/~/git/
myphpapp.git/
   e368126..9dfe837  master -> master
```

Once you have pushed the changes to the remote repository, OpenShift Online will be notified about the new file(s) and will then redeploy your application. View your new source file by opening the page in a web browser at the following URL, ensuring that you use the correct namespace for your account:

`http://myphpapp-YourNamespace.rhcloud.com/hello.php`

>
> You may have noticed that OpenShift Online stops Apache during the deployment process. If you are familiar with PHP, you know that this step is not necessary. To ensure that your application does not experience downtime during a new deployment, learn how to take advantage of the hot deploy feature by referring to *Chapter 11, Using the Marker and Action Hook System*.

You now know the basic building blocks and workflow to create and deploy applications to OpenShift. You need to follow these basic steps:

1. Create an application using `rhc app create`.
2. Add new source files with `git add`.
3. Commit changes using `git commit`.
4. Push and deploy changes using `git push`.

>
> If you are not familiar with the Git revision control system, a good reference on the system is located at `http://gitref.org/index.html`.

Using the web console

Up to this point, we have focused exclusively on interacting with the OpenShift Online service purely from the command line. During this section, we are going to use the feature-rich web console that is provided for users to create and manage all applications from inside of their favorite web browser. We will now use the web console to deploy a WordPress application to the platform.

Creating Your First OpenShift Application

To get started, open up your web browser and go to `http://www.openshift.com`. Once the page is loaded, click on the **MY APPS** button at the top-right corner of the page and authenticate to the OpenShift Online platform using the username and password you created earlier in this chapter.

After you have authenticated, you will be placed on the application dashboard where you should see the `myphpapp` application that we created previously in this chapter. Click on the **Add Application...** button that is located under your application list.

On the next screen, look for the **Instant App** section and choose **WordPress 3.x**.

Chapter 1

After you select to create a WordPress instant application, you will be presented with a screen where you will need to specify the name of the application you are creating. For the name, enter in `myblog` and click on the **Create Application** button at the bottom of the screen.

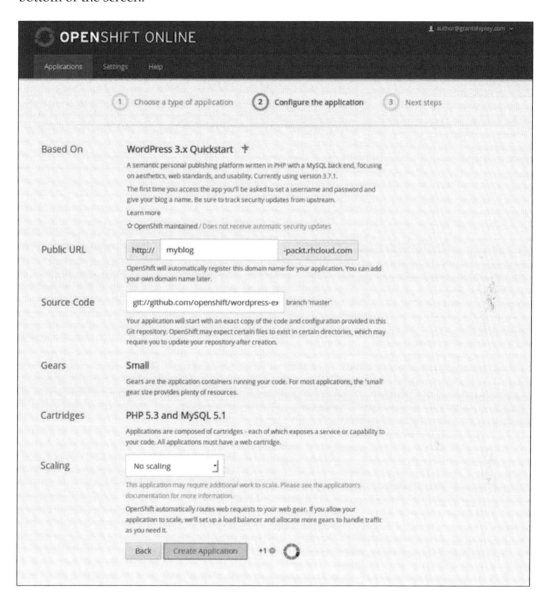

After the application creation process is complete, you will be presented with a confirmation page that includes important information about the WordPress deployment, which includes information on the database connection authentication.

You now have a fully functioning WordPress installation that you created in about two minutes. Don't believe me? Open up your web browser and enter in the URL for the application that you just created. Once you load the site for the first time, you will be prompted to enter some basic information about the blog site as well as to create the username and password that will be the administrator of the site. Pretty neat stuff!

 In *Chapter 9*, *Using the OpenShift Web Console*, we will learn how to create our own instant application, such as the one we just deployed, which will enable you to quickly spin up preconfigured applications in a matter of minutes.

The web console comes in handy when you want to create an application very quickly without having to use the command line. However, you will often find that once you create an application using the web console, you need to modify the source code of the application that you deployed. Let's go back to the command line to show you that we can clone the source code repository of the myblog application that we just created. Open up a new terminal window and change to your code directory that we created previously in this chapter:

```
$ cd ~/code
```

Once you are in this directory, we can use the rhc app show command to list the information about the WordPress deployment:

```
$ rhc app show myblog
myblog @ http://myblog-packt.rhcloud.com/ (uuid: 52bf71fc5973ca055f0003b7)
--------------------------------------------------------------------------
  Domain:          packt
  Created:         5:51 PM
  Gears:           1 (defaults to small)
  Git URL:         ssh://52bf71fc5973ca055f0003b7@myblog-packt.rhcloud.com/~/git/myblog.git/
  Initial Git URL: git://github.com/openshift/wordpress-example.git
  SSH:             52bf71fc5973ca055f0003b7@myblog-packt.rhcloud.com
  Deployment:      auto (on git push)

  php-5.3 (PHP 5.3)
```

```
------------------
  Gears: Located with mysql-5.1

mysql-5.1 (MySQL 5.1)
--------------------
  Gears:             Located with php-5.3
  Connection URL: mysql://$OPENSHIFT_MYSQL_DB_HOST:$OPENSHIFT_MYSQL_DB_
PORT/
  Database Name:     myblog
  Password:          mG3SasTv-mRL
  Username:          adminNyyHHvA
```

If you examine the output, you will notice that part of the information provided is the Git URL for your application. In the preceding example, the Git URL for the application is as follows:

`ssh://52bf71fc5973ca055f0003b7@myblog-packt.rhcloud.com/~/git/myblog.git/`

> You can use a combination of `rhc app show` and `grep` to list only the URL of your Git repository with the following command:
> `$ rhc app show myblog|grep 'Git URL:'`

Now that we know the URL of our remote Git repository, we can clone the repository by using the `git clone` command:

`$ git clone ssh://52bf71fc5973ca055f0003b7@myblog-packt.rhcloud.com/~/git/myblog.git/`

> The Git URL shown previously is an example that is based on the application that I created. The Git URL for your WordPress application will be different. Make sure that you use the correct URL when cloning the repository.

However, the suggested way to clone a Git repository from the OpenShift Online platform is to use the `rhc git-clone` command, as shown in the following command:

`$ rhc git-clone myblog`

This will create a directory under your `~/code` directory, named `myblog`. If you are curious, switch to that directory and take a look around the source code for your newly created blog.

The same application workflow that we learned about previously in this chapter holds true for applications that you create with the web console. For instance, if you wanted to manually install plugins and themes for your blog, you would deploy them using the following:

- Adding new templates or themes with `git add`
- Committing changes using `git commit`
- Pushing and deploying changes using `git push`

Summary

In this chapter, we built the foundation for interacting with OpenShift Online, and we will continue to expand on this throughout the remainder of this book. Laying this groundwork is essential to ensure that your local system is configured properly in order to communicate with the platform.

We created a user account, installed the client tools, and created two applications. We also learned the basic application creation and deployment workflow that will be the cornerstone for every application that we create in the future.

In the next chapter, we will learn about the essential commands for the RHC client tools. We will also explore the embedded cartridge system that will enable us to add additional functionalities to our applications, such as databases, metrics, and task scheduling.

2
Creating and Managing Applications

We got our feet wet in *Chapter 1*, *Creating Your First OpenShift Application*, by creating and deploying a simple sample application to the OpenShift Online platform. In this chapter, we are going to dive all the way in and learn the essential commands for the RHC client tools that will allow us to effectively create and manage applications. We will also explore the embedded cartridge system that will enable us to add additional functionality, such as databases and task scheduling, to our applications. Having these skills and building blocks will allow us to move beyond a simple static application into the world of creating interactive applications that can save application state.

Learning the essential RHC commands

As you learned in the previous chapter, the RHC tool is an umbrella command that will allow us to perform many different operations on the OpenShift platform. It is critical that you understand the most commonly used parameters in order to be effective with the OpenShift Online platform. Developers interact with the RHC toolset using the convention of the following command:

```
$ rhc command action arguments
```

The essential commands that we will cover in this chapter are `app` and `cartridge`. The `app` command will allow us to create and manage applications on the platform, while the `cartridge` command will allow us to add and manage embeddable cartridges. Given that the conventions are listed, we can further build out the entered text we issue by adding the command that we want to perform an action on. For instance, if we want to perform an action on an application, the command will be as follows:

```
$ rhc app action
```

Now that we have specified the command (app) that we want to perform an action on, we can then specify the action that we want by using the correct argument associated with the command. The available actions for the app command are listed in the following table:

Action	Description
configure	This allows the developer to modify configuration items for an application such as auto-deployment, namespace, and deployment type.
create	This allows the developer to create a new application on the OpenShift Online Platform.
delete	This allows the developer to delete an application from the OpenShift Online server. The Git repository on the local filesystem will not be modified.
deploy	This deploys a Git reference or binary file.
force-stop	This forces the stopping of all application processes.
reload	This reloads the application configuration.
restart	This restarts the application.
show	This shows information about the application such as domain, date created, the Git URL, and cartridges in use by the application.
start	This starts the application.
stop	This stops the application.
tidy	This allows the developer to clean the application logs, tmp directories, and the Git repository on the OpenShift server.

> You can view a list of all actions available for the rhc app command by entering in the following command:
> $ rhc app

Displaying information about an application

Let's test out the new commands you have just learned by displaying the information for the application we created in the previous chapter. Open up your terminal prompt and enter in the following command:

$ rhc app show

After entering in this command, you probably saw an error message. Why is this? In order for the RHC tool to know which application you want to display information about, you must also provide the name of the application. Given that we named our application myphpapp in the previous chapter, let's modify the command to include the application name:

```
$ rhc app show myphpapp
```

> The RHC tool is context aware, which means that if you are in the directory that contains the Git source code repository, you will not need to specify the application name. It will default to the application of the directory you are currently working from.
>
> If you have forgotten the name of your application, or just want to view a list containing all of your applications, you can enter in the follow command:
>
> ```
> $ rhc apps
> ```

Once the command has been executed, you should see an output that is similar to the following:

```
myphpapp @ http://myphpapp-packt.rhcloud.com/ (uuid: 52bf4758e0b8cd189d0000d9)
---------------------------------------------------------------------
  Domain:     packt
  Created:    Jan 10, 2014  8:49 PM
  Gears:      1 (defaults to small)
  Git URL:    ssh://52bf4758e0b8cd189d0000d9@myphpapp-packt.rhcloud.com/~/git/myphpapp.git/
  SSH:        52bf4758e0b8cd189d0000d9@myphpapp-packt.rhcloud.com
  Deployment: auto (on git push)

  php-5.3 (PHP 5.3)
  -----------------
    Gears: 1 small
```

The essential information that a developer would want to know about their application is displayed in the output provided. Given this output, a developer will have the necessary information required to SSH to the application gear, clone the Git source repository, and know the cartridges that the application gear is consuming.

Deleting applications

OpenShift Online is a great platform for quickly spinning up a new development stack in order to try out a new piece of technology or to prototype ideas rapidly. While this is a great use of the platform, you have to keep in mind that while on the free tier, you are limited to having three gears at any point in the time. In order to manage your system usage appropriately, the RHC toolset provides users a way to delete applications once they are no longer in use. This will free up a gear on the server that has been allocated to your account, which in turn will allow you to have room to create a new application. In the previous chapter, we created two applications that we will no longer use. Let's free up the resources for our account by deleting both of them. In order to delete an application, issue the following command in your terminal prompt:

```
$ rhc app delete myphpapp
```

Deleting an application cannot be reversed. While the source code repository on your local machine will not be altered, it is important to understand that once you delete an application, it is completely removed from the OpenShift servers.

After you enter in the previous command, the system will prompt you to ensure that you want to delete the application. Type `yes` to confirm that you want to delete it and press the *Enter* key. After the application has been deleted, you will see an output message that confirms the delete operation was successful.

The `rhc app delete` command can also be passed a flag that will notify the system that you want to bypass the confirmation message prompt. Let's delete the blog application we created in the previous chapter while bypassing the confirmation prompt:

```
$ rhc app delete myblog --confirm
```

If you no longer need the source code for the application you deleted, make sure you remove the directories from your local filesystem.

Understanding cartridges

When I hear the word cartridge, I often think back to when I was kid and all the enjoyment I had while playing the original 8-bit **Nintendo Entertainment System** (**NES**). One of the great things about the NES was the ability to play a plethora of games simply by inserting a new game cartridge into the system. Plugging one of the game cartridges into the console changed the state of the system by allowing the consumer to utilize added functionality on top of the core console. The cartridge was the delivery mechanism for the game software that made the system usable. Without a game cartridge, NES would have been a pretty boring game console.

Just as with video game consoles that most people have played, OpenShift supports a cartridge system that will allow developers to change the state of the platform to meet their specific needs and requirements. Using one of these cartridges is what makes the platform usable.

There are two types of cartridges that are available for the OpenShift Online platform:

- Web cartridges
- Add-on cartridges

Web cartridges

You can think of a web cartridge as the language runtime (server) that you will be using for your application development. A common example for Java-based applications would be the Tomcat web cartridge. Each application that you create on the platform must include one web cartridge. At the time of writing, the available web cartridges for use by developers are shown in the following table:

Cartridge name	Developers
jbossas-7	JBoss Application Server 7
jbosseap-6	JBoss Enterprise Application Platform 6
jenkins-1	Jenkins servers that provides continuous integration functionality
nodejs-0.10	Version .10 of the popular node.js runtime
zend-6.1	The popular Zend Server for PHP applications
php-5.3	PHP 5.3
php-5.4	PHP 5.4
ruby-1.8	Ruby 1.8
ruby-1.9	Ruby 1.9
perl-5.10	Perl 5.10

Cartridge name	Developers
python-2.6	Python 2.6
python-2.7	Python 2.7
python-3.3	Python 3.3
jbossews-1.0	Tomcat 6
jbossews-2.0	Tomcat 7
diy-0.1	This is an empty gear that will allow you to install and run a custom runtime

Keep in mind that the version number of a specific application runtime that is offered is a fast moving target. Don't be surprised if newer versions of a runtime show up once they are generally available to the public.

Add-on cartridges

To further expand the functionality of the web cartridge, a developer can also embed an add-on cartridge to their application gear. These add-on cartridges provide features that complement the core web cartridge that you have chosen for your application. For example, most modern web applications rely on a database to store and retrieve information that is required for the application to run. Common examples of add-on cartridges will include databases, database management tools, and job schedulers.

A developer may embed multiple add-on cartridges into a single application. For instance, you can use both the MySQL and MongoDB databases with the same application.

At the time of writing, the available add-on cartridges for use by developers are shown as follows:

Cartridge name	Description
10gen-mms-agent-0.1	This is a tenth generation Mongo Monitoring Service Agent
cron-1.4	This is the popular task schedule for Unix-based systems
jenkins-client-1	This Jenkins client is used with continuous integration
mongodb-2.4	This is Version 2.4 of the popular MongoDB NoSQL database
mysql-5.1	This is Version 5.1 of the MySQL database
mysql-5.5	This is Version 5.5 of the MySQL database

Cartridge name	Description
phpmyadmin-4	This is a popular web-based frontend for the MySQL database
postgresql-8.4	This is Version 8.4 of the popular PostgreSQL relational database
postgresql-9.2	This is Version 9.2 of the popular PostgreSQL relational database
rockmongo-1.1	This is a web frontend to manage an embedded MongoDB database

To view a complete list of all cartridges currently available on the platform, you can issue the following command:
`$ rhc cartridge list`

Using cartridges

Now that you understand that a cartridge allows the developers to change the features available on the platform, let's dig in and learn some of the basic cartridge commands. To interact with cartridges, use the following syntax:

`$ rhc cartridge action`

The available actions for the `cartridge` command are listed in the following table:

Action	Description
add	This allows the developer to add a cartridge to an existing application.
list	This lists all of the available supported cartridges on the platform.
reload	This allows the developer to reload the configuration for the cartridge.
remove	This allows the developer to remove a cartridge from an existing application.
scale	This allows the developer to specify the configuration for how many gears the application can consume while scaling.
show	This shows information about a cartridge. For instance, if you issue the command to show information about a database cartridge, such as mysql, the username and password for the database will be displayed.
start	This allows the developer to start the cartridge.
status	This displays the current status of the cartridge state, for instance, if the cartridge is in a running or stopped state.
stop	This stops the cartridge.
storage	This allows the developer to view and modify the storage configuration for the cartridge.

> You can view a list of all actions available for the `rhc cartridge` command by entering in the following command:
>
> `$ rhc cartridge`

Adding cartridges

One of the most popular development stacks in existence today is called the LAMP stack. During the remainder of this chapter, we will build out a full LAMP stack using the OpenShift Online platform.

> The LAMP acronym refers to the first letters of each technology that is used for one of the most popular programming stacks in existence. The technologies that commonly make up the LAMP stack are Linux, Apache, MySQL, and PHP, Perl, or Python.

The first thing we need to do in order to build this stack is to create a new application using the PHP runtime. Open up your terminal window and enter in the following command, ensuring that you are in the directory where you want the source code repository to reside:

`$ rhc app create lampstack php-5.4`

Given the information you learned previously in this chapter, we can map this command to the standard convention of the RHC command action arguments as follows:

Component	Type	Description
rhc	Umbrella command	This is the umbrella command for all RHC tools
app	Command	This notifies the RHC toolset that is going to perform actions for applications
create	Action	This specifies that we want the create action to spin up a new application gear
lampstack	Argument	This is the argument that specifies we are going to name our application `lampstack`
php-5.4	Argument	This is the argument that specifies we are going use the PHP-5.4 web cartridge

The previous command created a new application with all of the components required for a LAMP stack, except for the MySQL database. In order to add this functionality to our application stack, we can embed the MySQL add-on cartridge with the following command:

```
$ rhc cartridge add mysql-5.5 -a lampstack
```

Once the previous command has completed successfully, you will see an output that is similar to the following:

```
MySQL 5.5 database added.  Please make note of these credentials:

      Root User: adminbrePNb2
  Root Password: FMsgJpTHEwYd
  Database Name: lampstack


Connection URL: mysql://$OPENSHIFT_MYSQL_DB_HOST:$OPENSHIFT_MYSQL_DB_PORT/


You can manage your new MySQL database by also embedding phpmyadmin.
The phpmyadmin username and password will be the same as the MySQL credentials above.
```

Congratulations! You have just spun up an entire LAMP stack in a record amount of time.

> The RHC toolset is a very powerful command line utility. One of the features it provides is the ability to chain cartridges together. For instance, to create a complete LAMP stack with a single command, we can use the following syntax:
> ```
> $ rhc app create lampstack php-5.4 mysql-5.5
> ```

Using databases with your application

In the previous section, we created a new application called `lampstack` and deployed it to the public cloud. In this section, we are going make use of the MySQL database cartridge that we added by creating a web application that will display information that our application code retrieves from this embedded cartridge. We are also going to embed a popular MySQL database management tool called phpMyAdmin.

 Although we will be using the phpMyAdmin tool during this section, it is important to remember that you can use any database management tool, including the MySQL command line utility, to connect to and manage your database.

Adding the phpMyAdmin add-on cartridge

As you learned previously in this chapter, OpenShift Online provides a wide assortment of cartridges that you can use to provide more functionality to your web applications. A common application that most PHP developers use to manage their database is called phpMyAdmin. In this section, we are going to embed this popular application to our `lampstack` application. In order to add this cartridge to our application, open up your terminal prompt and enter in the following command:

```
$ rhc cartridge add phpmyadmin-4 -a lampstack
```

After the command has executed, make a note of the username and password that is provided. The output provided should look similar to the following:

```
Adding phpmyadmin-4 to application 'lampstack' ... done

phpmyadmin-4 (phpMyAdmin 4.0)
-----------------------------
  Gears:          Located with php-5.4, mysql-5.5
  Connection URL: https://lampstack-packt.rhcloud.com/phpmyadmin/

Please make note of these MySQL credentials again:
  Root User: adminRapRWMM
  Root Password: JerElgadNgFP
URL: https://lampstack-packt.rhcloud.com/phpmyadmin/
```

Open up your web browser and point the location to the URL that is provided in the output.

 Ensure that you are using the correct URL and not the one provided previously as an example.

Once the web page has loaded, you will be presented with an authentication dialog box where you will need to enter in the credentials provided when you added the cartridge to your application. For example, in the previous output, the username is `adminRapRWMM` and the password is `JerElgadNgFP`.

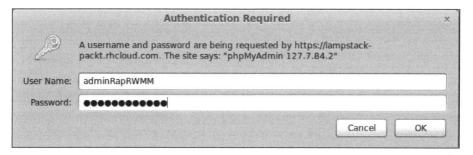

After you have authenticated to the phpMyAdmin application, you will see the main dashboard for the application, which lists all of the available databases for your MySQL instance. You will notice that OpenShift created a default database for you with the same name as the application you created, `lampstack`. This default database can be seen on the left hand side of the screen as shown in the following screenshot:

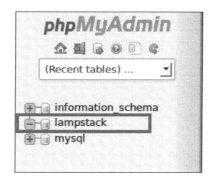

Creating and Managing Applications

Click on the database named `lampstack` so that we can create a new table that will hold the information we want to display from our web application. Create a table named `users` with two columns and click on the **Go** button.

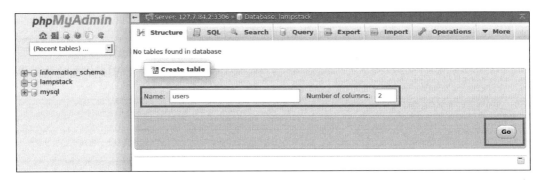

After creating the table, phpMyAdmin will present you with a screen where you will need to define the columns that the table will contain. We want to create a basic users table that will only hold the username and e-mail address of a user. In order to accomplish this, create a `username` column of type `varchar` with a length of `50`, create an `email` column of type `varchar` with a length of `150`, and then click on the **Save** button, as shown in the following screenshot:

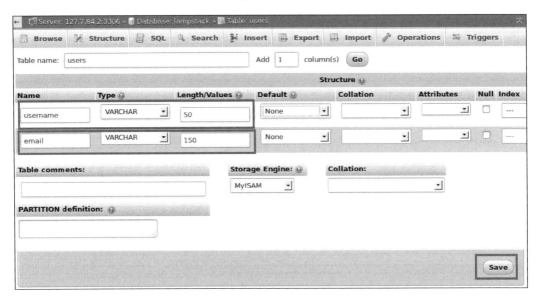

Chapter 2

Now that we have a `users` table created, we can insert a few basic rows. Click on the **SQL** tab at the top of the screen in order to open up an interactive SQL command window where we can perform database statements, as shown in the following screenshot:

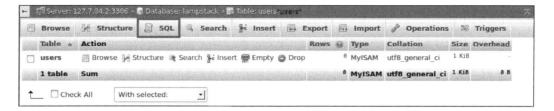

Enter in the following SQL statements to create a few rows in the `users` table and then click on the **Go** button:

```
INSERT INTO users VALUES ('author', 'author@grantshipley.com');
INSERT INTO users VALUES ('OpenShift Help', 'openshift@redhat.com');
```

> **Downloading the example code**
>
> You can download the example code files for all Packt books you have purchased from your account at http://www.packtpub.com. If you purchased this book elsewhere, you can visit http://www.packtpub.com/support and register to have the files e-mailed directly to you.

Creating and Managing Applications

Once you click on the **Go** button, you can verify that the records were saved to the database by clicking on the **Browse** button at the top of the screen, as shown in the following screenshot:

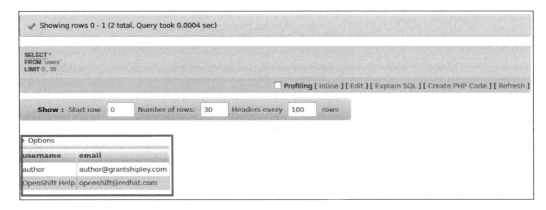

Now we have some information in the database, we can create a simple application that will display the results to the user.

> This section only touches the surface of the phpMyAdmin tool. For a more comprehensive tutorial on learning this application, you can read *Mastering phpMyAdmin 3.4 for Effective MySQL Management*, Marc Delisle, Packt Publishing.

Developing the application

At this point, we should have a LAMP stack fully deployed as well as a database that contains a few records. We will now develop a simple PHP application that authenticates to the database and displays the information contained in the `users` table that we created in the previous section.

Change to the root directory of your `lampstack` application by using the following command:

```
$ cd ~/code/lampstack
```

Once you are in this directory, create a new file called `hellodb.php` using the text editor of your choice, with the following source code:

```
<?php
$dbhost = getenv("OPENSHIFT_MYSQL_DB_HOST");
$dbuser = getenv("OPENSHIFT_MYSQL_DB_USERNAME");
```

```
$dbpassword = getenv("OPENSHIFT_MYSQL_DB_PASSWORD");
$dbname = getenv("OPENSHIFT_APP_NAME");

mysql_connect($dbhost, $dbuser, $dbpassword) or die(mysql_error());
mysql_select_db($dbname) or die(mysql_error());
$result = mysql_query("SELECT * FROM users") or die(mysql_error());

echo "<table border cellpadding=3>";
echo "<tr><td>Username</td>";
echo "<td>Email Address</td></tr>";

while($currentRow = mysql_fetch_array( $result ))
{
  echo "<tr>";
  echo "<td>".$currentRow['username']."</td>";
  echo "<td>".$currentRow['email']."</td>";
  echo "</tr>";
}

echo "</table>";
```

Save your changes and then perform the following commands to deploy your new source file to your OpenShift gear:

`$ git add .`

`$ git commit -am "Adding a file to print information from the users database table"`

`$ git push`

If this is the first time you are using Git on your machine, you may see the following error message:

`*** Please tell me who you are.`

Run

```
  git config --global user.email "you@example.com"
  git config --global user.name "Your Name"
```

to set your account's default identity.
Omit --global to set the identity only in this repository.

`fatal: unable to auto-detect email address (got 'gshipley@author-workstation.(none)')`

With a newer version of the Git revision control system, you need to identify yourself before you can commit changes to your repository. In order to do this, enter in the following command supplying your correct e-mail address:

```
$ git config --global user.email "author@grantshipley.com"
```

Once your application has deployed, open your web browser and point it to the `http://lampstack-youNameSpace.rhcloud.com/hellodb.php` URL of your application.

Once the page loads, you should see the following output:

Understanding the code

Now that we have created the new source file and deployed the changes, let's take a closer look at the code so that you understand all of the pieces.

The first block of code that we need to examine and understand is where we define our connection information for the database, as shown in the following code:

```
$dbhost = getenv("OPENSHIFT_MYSQL_DB_HOST");
$dbuser = getenv("OPENSHIFT_MYSQL_DB_USERNAME");
$dbpassword = getenv("OPENSHIFT_MYSQL_DB_PASSWORD");
$dbname = getenv("OPENSHIFT_APP_NAME");
```

This probably looks a bit strange to you in that we are not actually specifying the connection information that has been provided to us. What we are doing instead is referencing environment variables that the OpenShift Online platform created for us to reference the resources available to our application. This is an important concept to understand, because it is suggested that you never hardcode any IP addresses or authorization credentials in your application. The reason for this is that if your application scales, the IP information for your particular host may change. Using environment variables also provides the mechanism that makes your application portable to a new host.

 We will discuss the available environment variables in more depth in the next chapter.

```
mysql_connect($dbhost, $dbuser, $dbpassword) or die(mysql_error());
mysql_select_db($dbname) or die(mysql_error());
```

In the previous two statements, we connect to our database, providing the information from the environment variables as well as printing out an error message if the application code could not establish a connection. We then specify the database name that we will be working with for our queries.

> The database name we get from the OPENSHIFT_APP_NAME environment variable is the name of our application, lampstack.

The next thing we want to do is to execute a query on the database server that will return all of the users:

```
$result = mysql_query("SELECT * FROM users") or die(mysql_error());
```

The previous command line is where we actually perform the SQL query that will return all rows and columns from the **users** tables. We store the returned values in a variable named result. The code is as follows:

```
echo "<table border cellpadding=3>";
echo "<tr><td>Username</td>";
echo "<td>Email Address</td></tr>";
```

The next three lines of code is some simple markup to lay out the information we are going to present to the user in HTML. We create a table and then specify the header information for the columns using the following code:

```
while($currentRow = mysql_fetch_array( $result ))
{
  echo "<tr>";
  echo "<td>".$currentRow['username']."</td>";
  echo "<td>".$currentRow['email']."</td>";
  echo "</tr>";
}
```

Once we have our database connection and the simple markup defined, we are going to iterate over each of the rows returned from the database. For each row that has been returned, we create a new table row and output the username and e-mail address for each entry in our database, as shown in the following code:

```
echo "</table>";
```

The last thing we do is close our table tag and end the PHP script.

The cron cartridge

Developers routinely come across a scenario when they need to perform a job at certain time intervals. One popular example that I come across is the need to send an e-mail communication out to users at a scheduled frequency. Some language frameworks include this scheduling ability as part of the core distribution while other languages require that you download additional packages to achieve this functionality.

OpenShift Online provides an add-on cartridge that will allow you to schedule jobs at the operating system level using the popular `cron` utility that is standard on most Linux distributions. To demonstrate the cron add-on cartridge, we are going to create a simple job that will add the current date and time to a file that we can view in the web browser.

Adding the cron cartridge

To get started with the cron add-on cartridge, the first thing we need to do is embed it into our `lampstack` application. This can be achieved using the following command:

```
$ rhc cartridge add cron-1.4 -a lampstack
```

Once you have executed that command, you should get the following output:

```
Adding cron-1.4 to application 'lampstack' ... done

cron-1.4 (Cron 1.4)
-------------------
  Gears: Located with php-5.4, mysql-5.5, phpmyadmin-4

To schedule your scripts to run on a periodic basis, add the scripts to
your application's .openshift/cron/{minutely,hourly,daily,weekly,monthly}/
directories (and commit and redeploy your application).

Example: A script .openshift/cron/hourly/crony added to your application
         will be executed once every hour.
         Similarly, a script .openshift/cron/weekly/chronograph added
         to your application will be executed once every week.
```

Once you have embedded the cron add-on cartridge into your application, you can create a job by placing an executable script in the appropriate directory for the schedule that you want to create. The cartridge looks for these files under the `.openshift/cron` directory in your applications root folder. If we take a closer look at the directory structure of the `.openshift/cron` directory, we will see the options shown in the following screenshot:

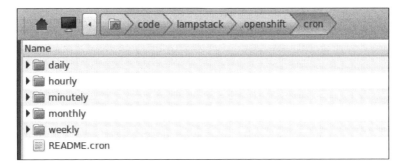

 If you don't see the `.openshift` directory in your file browser, it is because the directory is a hidden one. In order to see this directory, you will need to enable the visibility of hidden directories on your operating system. If using the command line on Linux or OS X, you can list all of the files—including hidden ones—with the following command:

```
$ ls -a
```

As we can see in the previous screenshot, we have directories available for scheduling jobs based upon minutes, hours, days, weeks, and months. This system provides all of the available options that you would need to schedule your job at the appropriate time interval.

Adding a cron job

Change to the `lampstack/.openshift/cron/minutely` directory by using the following command:

```
$ cd ~/code/lampstack/.openshift/cron/minutely
```

Once you are inside of this directory, create a new file called `crondate.sh` and add the following content:

```
date >> $OPENSHIFT_REPO_DIR/crontest.txt
```

The previous command will create a new file, if required, and append the current output of the Linux `date` command. Once you have created and saved this file, add it to your repository and deploy the change:

```
$ git add .
$ git commit -am "Adding cron job to echo the date"
$ git push
```

After you have deployed the change, open up your web browser and view the output by pointing your browser to the following URL:

`http://lampstack-yourNameSpace.rhcloud.com/crontest.txt`

Keep refreshing the page to see new entries added every minute as the scheduled job is executed by the platform as shown in the following screenshot:

> Note that the date is the server date/time and not the value from your local machine. Keep this is mind when developing applications that relies on timestamps.

Summary

In this chapter, you got a lot of information that is critical to being effective while using the OpenShift Online platform. You learned the essential RHC commands to create and interact with applications and cartridges. You also learned the difference between web and add-on cartridges as well as how to add cartridges to an existing application. We discussed the OpenShift provided environment variables and why it is good practice to use these variables instead of hardcoding the authorization credentials and host information for your application. You also learned how to use the `cron` cartridge in order to add scheduled job to an application.

In the next chapter, we will go more in depth and discuss the common application maintenance operations, such as viewing logfiles and connecting to the remote gear via SSH. We will also explore environment variables on the OpenShift Online platform.

3
Application Maintenance

In both the previous chapters, we learned how to create applications as well as how to add additional cartridges to enhance the functionality of the platform. In this chapter, we are going to learn more tricks to maintain and manage the applications that we deploy to the OpenShift platform.

The first part of this chapter will focus on stopping and starting applications as well as cartridges and then progress to viewing logfiles of running gears. After that, we will learn how to back up and restore applications and then how to remotely connect to our application gears using SSH.

Stopping and starting applications

In the last chapter, we created an application named `lampstack` that included the phpMyAdmin management console as well as a MySQL database. There may be times when you want to stop a particular cartridge so that it is not consuming system resources while not in use.

1. Open your web browser and go to the URL of the phpMyAdmin cartridge that we embedded in the previous chapter.
2. Ensure the application is responding to requests as expected.
3. Once you have verified the application is up and running, issue the following command at your terminal prompt:

   `$ rhc cartridge stop phpmyadmin -a lampstack`

4. Now, refresh the page for phpMyAdmin and you should see an error message stating that the service is temporarily unavailable. If you change the URL to point to the `hellodb.php` file we created in *Chapter 2, Creating and Managing Applications*, you will notice that the core application as well as the MySQL database is still running.

Application Maintenance

5. Now, let's stop the MySQL database to see how the `hellodb.php` script behaves when it cannot connect to the database using the following command:

   `$ rhc cartridge stop mysql-5.5 -a lampstack`

6. Reload the `hellodb.php` page and you should see an error stating that the connection to MySQL could not be established.

7. While we are stopping services, let's go ahead and stop the core application server as well with the following command:

   `$ rhc app stop lampstack`

8. Once the command is executed, you will see a confirmation message that the `lampstack` application has been stopped. To verify this, open up your web browser and navigate to the URL of your application. If the `stop` command was successful, you should see an error message indicating that the server is temporarily unavailable.

9. Go ahead and start the application back up using the following command:

   `$ rhc app start lampstack`

Once the `start` command has executed, verify that the application is deployed and it is responding to requests by refreshing the application URL in your web browser.

> When you start an application, all of the cartridges associated with the application are also started, including the ones that were stopped when the application was stopped. You can verify this by viewing the `hellodb.php` script.

Viewing application logfiles

Viewing the logfiles for an application is a critical task when trying to troubleshoot errors or to monitor the health of your application. Having access to these logs is an important part of the development life cycle and OpenShift makes viewing these files a straightforward task. The RHC toolset provides a command that will display all of the logfiles available for your application from the Shell prompt. To try this out, use the following syntax:

`$ rhc tail lampstack`

The previous example will open up a Linux tail command on the remote gear and display all information as it is logged into the appropriate logfiles.

> To exit the `rhc tail` command, you must press *Ctrl + c* on your keyboard.

While you have the `rhc tail` command running, open your web browser and refresh the `hellodb.php` script. Once your browser makes the GET request to the web server, you will see the following line in the logs to indicate the action:

```
72.208.43.224 - - [16/Jan/2014:22:38:55 -0500] "GET /hellodb.php HTTP/1.1" 200 203 "-" "Mozilla/5.0 (X11; Ubuntu; Linux x86_64; rv:24.0) Gecko/20100101 Firefox/24.0"
```

> If you leave the tail command open, you will also see the Cron job that runs every minute, which we created in the previous chapter.

If you are familiar with the Linux `tail` command, the `-f` option is passed by default when viewing the logfiles. Since this is running the Linux command under the covers, you can also pass any option to the command just as you would if you were executing it on a local server. For example, to view the last 50 lines of the logfile, you can specify the `-o` argument:

```
$ rhc tail lampstack -o '-n 50'
```

Creating your own logfiles

Most software projects today will log activity to help troubleshoot problems in the application as and when they arise. As we have learned previously in this chapter, you can view the standard logfiles with a simple `rhc tail` command. This command will display all information in the standard log directories for your application. It is good practice to create your own logfiles instead of writing to the standard HTTP access logs. Let's modify the `hellodb.php` source file that we created in the previous chapter to add logging capabilities.

> Most frameworks will include a standard convention for writing logfiles. It is good practice to follow the convention of the framework you are using.

Open up the source file and modify the contents to reflect the following source code:

```
$dbhost = getenv("OPENSHIFT_MYSQL_DB_HOST");
$dbuser = getenv("OPENSHIFT_MYSQL_DB_USERNAME");
$dbpassword = getenv("OPENSHIFT_MYSQL_DB_PASSWORD");
$dbname = getenv("OPENSHIFT_APP_NAME");
$logdir = getenv("OPENSHIFT_LOG_DIR");
$logfile = fopen($logdir."lampstacklog", 'a');
```

Application Maintenance

The first modification is the last two lines in the previous code, where we created a new variable named `log` that contains the path to our application's log directory. We then open a file named `lampstacklog` and set the parameter to append to the file:

```
mysql_connect($dbhost, $dbuser, $dbpassword) or die(mysql_error());
fwrite($logfile, date("m/d/Y h:i:s a", time())." Connected to
database.\n");
```

The second modification will write a log entry to the file that contains the date and time as well as a message stating that we have successfully connected to the database:

```
mysql_select_db($dbname) or die(mysql_error());
$result = mysql_query("SELECT * FROM users") or die(mysql_error());
fwrite($logfile, date("m/d/Y h:i:s a", time())." Ran query SELECT *
FROM users\n");
```

The third modification is made in another log statement that states we have successfully run the SQL query:

```
echo "<table border cellpadding=3>";
echo "<tr><td>Username</td>";
echo "<td>Email Address</td></tr>";

while($currentRow = mysql_fetch_array( $result ))
{
  echo "<tr>";
  echo "<td>".$currentRow['username']."</td>";
  echo "<td>".$currentRow['email']."</td>";
  echo "</tr>";
}

echo "</table>";
fwrite($logfile, date("m/d/Y h:i:s a", time())." Returned results to
browser\n");
fclose($logfile);
```

The final modification contains a log statement, which indicates that the results have been returned to the browser. Then, we close the file.

Save the changes to the file and then deploy the changes using the standard workflow:

```
$ git commit -am "Adding logging to our application"
$ git push
```

Once your application has been deployed, run the following command:

```
$ rhc tail lampstack
```

Open up your web browser, load the `hellodp.php` file again, and view the contents of the `tail` command on your terminal prompt. You will see the following entries in the log:

```
==> app-root/logs/lampstacklog <==
01/17/2014 04:19:20 am Connected to database.
01/17/2014 04:19:20 am Ran query SELECT * FROM users
01/17/2014 04:19:20 am Returned results to browser
```

Viewing a single logfile

I often find that when I am troubleshooting an issue, I want to focus on one logfile. By default, the `rhc tail` command will display all entries for every file that our application is using. If we want to narrow down the scope of the files that we view, we can use the `-f` option of the command while specifying the logfile that we want to view. For example, to view only the `lampstacklog` logfile that we created for our application, enter the following command:

```
$ rhc tail -f app-root/logs/lampstacklog
```

You can also pass in wildcards as an option if you are interested in viewing all logfiles in a given directory:

```
$ rhc tail -f app-root/logs/*
```

> For a complete list of options you can pass to the command, you can run the following command:
> ```
> $ rhc tail --help
> ```

Backing up and restoring applications

OpenShift Online does not keep or restore backups of a user's applications that developers have deployed to the platform. Due to security and privacy concerns, this task is left up to the user of the system to perform and maintain. Fortunately, the RHC toolset provides an easy-to-use utility to perform this function. In this section, we are going to take a snapshot of our application and then modify the source code that will break the database connection. We will then restore the snapshot to bring back the application to a working state.

Creating a snapshot

Create a new directory named `backups` under your `code` directory and change to the newly created directory using the following command:

```
$ cd ~/code
$ mkdir backups
$ cd backups
```

Once you are in this directory, you can create a snapshot of the `lampstack` application with the following command:

```
$ rhc snapshot save lampstack
```

This will create a new file on your local system that contains the complete snapshot of your application. This includes every piece of information that you need to get your application up and running, including your database. Having this snapshot makes it possible and extremely easy to recreate your application on OpenShift or to move it to a larger gear instance with more memory.

You will notice that, by default, the `snapshot` utility created a new file named `lampstack.tar.gz` when you make the snapshot. The next time you create a snapshot, this file will be overwritten with the contents of the new archive. With a little command-line jujitsu, we can modify the snapshot command to create a file with the current date and time for our backup. This is useful if you want to keep a history of snapshots for your application or if you want to set up a cron job that automatically creates a backup of your application.

> It is important to know when taking a snapshot of your application that the platform stops your gear while performing the back up. If you create a snapshot, your application will experience downtime while the snapshot is saving.

To create a new snapshot with a timestamp, execute the following command:

```
$ rhc snapshot save lampstack -f ./$( date '+%Y-%m-%d_%H-%M-%S' ).lampstack.tar.gz
```

Chapter 3

Once the command is executed, you will see the following output on the screen to notify you that a new snapshot is being saved:

```
Pulling down a snapshot to ./2014-07-14_22-04-48.lampstack.tar.gz...
Creating and sending tar.gz
```

```
RESULT:
Success
```

> While the OpenShift Online platform is creating your snapshot, your application will be unavailable, as it stops all of the processes in order to get a clean backup.

Restoring a snapshot

Let's create a mock scenario where a critical source file was deleted from our application and it is necessary that we restore it. I am sorry to admit that this situation has happened to me in the past and I didn't have a backup of the missing file. Let's create this mock example by deleting the `hellodb.php` source file from the previous chapter. Open up your command line or file browser and delete the file. Once you have deleted the file, push the changes to the OpenShift servers using the standard workflow:

```
$ git commit -am "removing source file"
$ git push
```

Verify that the file has been deleted on the server by opening the file in your web browser. If the file was deleted correctly, you should see a 404 error page, as shown in the following screenshot:

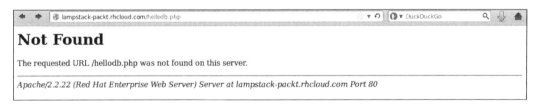

To restore the source file as well as the entire application to the last-known good backup state, change to the directory where you stored the last backup and issue the following command:

```
$ rhc snapshot restore -f lampstack.tar.gz -a lampstack
```

Application Maintenance

After entering the previous command, you will see the following output on the screen, which states the steps that are currently being taken to restore the application:

```
Restoring from snapshot lampstack.tar.gz to application 'lampstack' ...
done
```

Once the process has finished, refresh the `hellodb.php` page to ensure that the file has been restored and is able to display information from the database.

> The `restore` option also restores the database and all of its content to the information that was saved when taking the snapshot. This means that any data in the database that was saved between snapshots will be rolled back. Given this information, a good use case to restore a snapshot is if you accidentally drop a database table from the application.

It is important to understand that once you restore a snapshot, your current Git repository is out of date with the repository on the OpenShift server. This makes sense because the snapshot is a complete backup of the entire application gear, including the Git repository. Since we deleted the `hellodb.php` file and then committed the change to our local repository, it is ahead of the newly restored Git repository. You can correct this scenario in one of the following two ways:

- Remove your `lampstack` directory and recreate it using the following command:

    ```
    $ rhc git-clone lampstack
    ```

- Reset your local Git repository to match with the OpenShift server using the following commands:

    ```
    $ cd ~/code/lampstack
    $ git reset origin --hard
    ```

Secure shell and your application

When a developer creates an application on the OpenShift Online platform, a Linux user account is also created on the server that the application is deployed on. Having this user account on the system allows a developer to secure shell or SSH to the application gear. However, because OpenShift uses SELinux and Linux control groups, the user account is limited in what actions can be executed. For instance, you can't install new system packages on the server, but you do have access to view logfiles, securely copy files, and perform maintenance tasks for your application.

Let's start learning some of the things we can do while connected to the remote server via SSH by connecting to the `lampstack` application gear. This can be done using the RHC tool with the following command:

```
$ rhc ssh lampstack
```

Once you enter the previous command, you will be connected to the container that your application code is deployed to. You should see the following output confirming the SSH command was successful:

```
gshipley@author-workstation - $ rhc ssh lampstack
Connecting to 52d5d7c05973ca5f33000015@lampstack-packt.rhcloud.com ...

************************************************************************

    You are accessing a service that is for use only by authorized users.
    If you do not have authorization, discontinue use at once.
    Any use of the services is subject to the applicable terms of the
    agreement which can be found at:
    https://www.openshift.com/legal

************************************************************************

    Welcome to OpenShift shell

    This shell will assist you in managing OpenShift applications.

    !!! IMPORTANT !!! IMPORTANT !!! IMPORTANT !!!
    Shell access is quite powerful and it is possible for you to
    accidentally damage your application.  Proceed with care!
    If worse comes to worst, destroy your application with "rhc app delete"
    and recreate it
    !!! IMPORTANT !!! IMPORTANT !!! IMPORTANT !!!

    Type "help" for more info.

    *** This gear has been temporarily unidled. To keep it active, access
    *** your app @ http://lampstack-packt.rhcloud.com/

[lampstack-packt.rhcloud.com 52d5d7c05973ca5f33000015]\>
```

Now that you are connected to the remote server, I know the first instinct is to look around and see what permissions you have. Go ahead and take a few minutes to try some things out.

Back already? If you are like me, the first thing you probably tried was getting root level permissions with the following command:

```
$ sudo su
```

Application Maintenance

Once you entered the preceding command, you were notified that you don't have permission to the `sudo` command, as shown in the following command:

`bash: /usr/bin/sudo: Permission denied`

You probably also found out that your home directory is not in a standard location such as `/home`, but is located at `/var/lib/openshift`. Then, you tried to list all of the other applications that may be sharing the same server as your application code:

`$ cd /var/lib/openshift`
`$ ls`

At this point, you were greeted with another `Permission denied` error message as follows:

`ls: cannot open directory .: Permission denied`

Understanding and viewing the /etc/passwd file

If you are really devious, you probably tried viewing the `/etc/passwd` file to see all of the user accounts that exist on the system. If you didn't try that, you can do so now with the following command:

`$ cat /etc/passwd`

The `/etc/passwd` file is a text file that contains information about all users that can log in to the system. The file contains seven fields that are delimited by the `:` character. The fields in order are as follows:

- The username for the account.
- The hashed password for the account. In most modern use cases, this field is simply an `x` because the actual hashed password is stored in the `/etc/shadow` file.
- The user ID for the account.
- The group ID for the account.
- The descriptive identifier for the account to state the user's real name. All OpenShift accounts will have the real name of OpenShift Guest.
- The location of the user's home directory.
- The executable code that will be run every time the specified user logs in to the system. This is typically the Shell environment that the user will be working with such as Bash or Zsh. All OpenShift accounts will be running the `oo-trap-user` command.

You may be wondering why users have access to view the /etc/passwd file, while great lengths have been taken to ensure that applications are secure and not visible to other users on the system. One of the main reasons for visibility of this file is the expectation by some applications to have access to read information from this file (such as home directory) in order to function correctly.

Understanding and viewing cgroup information

OpenShift Online uses Linux control groups to manage availability of system resources for your application. In order to view the resources that your application is currently consuming as well as the resources the application has access to, we can use the oo-cgroup-read command. To list all of the information that we can view, issue the following command on the OpenShift Online server:

```
$ oo-cgroup-read all
```

```
[lampstack-packt.rhcloud.com 52d5d7c05973ca5f33000015]\> oo-cgroup-read all
cgroup.procs
cpu.cfs_period_us
cpu.cfs_quota_us
cpu.rt_period_us
cpu.rt_runtime_us
cpu.shares
cpu.stat
cpuacct.stat
cpuacct.usage
cpuacct.usage_percpu
freezer.state
memory.failcnt
memory.limit_in_bytes
memory.max_usage_in_bytes
memory.memsw.failcnt
memory.memsw.limit_in_bytes
memory.memsw.max_usage_in_bytes
memory.memsw.usage_in_bytes
memory.move_charge_at_immigrate
memory.oom_control
memory.soft_limit_in_bytes
memory.stat
memory.swappiness
memory.usage_in_bytes
memory.use_hierarchy
net_cls.classid
notify_on_release
tasks
[lampstack-packt.rhcloud.com 52d5d7c05973ca5f33000015]\>
```

We can then view detailed information for any item by specifying the item name in conjunction with the `oo-cgroup-read` command. For instance, if we want to view the current limit of memory that your application is allowed to consume, we can issue the following command:

```
$ oo-cgroup-read memory.limit_in_bytes
```

Go ahead and play around with some of the other items by viewing them with the `oo-group-read` command.

Setting the timeout parameter and viewing logfiles

While working on the remote server with SSH, you probably noticed that the system will automatically log you out after a period of time when no commands are entered. This was implemented to automatically disconnect users who may have forgotten they were connected to the remote server. While this is a good thing, it can also be annoying when you want to leave the session connected for longer periods of time. Fortunately, the parameter that specifies the amount of time before disconnecting a user is configurable by the user. To view the current value, you can issue the following command:

```
$ echo $TMOUT
```

The previous command will output the value of the TMOUT environment variable. This variable is used to determine how long a user can be inactive before automatically disconnecting the session. To modify this environment variable, issue the following command to change the value to 3600, which is 1 hour:

```
$ export TMOUT=3600
```

Alternatively, you can disable the timeout altogether with the following command:

```
$ unset TMOUT
```

Previously in this chapter, we learned how to view logfiles for the `lampstack` application by using the `rhc tail` command. You can also view logfiles while connected to the remote server via SSH. For example, to view the custom logfile that we created earlier in the chapter, issue the following command:

```
$ cat ~/app-root/logs/lampstacklog
```

Understanding environment variables

OpenShift Online brings a lot of convenience and flexibility to our applications by managing the hardware tier and even some of the software tier for us so that we can focus on the application development. However, having this convenience also changes the way you would typically address certain types of development tasks, such as where to store and retrieve authentication information for databases.

We saw how quickly you can spin up a Wordpress-based application with the database connection already configured for the application. Having this auto-wiring is crucial to reuse and redeploy a new instance of your application. A lot of this perceived magic is actually just system environment variables hard at work. The platform stores such things and IP addresses and database credentials as environment variables so that your application code can reference these variables without having to know the actual value. This is an extremely powerful concept because it makes your application code portable to another server without having to change a single line of code. It also allows the OpenShift platform to scale up the number of servers hosting your application without the developer having to modify the IP addresses associated with the application.

To better understand this concept, let's list all of the environment variables that contain information about the MySQL database that we added to our `lampstack` application. In order to do this, SSH to the `lampstack` application and then perform the `env` command. The steps are as follows:

```
$ rhc ssh lampstack
```

Once connected to the remote server, run the following command:

```
$ env |grep OPENSHIFT_MYSQL
```

The following output will be displayed on the screen:

```
OPENSHIFT_MYSQL_DIR=/var/lib/openshift/52d5d7c05973ca5f33000015/mysql/
OPENSHIFT_MYSQL_DB_PORT=3306
OPENSHIFT_MYSQL_DB_HOST=127.7.84.2
OPENSHIFT_MYSQL_DB_PASSWORD=JerElgadNgFP
OPENSHIFT_MYSQL_IDENT=redhat:mysql:5.1:0.2.6
OPENSHIFT_MYSQL_DB_USERNAME=adminRapRWMM
OPENSHIFT_MYSQL_DB_SOCKET=/var/lib/openshift/52d5d7c05973ca5f33000015/mysql//socket/mysql.sock
OPENSHIFT_MYSQL_DB_URL=mysql://adminRapRWMM:JerElgadNgFP@127.7.84.2:3306/
OPENSHIFT_MYSQL_DB_LOG_DIR=/var/lib/openshift/52d5d7c05973ca5f33000015/app-root/logs/
```

Application Maintenance

As you can see, all of the information that you would need to know in order to connect to the database is stored inside the environment variables. Most modern programming languages provide an API in order to read values that are stored as system environment variables. For example, in PHP, you would reference the `OPENSHIFT_MYSQL_DB_URL` environment variable with the following code:

```
$mysqlURL = getenv('OPENSHIFT_MYSQL_DB_URL');
```

The result of the previous syntax would be a variable named `mysqlURL` that contains `mysql://adminRapRWMM:JerElgadNgFP@127.7.84.2:3306/` as the value.

Another popular environment variable that is used inside of application code is the ability to find out the full URL for the running application. This can be found by referencing the `OPENSHIFT_APP_DNS` environment variable with the following command:

```
$ env |grep OPENSHIFT_APP_DNS
```

If you just want to get the name of application that you are working with, you can run the following command:

```
$ env |grep OPENSHIFT_APP_NAME
```

For a complete list of all available environment variables, run the following command:

```
$env |grep OPENSHIFT
```

The output that you see from the previous command will look similar to the following screenshot:

Chapter 3

```
[lampstack-packt.rhcloud.com 52d5d7c05973ca5f33000015]\> env | grep OPENSHIFT
OPENSHIFT_SECRET_TOKEN=zHpTeHvA6ZnwkSafswIkMcuoXRHAhdnn-aQoXQwlrwmzHeDQeZtxFFEk8-IH0xCmnTUNJiuJbXJZM44HGM8_wJgzhJt4AymJWv5UC
oke7ZkxzvbVr_IgEdg95Wgyq6gF
OPENSHIFT_PHP_IDENT=redhat:php:5.3:0.0.10
OPENSHIFT_GEAR_MEMORY_MB=512
OPENSHIFT_MYSQL_DIR=/var/lib/openshift/52d5d7c05973ca5f33000015/mysql/
OPENSHIFT_DEPLOYMENT_TYPE=git
OPENSHIFT_PHP_LOG_DIR=/var/lib/openshift/52d5d7c05973ca5f33000015/php//logs/
OPENSHIFT_DEPLOYMENTS_DIR=/var/lib/openshift/52d5d7c05973ca5f33000015/app-deployments/
OPENSHIFT_METRICS_DIR=/var/lib/openshift/52d5d7c05973ca5f33000015/metrics/
OPENSHIFT_TMP_DIR=/tmp/
OPENSHIFT_MYSQL_DB_PORT=3306
OPENSHIFT_REPO_DIR=/var/lib/openshift/52d5d7c05973ca5f33000015/app-root/runtime/repo/
OPENSHIFT_HOMEDIR=/var/lib/openshift/52d5d7c05973ca5f33000015/
OPENSHIFT_GEAR_NAME=lampstack
OPENSHIFT_PHPMYADMIN_IP=127.7.84.3
OPENSHIFT_MYSQL_DB_HOST=127.7.84.2
OPENSHIFT_PYPI_MIRROR_URL=http://mirror1.ops.rhcloud.com/mirror/python/web/simple
OPENSHIFT_CRON_DIR=/var/lib/openshift/52d5d7c05973ca5f33000015/cron/
OPENSHIFT_MYSQL_DB_PASSWORD=JerElgadNgFP
OPENSHIFT_APP_SSH_PUBLIC_KEY=/var/lib/openshift/52d5d7c05973ca5f33000015/.openshift_ssh/id_rsa.pub
OPENSHIFT_CLOUD_DOMAIN=rhcloud.com
OPENSHIFT_MYSQL_IDENT=redhat:mysql:5.1:0.2.7
OPENSHIFT_PHPMYADMIN_VERSION=4
OPENSHIFT_BUILD_DEPENDENCIES_DIR=/var/lib/openshift/52d5d7c05973ca5f33000015/app-root/runtime/build-dependencies/
OPENSHIFT_METRICS_PORT=8080
OPENSHIFT_MYSQL_DB_USERNAME=adminRapRWMM
OPENSHIFT_PHP_PATH_ELEMENT=/var/lib/openshift/52d5d7c05973ca5f33000015/php/phplib/pear/pear
OPENSHIFT_MYSQL_DB_SOCKET=/var/lib/openshift/52d5d7c05973ca5f33000015/mysql//socket/mysql.sock
OPENSHIFT_METRICS_LOG_DIR=/var/lib/openshift/52d5d7c05973ca5f33000015/metrics//logs/
OPENSHIFT_LAMPSTACK_DEBUG=1
OPENSHIFT_PHP_DIR=/var/lib/openshift/52d5d7c05973ca5f33000015/php/
OPENSHIFT_MYSQL_DB_URL=mysql://adminRapRWMM:JerElgadNgFP@127.7.84.2:3306/
OPENSHIFT_PHPMYADMIN_LOG_DIR=/var/lib/openshift/52d5d7c05973ca5f33000015/phpmyadmin//logs/
OPENSHIFT_PHPMYADMIN_DIR=/var/lib/openshift/52d5d7c05973ca5f33000015/phpmyadmin/
OPENSHIFT_APP_DNS=lampstack-packt.rhcloud.com
OPENSHIFT_PRIMARY_CARTRIDGE_DIR=/var/lib/openshift/52d5d7c05973ca5f33000015/php/
OPENSHIFT_GEAR_DNS=lampstack-packt.rhcloud.com
OPENSHIFT_CRON_IDENT=redhat:cron:1.4:0.0.9
OPENSHIFT_CARTRIDGE_SDK_BASH=/usr/lib/openshift/cartridge_sdk/bash/sdk
OPENSHIFT_APP_SSH_KEY=/var/lib/openshift/52d5d7c05973ca5f33000015/.openshift_ssh/id_rsa
OPENSHIFT_LAMPSTACK_DEBUG_LEVEL=DEBUG
OPENSHIFT_PHP_PORT=8080
OPENSHIFT_DEPLOYMENT_BRANCH=master
OPENSHIFT_PHPMYADMIN_IDENT=redhat:phpmyadmin:4:0.0.7
OPENSHIFT_PHP_VERSION=5.3
OPENSHIFT_DEPENDENCIES_DIR=/var/lib/openshift/52d5d7c05973ca5f33000015/app-root/runtime/dependencies/
OPENSHIFT_KEEP_DEPLOYMENTS=1
OPENSHIFT_APP_NAME=lampstack
OPENSHIFT_LAMPSTACK_LOGLEVEL=INFO
OPENSHIFT_METRICS_IP=127.7.84.4
OPENSHIFT_MYSQL_DB_LOG_DIR=/var/lib/openshift/52d5d7c05973ca5f33000015/mysql//log/
OPENSHIFT_DATA_DIR=/var/lib/openshift/52d5d7c05973ca5f33000015/app-root/data/
OPENSHIFT_NAMESPACE=packt
OPENSHIFT_AUTO_DEPLOY=true
OPENSHIFT_GEAR_UUID=52d5d7c05973ca5f33000015
OPENSHIFT_METRICS_IDENT=redhat:metrics:0.1:0.0.5
OPENSHIFT_BROKER_HOST=openshift.redhat.com
OPENSHIFT_APP_UUID=52d5d7c05973ca5f33000015
OPENSHIFT_PHPMYADMIN_PORT=8080
OPENSHIFT_UMASK=077
OPENSHIFT_CARTRIDGE_SDK_RUBY=/usr/lib/openshift/cartridge_sdk/ruby/sdk.rb
OPENSHIFT_PHP_IP=127.7.84.1
[lampstack-packt.rhcloud.com 52d5d7c05973ca5f33000015]\>
```

The usernames, passwords, and IP address information that is displayed for your application will be slightly different from the output shown in the previous screenshot to reflect the specific server and generated credentials that your application is using.

Application Maintenance

Setting your own environment variables

The OpenShift Online platform allows developers to set their own environment variables that can be referenced from their application code. One use case might be to set a logging level variable that your application code reads to determine the amount of logging to perform. To illustrate this particular use case, we are going to modify the `hellodb.php` file to read an environment variable that will determine the logging level we want to use.

The first thing we need to do is to create, set an environment variable named `OPENSHIFT_LAMPSTACK_LEVEL`, and set the value to `DEBUG`. We can do this by using the RHC tool that we have installed on our local machine. Open up your local terminal prompt and set the variable with the following command:

```
$ rhc set-env OPENSHIFT_LAMPSTACK_LOGLEVEL=DEBUG -a lampstack
```

Verify that the environment variable was set correctly by connecting to your application gear with SSH and viewing the contents of the variable:

```
$ rhc ssh lampstack
```
```
$ echo $OPENSHIFT_LAMPSTACK_LOGLEVEL
```

The output from the previous command should be `DEBUG`.

Now that the environment variable has been created on the remote server, let's modify the `hellodb.php` file to look like the following code:

```php
<?php
$dbhost = getenv("OPENSHIFT_MYSQL_DB_HOST");
$dbuser = getenv("OPENSHIFT_MYSQL_DB_USERNAME");
$dbpassword = getenv("OPENSHIFT_MYSQL_DB_PASSWORD");
$dbname = getenv("OPENSHIFT_APP_NAME");
$logdir = getenv("OPENSHIFT_LOG_DIR");
$logDebug = getenv("OPENSHIFT_LAMPSTACK_LOGLEVEL") === "DEBUG" ? true : false;
```

The first modification we add is a new PHP variable that is set to true if the value of the `OPENSHIFT_LAMPSTACK_LOGLEVEL` environment variable is `DEBUG`. If it has any other value, or is not set, the `$logDebug` variable will be `false`:

```php
$logfile = fopen($logdir."lampstacklog", 'a');

mysql_connect($dbhost, $dbuser, $dbpassword) or die(mysql_error());
if($logDebug) {fwrite($logfile, date("m/d/Y h:i:s a", time())." Connected to database.\n");}
```

[64]

The next modification, which we need to make to the source, will check if the value of the `$logDebug` variable is `true`. If it is, we will then print a message to indicate that a connection to the database was successfully established:

```
mysql_select_db($dbname) or die(mysql_error());
$result = mysql_query("SELECT * FROM users") or die(mysql_error());
if ($logDebug) {fwrite($logfile, date("m/d/Y h:i:s a", time())." Ran query SELECT * FROM users\n");}
```

The next modification we make is to only print the database query log message if the `$logDebug` variable is `true`:

```
echo "<table border cellpadding=3>";
echo "<tr><td>Username</td>";
echo "<td>Email Address</td></tr>";

while($currentRow = mysql_fetch_array( $result ))
{
  echo "<tr>";
  echo "<td>".$currentRow['username']."</td>";
  echo "<td>".$currentRow['email']."</td>";
  echo "</tr>";
}

echo "</table>";
if($logDebug) {fwrite($logfile, date("m/d/Y h:i:s a", time())." Returned results to browser\n");}
```

The next modification we make is to only print the log message indicating that results were returned to the browser if the `$logDebug` variable is `true`:

```
fclose($logfile);
```

Once you have made the previous changes and saved the source file, push your changes to the server using the following commands:

```
$ git commit -am "adding debug level log check"
$ git push
```

Once the changes have been deployed to your server, open up the logfile using the information you learned previously in this chapter with the following command:

```
$ rhc tail -f app-root/logs/lampstacklog
```

Try setting the environment variable to a different value and then refresh the `hellodb.php` file to ensure that information is not being logged. To do this, run the following commands:

```
$ rhc set-env OPENSHIFT_LAMPSTACK_LOGLEVEL=INFO -a lampstack
```

```
$ rhc app stop -a lampstack
$ rhc app start -a lampstack
```

The Apache process that serves PHP source code loads the system environment variables when the `httpd` server is started. When changing environment variables, you will need to stop and restart your application gear in order for Apache to pick up the new changes.

Summary

In this chapter, you learned some essential tools and commands that will help you maintain applications that you have deployed on the OpenShift platform. Specifically, you have learned key concepts such as how to stop and start applications, how to view logfiles (including ones that you create and write information to from your application code), how to back up and restore application snapshots, how to use SSH in order to connect to your application gears that are deployed to OpenShift Online, and learned about system environment variables and how to create and use them.

In the next chapter, we will take a break from the command line and application maintenance and dig a bit deeper into the application development aspect of the platform. We will focus on integrating OpenShift Online with integrated development environments.

4
Using an Integrated Development Environment

In this chapter, we are going to look at the software development aspects of the OpenShift platform by exploring how to use **integrated development environments (IDEs)** to interact with the OpenShift service. Developers are often passionate about their software development environment of choice and I can't possibly cover each environment in the scope of this chapter. However, we will be examining the most popular IDE in use by developers today, Eclipse. We will learn how to download, install, and configure the Eclipse IDE as well and how to install and configure the OpenShift Eclipse plugin that is provided as part of the JBoss Tools project. After we have our development environment configured, we will explore how to interact with the OpenShift platform from within the IDE in order to create, delete, and manage applications.

To use an IDE or not to use an IDE is the question

There are often two types of software developers today: those that benefit from using a full IDE and those that prefer a lightweight approach such at VI, EMACS, or Sublime Text. If you are expecting me to preach the merits of using a simple text editor for software development, you will be disappointed with the content of this chapter.

While I am a huge fan of using VI or Sublime Text for small single-page applications or to make a quick change to a file, I am convinced that using an IDE is the most productive way to work on large software projects. I equate using an IDE for development to using a hammer to drive nails. Sure, you could use a brick or some other blunt object with a nail, but a hammer was designed for the specific purpose of driving nails.

Likewise, IDEs are designed for one purpose: to make the life of a software developer more productive. This is accomplished by providing a tight integration with the language runtime, providing code insight, looking for compile errors as you write software, and even integrating with source code revision systems.

Another benefit of using an IDE, when working on software projects that you intend to deploy to the OpenShift platform, is the ability to have full control over all aspects of your application from the same environment that you use to write the code. The OpenShift IDE plugin allows you to create applications, view logfiles of your application, debug your application code, use port forwarding to connect to your remote databases, deploy code to the remote server, and many other features. By the end of this chapter, you will understand the convenience of having this tightly coupled integration with the Eclipse IDE.

Installing and configuring Eclipse

The Eclipse IDE is one of the most popular development environments in existence and is often the primary editor for Java developers. Over the years, the Eclipse platform has grown to support most programming languages including C++, PHP, and others. In fact, a lot of newer IDEs are based on the Eclipse source code because it has the reputation of being stable and performant as well as the ability to run on most operating systems including Windows, Linux, and Mac OSX.

Downloading and installing Eclipse

To get started with the Eclipse platform, we first need to download the software package. One of the great things about the Eclipse platform is that it is open source software and is therefore free to both download and use. For this chapter, we will be downloading the Kepler version of Eclipse from `http://www.eclipse.org/downloads/`.

> Even though I am showing the usage of the Kepler version of Eclipse, the newest version named Luna will also work with the same instructions.

Once the page has loaded in your browser, download the Eclipse IDE for Java EE Developers by selecting the correct version for your operating system, as shown in the following screenshot:

This will download a compressed archive of the Eclipse platform to your local filesystem. Once the download has completed, extract the contents of the archive using the correct command for your operating system. As an example, I am using the Linux operating system; the archive for that platform is a `.tar.gz` file. To extract the contents of the archive, I would open up a terminal prompt and change to the location of the downloaded file. Once I am in that directory, I would issue the following command:

```
$ tar zxvf eclipse-jee-kepler-SR1-linux-gtk-x86_64.tar.gz
```

Using an Integrated Development Environment

Once the contents have been extracted, the binary used to run the IDE is located inside the **eclipse** directory. For example, if you extracted the contents to the **Downloads** directory, you would see what is shown in the following screenshot:

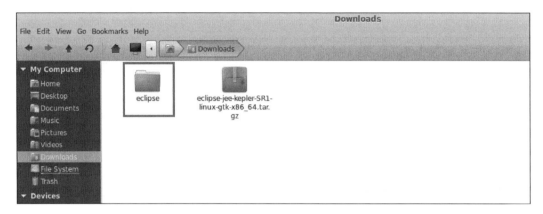

Open the **eclipse** directory and launch the environment by double-clicking on the Eclipse executable file, as follows:

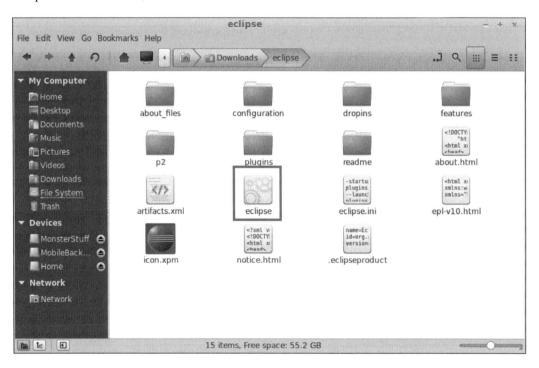

Chapter 4

The first thing the IDE will ask you is what workspace you would like to use. If you are not familiar with the concept of a workspace, don't worry as it's not that complicated. A workspace is simply a directory on your filesystem where Eclipse stores the settings and configurations that you are working with for the given workspace. If this is the first time you are using Eclipse, my advice is to use the default workspace that is provided by clicking on the **OK** button, as shown in the following screenshot:

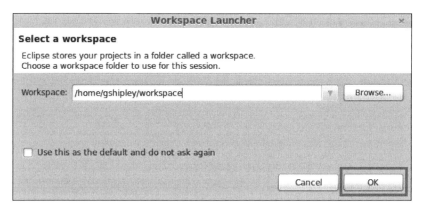

If the download and installation were successful, you should see the following welcome screen after selecting the default workspace:

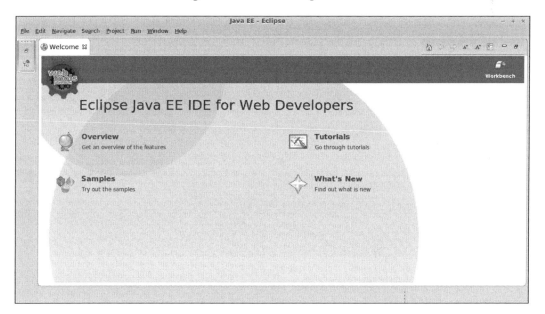

Downloading and installing the OpenShift plugin

Now that our Eclipse IDE is installed and running, the next thing we want to do is download and install the OpenShift plugin for the IDE. The OpenShift plugin is packaged as part of the JBoss Tools project that is provided by the JBoss team at Red Hat. In order to download, install, and use this plugin, open up your browser and go to `https://tools.jboss.org/downloads`.

> Alternatively, if you are familiar with the Eclipse Marketplace, you can simply search for JBoss Tools and install the plugin directly from within the IDE. This is probably the simplest way to get the plugin installed.

On this page, you will be able to download the correct package for the version of Eclipse that you have installed. Select the version of JBoss Tools that you would like to install and click on the **Download** button.

The team that works on JBoss Tools has made it extremely easy to install the plugin by simply dragging the install icon to your running Eclipse application. Move your mouse over the icon to view the instructions and then drag it to your Eclipse environment, as shown in the following screenshot:

The installation by dragging the **Install** icon may not work on some systems. If this is the case with your particular installation, you can manually install the package by clicking on **Help** and then on **Install New Software...** from within the Eclipse IDE, as shown in the following screenshot:

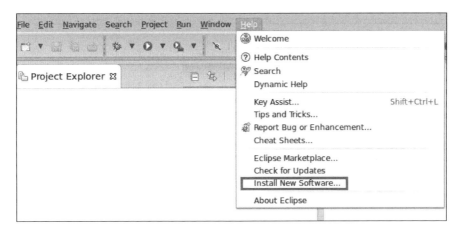

This will open up a dialog window that will allow you to add a new repository to install packages from. Click on the **Add** button and then name the repository `JBoss Tools` and provide `http://download.jboss.org/jbosstools/updates/stable/kepler/` for the location, as shown in the following screenshot:

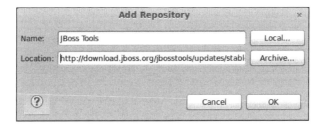

Once the new repository has been added, select all of the packages and then click on the **Next** button.

 Depending on the speed of your Internet connection, the installation may take a few minutes.

Once the installation of the plugin has completed, you will be prompted to restart the IDE.

Importing an existing OpenShift application

After the installation of the plugin has completed and you have restarted the IDE, the next step is to create a new project using the Eclipse IDE. In order to do this, navigate to **File** | **New** | **Other** and then expand the OpenShift selection, as shown in the following screenshot:

This will open up a new window where you can define a connection to the OpenShift Online service. This screen is fairly straightforward and only requires that you enter in the username and password combination that you used when creating your OpenShift account in *Chapter 1, Creating Your First OpenShift Application*.

Once you have authenticated to the OpenShift service and a new Eclipse connection has been defined, you will be presented with a dialog window that will allow you to either create a new application or to create an Eclipse-based project from an existing application. To showcase some of the capabilities of the Eclipse integration, let's choose to create a project from an existing application that we have already deployed to the OpenShift platform. In order to do this, select the checkbox next to **Use existing application** and then click on the **Browse** button. This will open up a dialog window that displays all the currently running applications that you have deployed on the OpenShift Cloud, as shown in the following screenshot:

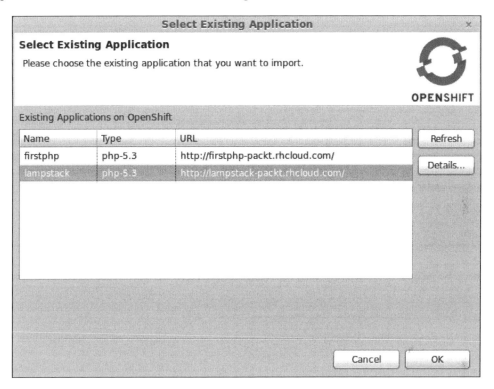

Using an Integrated Development Environment

Select the **lampstack** project that we created in *Chapter 2, Creating and Managing Applications*, as highlighted in the preceding screenshot, and click on the **OK** button. Once you click on this button, the dialog window will close and the previous window will be shown again. After clicking on the **Next** button, the plugin will allow you to define your project creation settings. Select the option of creating a new project and click on **Next**. Finally, you will be presented with a window where you need to define the location on disk where you want to create your Eclipse project files. Uncheck the box next to **Use default clone destination** and then click on the **Browse** button to specify the directory where you want your project source files to live, as shown in the following screenshot:

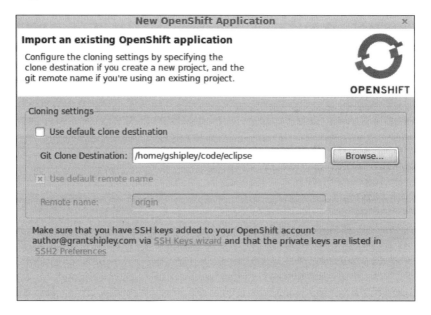

After clicking on the **Finish** button, the OpenShift plugin will create a new project using the existing source for the **lampstack** application. This is accomplished by cloning the remote Git repository that resides on your OpenShift gear and integrating the source code revision processes directly into the IDE. This will allow you to make changes and deploy your software code without having to leave the environment. This can be seen by expanding the **lampstack** folder under the **Project Explorer** view on the left-hand side of the screen. Note that the IDE displays the project's Git information next to the project's name to indicate which branch of the repository you are currently working with, as shown in the following screenshot:

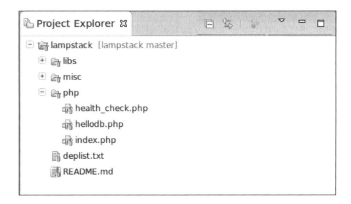

 To fully realize the power of the Eclipse IDE while working with PHP-based applications, you will need to download the Eclipse PDT plugin that offers native support for developing applications with the PHP language.

Creating and managing a new OpenShift application

Creating a new application is similar to the process that we have already explored; that is, using an existing OpenShift application. In order to see the full power of the OpenShift integration with Eclipse, we need to also explore how to create a new application. For this example, we are going to create a Java-based project while using the Tomcat server.

To create a new Java-based project, navigate to **File | New | Project**, and then select **OpenShift Application**. After authenticating to the OpenShift service, we will see the same dialog window that we saw previously, but this time we will want to select to create a new project called `JavaSample`. On the project creation dialog window, clicking on the **runtime** type field will display a list of all the available runtimes on the OpenShift platform. For this sample application, we will want to select **Tomcat 7 (JBoss EWS 2.0) (jbossews-2.0)** as shown in the following screenshot:

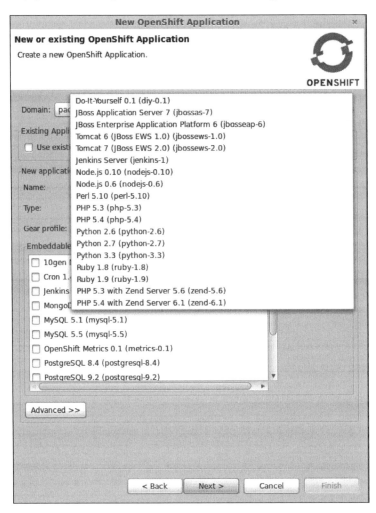

Chapter 4

The final two pieces of information that we want to define for our new application are the gear profile and any add-on cartridges that we want to add to our application. Select the **small** gear profile and the **MySQL 5.5 (mysql 5.5)** database for our application. After completing these steps, the dialog window should look similar to what's shown in the following screenshot:

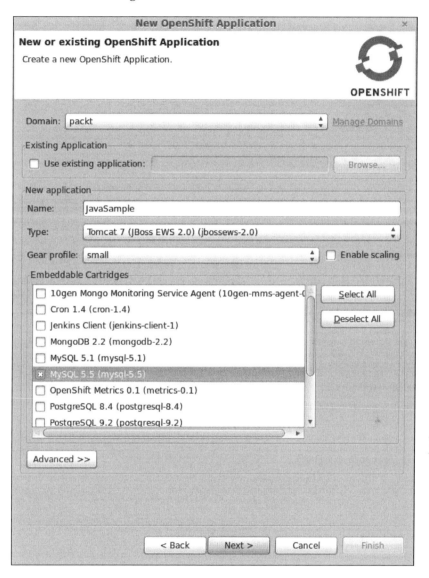

[79]

After defining your project options, follow the onscreen instructions to complete the project creation step. Once the project has been created, you will see two projects under the **Project Explorer** view on the left-hand side of the Eclipse IDE, as shown in the following screenshot:

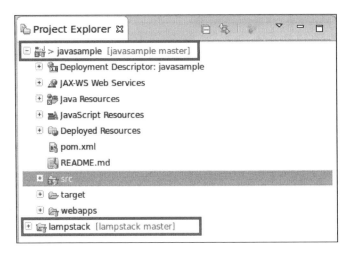

 The project creation process can take several minutes as it uses the Maven build system to compile the `JavaSample` application. This build process includes downloading several dependencies including the appropriate JAR files used to connect to and work with databases.

Deploying changes

One of the useful features of the JBoss Tools plugin, which provides OpenShift integration to the Eclipse IDE, is the ability to work on source code and then deploy those changes to the cloud without having to leave the familiar landscape of the IDE. To illustrate how this works, we are going to create a new JSP file that displays a message to the user. However, before we begin adding new software code, let's verify that our `JavaSample` application was compiled and deployed to the OpenShift platform during the project creation step.

Chapter 4

To verify that everything works correctly, we can use the internal web browser that is part of the Eclipse IDE by viewing our application inside of the OpenShift Explorer. To open this view, navigate to **Window** | **Show View** | **Other** and then select **OpenShift Explorer** under **JBoss Tools**, as shown in the following screenshot:

 You can also use the keyboard shortcut of *Cmd + 3* (OS X) or *Ctrl + 3* (Windows/Linux) and type `openshift`.

This will open up a new tab at the bottom of the screen that will display all of the applications that you have deployed to the OpenShift platform. Expand all of the applications and right-click on **JavaSample** and then select **Show in Web Browser**. This will open up the embedded web browser inside of Eclipse and point to the URL of your application.

[81]

Using an Integrated Development Environment

If the application was compiled and deployed successfully, you should see something similar to what's shown in the following screenshot inside the IDE:

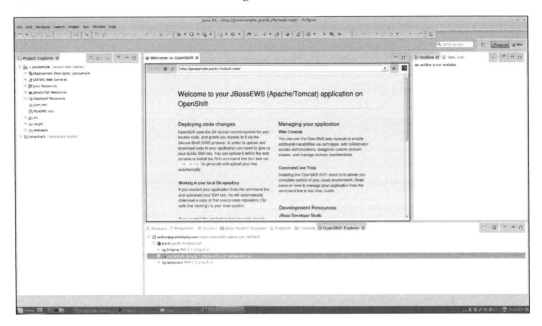

Now that we have verified that our application has been deployed correctly, let's create a new JSP file that will display a message to the user. Navigate to the **src | main | webapp** directory under the **Project Explorer** view and then right-click on the **webapp** directory. Once you right-click on this directory, you will be given the options to create a new JSP file, as shown in the following screenshot:

Name the new file `hello.jsp` and click on **Finish**. Once the file has been created, replace the contents with the following source code, which will greet the user and display the current system's date and time:

```
<%
out.println("Hello from Eclipse!");
out.println("The current date/time is " + new java.util.Date());
%>
```

Once the file has been saved, we need to perform three steps in order to deploy our changes to the OpenShift server:

1. Add our new file to the revision control system.
2. Commit our changes to the repository.
3. Push our changes to the remote upstream repository.

Luckily, the Git integration inside of Eclipse can tackle the first two steps at the same time. To add and commit our new file to the local repository, right-click on the **javasample** project under the **Project Explorer** view and then select **Team** and then finally choose **Commit**.

 You can also use the keyboard shortcut to commit changes to the Git repository using the *Ctrl* + *#* key combination.

This will open up a dialog window where we can input a message that will explain the changes that we are committing to the Git repository. Enter a commit message and then select the checkbox next to the **src/main/webapp/hello.jsp** file, as shown in the following screenshot, to indicate that this is the file we want to add and commit to the repository:

The last step is to push the changes we have made and committed to our local Git repository to the upstream OpenShift gear. You can do this by right-clicking on the **javasample** project and then selecting **Team** and finally **Push to Upstream**.

An alternative approach that is viewed by many as an easier way to commit and push changes to Git repositories is using the built-in **Git Staging** view that is part of the Eclipse IDE with OpenShift integration. To open this view, navigate to **Window | Show View | Other** and expand the **Git** folder to select the **Git Staging** view. This will open up a view at the bottom of the IDE that will allow you to drag unstaged changes to the staged area and then allow you to commit and push in one step. To try this out, make a small modification to the `hello.jsp` file and save the changes. For example:

```
out.println("Hello from Eclipse!");
```

The preceding line of code should be modified to read as follows:

```
out.println("Hello from OpenShift and Eclipse!");
```

Open up the **Git Staging** view and then drag the `hello.jsp` file to the **Staged Changed** box and enter a commit message. Lastly click on **Commit and Push** as shown in the following screenshot:

Viewing your application's logfiles

As we discussed previously, viewing the logfiles of your running application is an important tool in determining the current state of the application as well as a crucial tool in the debugging process when something is not working as expected. The OpenShift plugin for Eclipse provides the ability to view your application and server logfiles from right inside of the IDE. To view the logfiles for an application deployed on the OpenShift service, open up the **OpenShift Explorer** view and navigate to the application whose logfiles you want to view. Once you have located the application, you can simply right-click on it and then select to tail the files associated with it, as shown in the following screenshot:

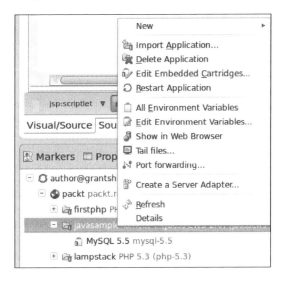

This will open up a dialog window that will allow you to specify any arguments that you want to pass to the remote tail command as well as allow you to specify what gears of the application you want to view. For most cases, using the defaults will provide the information that you are looking for when viewing the logfiles.

> Viewing logfiles for specific gears will be explained in *Chapter 12, Scaling Applications*, where we introduce the concept of automatic scaling of your application based upon the amount of web traffic your application receives. In short, the ability to view specific logs for a particular gear will allow you to isolate problems to a specific server while debugging application code.

Once you specify any arguments that you want to include, click on the **Finish** button to begin viewing the files. The contents of all the logfiles will be displayed in the **Console** tab at the bottom of the IDE, as shown in the following screenshot:

```
Markers  Properties  Servers  Data Source Explorer  Snippets  Console
javasample-packt.rhcloud.com [Tomcat 7 (JBoss EWS 2.0), MySQL 5.5 on gear #53016abce0b8cd13410004

==> jbossews/logs/catalina.out <==
Feb 16, 2014 10:02:04 PM org.apache.catalina.startup.Catalina start
INFO: Server startup in 32367 ms

==> jbossews/logs/localhost_access_log.2014-02-16.txt <==
127.12.250.1 - - [16/Feb/2014:22:02:18 -0500] "GET /hello.jsp HTTP/1.1" 200 74
127.12.250.1 - - [16/Feb/2014:22:11:06 -0500] "HEAD / HTTP/1.1" 200 -
127.12.250.1 - - [16/Feb/2014:22:11:06 -0500] "HEAD / HTTP/1.1" 200 -
```

Embedding add-on cartridges

As we discussed in *Chapter 2, Creating and Managing Applications*, embedding and using cartridges is an integral part of the application development and deployment process. Previously, we learned how to embed cartridges using the RHC command-line tools. Embedding add-on cartridges is also available from within the Eclipse IDE. If you recall, when we created the `JavaSample` application earlier in this chapter, we specified that the MySQL database cartridge should be included as part of the application creation process. We will now use the Eclipse IDE to add both the **Cron** and **phpMyAdmin** cartridges to our application.

To accomplish this task, right-click on your application from within the **OpenShift Explorer** view and select **Edit Embedded Cartridges...** as shown in the following screenshot:

Chapter 4

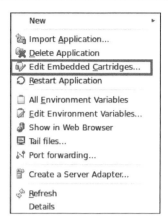

This will open up a dialog window that will display all of the available add-on cartridges that are applicable to your application. Select the **Cron 1.4 (cron-1.4)** and **phpMyAdmin 4.0 (phpmyadmin-4)** cartridges and click on **Finish**, as shown in the following screenshot:

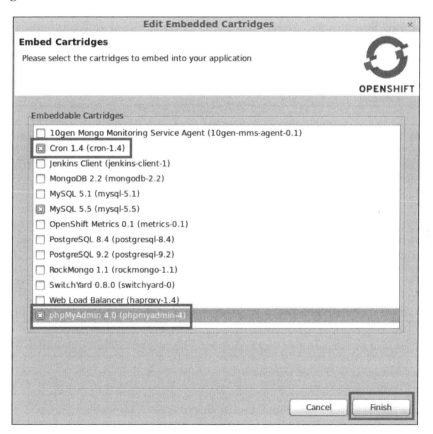

Once the **Cron** and **phpMyAdmin** cartridges have been added to your application, any authentication information needed for the newly added cartridges will be displayed on a dialog window that opens.

You can verify that the cartridges were successfully added by expanding your application in the **OpenShift Explorer** view where all of the cartridges that your application is consuming are displayed.

Viewing your application's environment variables

In *Chapter 3, Application Maintenance*, we discussed using environment variables as well as how to create your own environment variable. As part of that chapter, we created a new environment variable for our `lampstack` application called `OPENSHIFT_LAMPSTACK_LOGLEVEL`. We then used the value of that variable to determine the type of log output that we write to a custom logfile. The OpenShift plugin for Eclipse allows us to view and edit custom environment variables as well as the ability to view all system-level environment variables for our application. To demonstrate this, let's view the custom environment variable that we created in *Chapter 3, Application Maintenance*, using the Eclipse IDE instead of the RHC command-line tools. To do this, right-click on the **lampstack** application in the **OpenShift Explorer** view and then select **Edit Environment Variables**. This will open up a dialog window that will display any custom variables we have defined as well as the current value that is set for the variable. The following screenshot shows this in action:

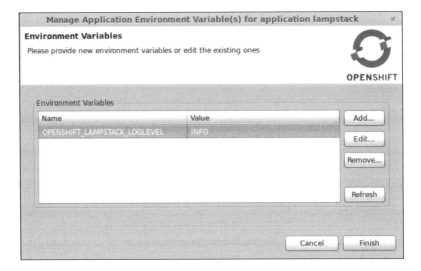

Using this dialog window, change the value of the **OPENSHIFT_LAMPSTACK_LOGLEVEL** variable by highlighting the variable and changing the value to **DEBUG**. Once you've changed the value, click on **Finish** to save your changes. Verify that the changes were deployed to your remote running application by either viewing the `hellodb.php` file from *Chapter 3*, *Application Maintenance*, or by viewing the environment variables again from inside of Eclipse.

Viewing the details of an application

In *Chapter 2*, *Creating and Managing Applications*, we explored how to use the `rhc app show` command to display all of the details for an application. For example, to view the details of the `lampstack` application using the RHC command-line tools, we would issue the following command at a terminal prompt:

```
$ rhc app show lampstack
```

As with most of the RHC command-line tools, there is an equivalent included as part of the OpenShift Eclipse plugin. To view the details of an application, right-click on the application name under the **OpenShift Explorer** view and select **Details**. This will open up a new window that displays the following information:

- The name of the application
- The public URL of the application that can be used to view the application inside of a web browser
- The type of runtime that is associated with the application, for example, PHP, JBoss EAP, and so on
- The date the application was first created and deployed to the OpenShift platform
- The user ID of the gear that your application code is deployed on
- The Git URL for the remote repository that resides on the OpenShift gear
- The connection information that allows you to connect to the remote OpenShift gear using the SSH protocol
- All add-on cartridges that are embedded in your application

Deleting an application

Previously in this chapter, we created an application called `JavaSample`. Since we will not be using this application in the future, we can safely remove it from the OpenShift service in order to free up resources in our account. To delete this application from inside of Eclipse, right-click on the application's name from within the **OpenShift Explorer** view and select **Delete Application**. The OpenShift plugin will display a dialog box asking you to confirm the operation since a delete operation cannot be reversed, as shown in the following screenshot:

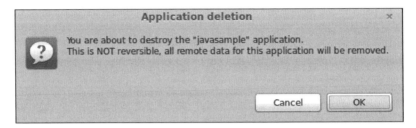

To verify that your application has been deleted, refresh the **OpenShift Explorer** view to ensure that the `JavaSample` application is no longer listed.

 To refresh the view, right-click on your account name and select **Refresh**.

You are probably wondering why the source code for the application we just deleted is still showing in the **Project Explorer** view. This is because when deleting an application, it only deletes the remote gear that your application has been deployed to, while leaving the local copy of your application's source code and repository intact. To fully delete the application and any source code on your local filesystem, you will need to also delete the Eclipse project associated with the application. To do this, right-click on your project and select the option of deleting it.

Integrating OpenShift with other IDEs

What happens if your preferred IDE is not Eclipse? I am happy to report that because of the popularity of the OpenShift platform, integration is also available for the majority of the popular IDEs in use by developers today. While the actual implementation of the OpenShift service may differ slightly in each IDE, the concepts are the same. Some of the popular integrations that I have used in the past are available for the following environments:

- JetBrains IntelliJ IDEA
- Zend Studio
- Appcelerator Titanium Studio
- Code Envy
- Cloud 9

Summary

In this chapter, we learned how to install and configure the popular Eclipse IDE in order to work with the OpenShift platform. Once we had our development environment installed and properly configured, we learned how to import existing applications as well as how to create new applications from within the Eclipse IDE. Next, we learned the essential workflow steps for creating, managing, and deploying applications with OpenShift while using Eclipse. This included how to add, commit, and deploy code changes to the OpenShift server. Lastly, we learned how to embed cartridges, view logfiles, and how to use environment variables with our application.

In the next chapter, we will learn how to use the OpenShift Online service to create and deploy Java EE applications using the JBoss Enterprise Application Platform application server.

5
Creating and Deploying Java EE Applications

In this chapter, we are going to learn how to use OpenShift in order to create and deploy Java-EE-based applications using the JBoss **Enterprise Application Platform (EAP)** application server. To illustrate and learn the concepts of Java EE, we are going to create an application that displays an interactive map that contains all of the major league baseball parks in the United States. We will start by covering some background information on the Java EE framework and then introduce each part of the sample application. The process for learning how to create the sample application, named `mlbparks`, will be started by creating the JBoss EAP container, then adding a database, creating the web services, and lastly, creating the responsive map UI.

The evolution of Java EE

I can't think of a single programming language other than Java that has so many fans while at the same time has a large community of developers that profess their hatred towards it. The bad reputation that Java has can largely be attributed to early promises made by the community when the language was first released and then not being able to fulfill these promises. Developers were told that we would be able to write once and run anywhere, but we quickly found out that this meant that we could write once and then debug on every platform. Java was also perceived to consume more memory than required and was accused of being overly verbose by relying heavily on XML configuration files.

Another problem the language had was not being able to focus on and excel at one particular task. We used Java to create thick client applications, applets that could be downloaded via a web browser, embedded applications, web applications, and so on. Having Java available as a tool that completes most projects was a great thing, but the implementation for each project was often confusing. For example, let's examine the history of GUI development using the Java programming language. When the language was first introduced, it included an API called the **Abstract Window Toolkit** (**AWT**) that was essentially a Java wrapper around native UI components supplied by the operating system. When Java 1.2 was released, the AWT implementation was deprecated in favor of the Swing API that contained GUI elements written in 100 percent Java. By this time, a lot of developers were quickly growing frustrated with the available APIs and to further complicate the frustration, yet another new toolkit called the **Standard Widget Toolkit** (**SWT**) was developed.

SWT was developed by IBM and is the Windowing toolkit in use by the Eclipse IDE. It is considered by most to be the superior toolkit when creating applications with a graphical user interface.

Another reason why developers began switching from Java to more attractive programming languages was the implementation of **Enterprise JavaBeans** (**EJB**). The first Java EE release occurred in December, 1999, and the Java community is just now beginning to recover from the complexity introduced by the language in order to create applications. If you were able to escape creating applications using early EJBs, consider yourself lucky, as many of your fellow developers were consumed by implementing large-scale systems using this new technology. It wasn't fun; trust me. I was there and experienced it firsthand.

When developers began abandoning Java EE, they seemed to go in one of two directions. Developers who understood that the Java language itself was quite beautiful adopted the Spring Framework methodology of having enterprise grade features while sticking with a **Plain Old Java Object** (**POJO**) implementation. Other developers were wooed away by languages that were considered more modern, such as Ruby and the popular Rails framework. While the rise in popularity of both Ruby and Spring was happening, the team behind Java EE continued to improve and innovate, which resulted in the creation of a new implementation that is both easy to use and a pleasure to develop with.

I am happy to report that if you haven't taken a look at Java EE in the last few years, now is the time to do so. Working with the language after a long hiatus has been a rewarding and pleasurable experience. By the end of this chapter, you will have the skills and knowledge to see past the legacy of Java and realize that it is an exciting and refreshing language to use to create both simple and enterprise class applications.

Introducing the sample application

For the remainder of this chapter, we are going to develop an application called mlbparks that displays a map of the United States with a pin on the map representing the location of each major league baseball stadium. The requirements for the application are as follows:

- A single map that a user can zoom in and out of
- As the user moves the map around, the map must be updated with all baseball stadiums that are located in the shown area
- The location of the stadiums must be searchable based on map coordinates that are passed to the REST-based API
- The data should be transferred in the JSON format
- The web application must be responsive so that it is displayed correctly regardless of the resolution of the browser
- When a stadium is listed on the map, the user should be able to click on the stadium to view details about the associated team

The end state application will look like the following screenshot:

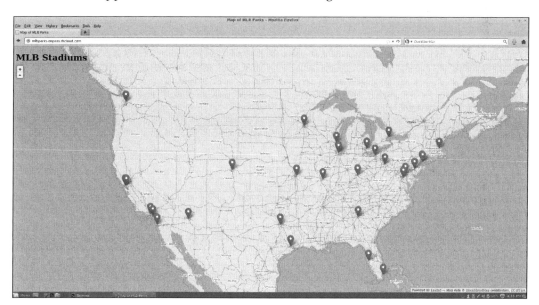

The user will also be able to zoom in on a specific location by double-clicking on the map or by clicking on the **+** zoom button in the top-left corner of the application. For example, if a user zooms the map in to the Phoenix, Arizona area of the United States, they will be able to see the information for the Arizona Diamondbacks stadium as shown in the following screenshot:

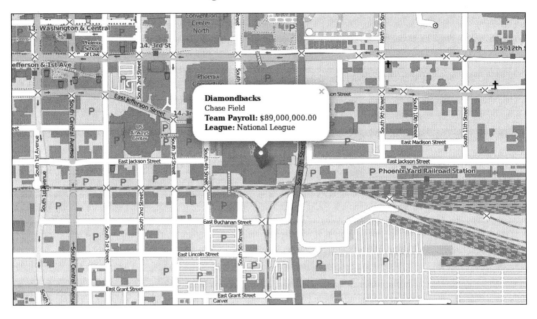

To view this sample application running live, open your browser and type `http://mlbparks-packt.rhcloud.com`.

Now that we have our requirements and know what the end result should look like, let's start creating our application.

Creating a JBoss EAP application

For the sample application that we are going to develop as part of this chapter, we are going to take advantage of the JBoss EAP application server that is available on the OpenShift platform.

> The JBoss EAP application server is a fully tested, stable, and supported platform for deploying mission-critical applications. Some developers prefer to use the open source community application server from JBoss called WildFly. Keep in mind when choosing WildFly over EAP that it only comes with community-based support and is a bleeding edge application server.

To get started with building the `mlbparks` application, the first thing we need to do is create a gear that contains the cartridge for our JBoss EAP runtime. For this, we are going to use the RHC tools, which we learned about in *Chapter 2, Creating and Managing Applications*. Open up your terminal application and enter in the following command:

```
$ rhc app create mlbparks jbosseap-6
```

Once the previous command is executed, you should see the following output:

```
Application Options
-------------------
Domain:     yourDomainName
Cartridges: jbosseap-6 (addtl. costs may apply)
Gear Size:  default
Scaling:    no


Creating application 'mlbparks' ... done
Waiting for your DNS name to be available ... done
Cloning into 'mlbparks'...
Your application 'mlbparks' is now available.
  URL:         http://mlbparks-yourDomainName.rhcloud.com/
  SSH to:      5311180f500446f54a0003bb@mlbparks-yourDomainName.rhcloud.com
  Git remote:  ssh://5311180f500446f54a0003bb@mlbparks-yourDomainName.rhcloud.com/~/git/mlbparks.git/
  Cloned to:   /home/gshipley/code/mlbparks


Run 'rhc show-app mlbparks' for more details about your app.
```

> If you have a paid subscription to OpenShift Online, you might want to consider using a medium- or large-size gear to host your Java-EE-based applications. To create this application using a medium-size gear, use the following command:
>
> ```
> $ rhc app create mlbparks jbosseap-6 -g medium
> ```

Adding database support to the application

Now that our application gear has been created, the next thing we want to do is embed a database cartridge that will hold the information about the baseball stadiums we want to map. Given that we are going to develop an application that doesn't require referential integrity but provides a REST-based API that will return JSON, it makes sense to use MongoDB as our database.

 MongoDB is arguably the most popular NoSQL database available today. The company behind the database, MongoDB, offers paid subscriptions and support plans for production deployments. For more information on this popular NoSQL database, visit www.mongodb.com.

As we learned in *Chapter 2, Creating and Managing Applications*, run the following command to embed a database into our existing `mlbparks` OpenShift gear:

```
$ rhc cartridge add mongodb-2.4 -a mlbparks
```

Once the preceding command is executed and the database has been added to your application, you will see the following information on the screen that contains the username and password for the database:

```
Adding mongodb-2.4 to application 'mlbparks' ... done


mongodb-2.4 (MongoDB 2.4)
-------------------------
  Gears:           Located with jbosseap-6
  Connection URL:  mongodb://$OPENSHIFT_MONGODB_DB_HOST:$OPENSHIFT_MONGODB_DB_PORT/
  Database Name:   mlbparks
  Password:        q_6eZ22-fraN
  Username:        admin
MongoDB 2.4 database added.  Please make note of these credentials:
  Root User:      admin
  Root Password:  yourPassword
  Database Name:  mlbparks
Connection URL: mongodb://$OPENSHIFT_MONGODB_DB_HOST:$OPENSHIFT_MONGODB_DB_PORT/
```

Importing the MLB stadiums into the database

Now that we have our application gear created and our database added, we need to populate the database with the information about the stadiums that we are going to place on the map. The data is provided as a JSON document and contains the following information:

- The name of the baseball team
- The total payroll for the team
- The location of the stadium represented with the longitude and latitude
- The name of the stadium
- The name of the city where the stadium is located
- The league the baseball club belongs to (National or American)
- The year the data is relevant for
- All of the players on the roster including their position and salary

A sample for the Arizona Diamondbacks looks like the following line of code:

```
{ "name":"Diamondbacks", "payroll":89000000, "coordinates":[ -112.066662, 33.444799 ], "ballpark":"Chase Field", "city":"Phoenix", "league":"National League", "year":"2013", "players":[ { "name":"Miguel Montero", "position":"Catcher", "salary":10000000 }, ............ ]}
```

In order to import the preceding data, we are going to use the `SSH` command, which we learned in *Chapter 3, Application Maintenance*. To get started with the import, `SSH` into your OpenShift gear for the `mlbparks` application by issuing the following command in your terminal prompt:

```
$ rhc app ssh mlbparks
```

Once we are connected to the remote gear, we need to download the JSON file and store it in the `/tmp` directory of our gear. To complete these steps, use the following commands on your remote gear:

```
$ cd /tmp
$ wget https://raw.github.com/gshipley/mlbparks/master/mlbparks.json
```

> Wget is a software package that is available on most Linux-based operating systems in order to retrieve files using HTTP, HTTPS, or FTP.

Once the file has completed downloading, take a quick look at the contents using your favorite text editor in order to get familiar with the structure of the document. When you are comfortable with the data that we are going to import into the database, execute the following command on the remote gear to populate MongoDB with the JSON documents:

```
$ mongoimport --jsonArray -d $OPENSHIFT_APP_NAME -c teams --type
json --file /tmp/mlbparks.json  -h $OPENSHIFT_MONGODB_DB_HOST --port
$OPENSHIFT_MONGODB_DB_PORT -u $OPENSHIFT_MONGODB_DB_USERNAME -p
$OPENSHIFT_MONGODB_DB_PASSWORD
```

If the command was executed successfully, you should see the following output on the screen:

```
connected to: 127.7.150.130:27017
Fri Feb 28 20:57:24.125 check 9 30
Fri Feb 28 20:57:24.126 imported 30 objects
```

What just happened? To understand this, we need to break the command we issued into smaller chunks, as detailed in the following table:

Command / argument	Description
`mongoimport`	This command is provided by MongoDB to allow users to import data into a database.
`--jsonArray`	This specifies that we are going to import an array of JSON documents.
`-d $OPENSHIFT_APP_NAME`	Specifies the database that we are going to import the data into. If you recall from *Chapter 3, Application Maintenance*, we are using a system environment variable to use the database that was created by default when we embedded the database cartridge in our application.
`-c teams`	This defines the collection to which we want to import the data. If the collection does not exist, it will be created.
`--type json`	This specifies the type of file we are going to to import.

Command / argument	Description
`--file /tmp/mlbparks.json`	This specifies the full path and name of the file that we are going to import into the database.
`-h $OPENSHIFT_MONGODB_DB_HOST`	This specifies the host of the MongoDB server.
`--port $OPENSHIFT_MONGODB_DB_PORT`	This specifies the port of the MongoDB server.
`-u $OPENSHIFT_MONGODB_DB_USERNAME`	This specifies the username to be used for authenticating to the database.
`-p $OPENSHIFT_MONGODB_DB_PASSWORD`	This specifies the password to be used for authenticating to the database.

To verify the data was loaded properly, you can use the following command that will print out the number of documents in the `teams` collection of the `mlbparks` database:

```
$ mongo -quiet $OPENSHIFT_MONGODB_DB_HOST:$OPENSHIFT_MONGODB_DB_PORT/$OPENSHIFT_APP_NAME -u $OPENSHIFT_MONGODB_DB_USERNAME -p $OPENSHIFT_MONGODB_DB_PASSWORD --eval "db.teams.count()"
```

The result should be **30**.

Lastly, we need to create a `2d` index on the `teams` collection to ensure that we can perform spatial queries on the data.

Geospatial queries are what allow us to search for specific documents that fall within a given location as provided by the latitude and longitude parameters.

To add the `2d` index to the `teams` collection, enter the following command on the remote gear:

```
$ mongo
$OPENSHIFT_MONGODB_DB_HOST:$OPENSHIFT_MONGODB_DB_PORT/$OPENSHIFT_APP_NAME
--eval 'db.teams.ensureIndex( { coordinates : "2d" } );'
```

Creating and Deploying Java EE Applications

Adding database support to our Java application

The next step in creating the `mlbparks` application is adding the MongoDB driver dependency to our application. OpenShift Online supports the popular Apache Maven build system as the default way of compiling the Java source code and resolving dependencies.

> Maven was originally created to simplify the build process by allowing developers to specify specific JARs that their application depends on. This alleviates the bad practice of checking JAR files into the source code repository and allows a way to share JARs across several projects. This is accomplished via a `pom.xml` file that contains configuration items and dependency information for the project.

In order to add the dependency for the MongoDB client to our `mlbparks` applications, we need to modify the `pom.xml` file that is in the root directory of the Git repository. The Git repository was cloned to our local machine during the application's creation step that we performed earlier in this chapter. Open up your favorite text editor and modify the `pom.xml` file to include the following lines of code in the `<dependencies>` block:

```
<dependency>
  <groupId>org.mongodb</groupId>
  <artifactId>mongo-java-driver</artifactId>
  <version>2.9.1</version>
</dependency>
```

Once you have added the dependency, commit the changes to your local repository by using the following command:

```
$ git commit -am "added MongoDB dependency"
```

Finally, let's push the change to our Java application to include the MongoDB database drivers using the `git push` command:

```
$ git push
```

> The first time the Maven build system builds the application, it downloads all the dependencies for the application and then caches them. Because of this, the first build will always take a bit longer than any subsequent build.

[102]

Creating the database access class

At this point, we have our application created, the MongoDB database embedded, all the information for the baseball stadiums imported, and the dependency for our database driver added to our application. The next step is to do some actual coding by creating a Java class that will act as the interface for connecting to and communicating with the MongoDB database. Create a Java file named `DBConnection.java` in the `mlbparks/src/main/java/org/openshift/mlbparks/mongo` directory and add the following source code:

```java
package org.openshift.mlbparks.mongo;

import java.net.UnknownHostException;
import javax.annotation.PostConstruct;
import javax.enterprise.context.ApplicationScoped;
import javax.inject.Named;
import com.mongodb.DB;
import com.mongodb.Mongo;

@Named
@ApplicationScoped
public class DBConnection {
  private DB mongoDB;
  public DBConnection() {
    super();
  }
  @PostConstruct
  public void afterCreate() {
    String mongoHost = System.getenv("OPENSHIFT_MONGODB_DB_HOST");
    String mongoPort = System.getenv("OPENSHIFT_MONGODB_DB_PORT");
    String mongoUser = System.getenv("OPENSHIFT_MONGODB_DB_USERNAME");
    String mongoPassword = System.getenv("OPENSHIFT_MONGODB_DB_PASSWORD");
    String mongoDBName = System.getenv("OPENSHIFT_APP_NAME");
    int port = Integer.decode(mongoPort);

    Mongo mongo = null;
    try {
      mongo = new Mongo(mongoHost, port);
    } catch (UnknownHostException e) {
      System.out.println("Couldn't connect to MongoDB: " + e.getMessage() + " :: " + e.getClass());
```

```
        }

        mongoDB = mongo.getDB(mongoDBName);
        if (mongoDB.authenticate(mongoUser, mongoPassword.toCharArray())
 == false) {
            System.out.println("Failed to authenticate DB ");
        }
    }
    public DB getDB() {
        return mongoDB;
    }
}
```

The preceding source code as well as all source code for this chapter is available on GitHub at `https://github.com/gshipley/mlbparks`.

The preceding code snippet simply creates an application-scoped bean that is available until the application is shut down.

The `@ApplicationScoped` annotation is used when creating application-wide data or constants that should be available to all the users of the application. We chose this scope because we want to maintain a single connection class for the database that is shared among all requests.

The next bit of interesting code is the `afterCreate` method that authenticates to the database using the system environment variables that we discussed in *Chapter 3, Application Maintenance*.

Once you have created the `DBConnection.java` file and added the preceding source code, add the file to your local repository and commit the changes as follows:

```
$ git add .
$ git commit -am "Adding database connection class"
```

Creating the beans.xml file

The `DBConnection` class we just created makes use of CDI for dependency injection.

CDI stands for Context Dependency Injection and is part of the official Java EE specification.

According to the official specification for CDI, an application that uses CDI must have a file called `beans.xml`. The file must be present and located under the `WEB-INF` directory. Given this requirement, create a file named `beans.xml` under the `mlbparks/src/main/webapp/WEB-INF` directory and add the following lines of code:

```xml
<?xml version="1.0"?>
<beans xmlns="http://java.sun.com/xml/ns/javaee" xmlns:xsi="http://www.w3.org/2001/XMLSchema-instance" xsi:schemaLocation="http://java.sun.com/xml/ns/javaee http://jboss.org/schema/cdi/beans_1_0.xsd"/>
```

After you have added the `beans.xml` file, add and commit it to your local Git repository:

```
$ git add .
$ git commit -am "Adding beans.xml for CDI"
```

Creating the domain model

The next step is to create our model class that will hold information on a specific baseball park. This model object is a POJO that is defined to contain the team name, position (the longitude and latitude), ballpark name, team payroll, and the league the team belongs to. Create a Java file named `MLBPark.java` under the `mlbparks/src/main/java/org/openshift/mlbparks/domain` directory and add the following source code:

```java
package org.openshift.mlbparks.domain;

public class MLBPark {
    private Object name;
    private Object position;
    private Object id;
    private Object ballpark;
    private Object payroll;
    private Object league;

    public Object getName() {
        return name;
    }
    public void setName(Object name) {
        this.name = name;
    }
    public Object getPosition() {
        return position;
```

```
    }
    public void setPosition(Object position) {
        this.position = position;
    }

}
```

 In the preceding code snippet, I have omitted the getters and setters for most of the variables. When creating your source file, make sure that you include a getter and setter for each variable in order to ensure that your application works correctly. Again, the complete source code for this application can viewed at https://github.com/gshipley/mlbparks.

Once you have created the `MLBPark.java` file and added the preceding listed source code, add the file to your local repository and commit the changes:

```
$ git add .
$ git commit -am "Adding MLBParks model object"
```

Creating the REST services

The application that we are developing will provide data to the user interface by providing a set of web services that will allow the code to make a request for all available baseball parks as well as the ability to query for stadiums within a given set of longitude and latitude parameters. We will be using the popular **Java API for RESTful Web Services (JAX-RS)** to provide this functionality. To get started with defining our available service, create a file named `JaxrsConfig.java` under the `mlbparks/src/main/java/org/openshift/mlbparks/rest` directory and add the following code snippet:

```
package org.openshift.mlbparks.rest;

import javax.ws.rs.ApplicationPath;
import javax.ws.rs.core.Application;

@ApplicationPath("/ws")
public class JaxrsConfig extends Application{
}
```

The preceding code snippet defines the URL path that clients will use to communicate with our REST web services. The definition occurs on the `@ApplicationPath("/ws")` line.

Considering the preceding line of explanation, the entry point for our REST services will be http://mlbparks-yourNameSpace.rhcloud.com/ws.

Now that we have our application path defined, we can begin to build the web services for our application. Create a file named MLBParkResource.java under the mlbparks/src/main/java/org/openshift/mlbparks/rest directory and add the following code snippet:

```
package org.openshift.mlbparks.rest;

import java.util.ArrayList;
import java.util.List;
import javax.enterprise.context.RequestScoped;
import javax.inject.Inject;
import javax.ws.rs.GET;
import javax.ws.rs.Path;
import javax.ws.rs.Produces;
import javax.ws.rs.QueryParam;
import org.openshift.mlbparks.domain.MLBPark;
import org.openshift.mlbparks.mongo.DBConnection;

import com.mongodb.BasicDBObject;
import com.mongodb.DB;
import com.mongodb.DBCollection;
import com.mongodb.DBCursor;
import com.mongodb.DBObject;
```

The preceding code snippet defines the package of the Java class as well as lists all the imports that are required for the class to function properly.

After you have added the package and import statements, we can begin building our class by defining the actual class as well as defining the database connection. Add the following code snippet directly after the last import statement in your source file:

```
@RequestScoped
@Path("/parks")
public class MLBParkResource {
   @Inject
   private DBConnection dbConnection;
```

The preceding code snippet creates a request-scoped bean with a default URL path of parks. It then defines a DBConnection variable that will be injected with an instance using CDI by leveraging the DBConnection class that we created previously in this chapter.

Next, we want to add two helper methods to our `MLBParkResource` class. We will use these to get our database collection as well as a method for populating the `MLBPark` model object. Add the following source code to the class directly after the definition of the `DBConnection` variable:

```
private DBCollection getMLBParksCollection() {
  DB db = dbConnection.getDB();
  DBCollection parkListCollection = db.getCollection("teams");
  return parkListCollection;
}

private MLBPark populateParkInformation(DBObject dataValue) {
  MLBPark thePark = new MLBPark();
  thePark.setName(dataValue.get("name"));
  thePark.setPosition(dataValue.get("coordinates"));
  thePark.setId(dataValue.get("_id").toString());
  thePark.setBallpark(dataValue.get("ballpark"));
  thePark.setLeague(dataValue.get("league"));
  thePark.setPayroll(dataValue.get("payroll"));

  return thePark;
}
```

Finally, we get to create our first actual web service using JAX-RS. The first service we are going to create will return all of the available baseball stadiums in the database. To add this method, modify your source code to include a `getMLBParksCollection()` method, as shown in the following source code:

```
@GET()
@Produces("application/json")
public List<MLBPark> getAllParks() {
  ArrayList<MLBPark> allParksList = new ArrayList<MLBPark>();

  DBCollection mlbParks = this.getMLBParksCollection();
  DBCursor cursor = mlbParks.find();
  try {
    while (cursor.hasNext()) {
      allParksList.add(this.populateParkInformation(cursor.next()));
    }
  }
  finally {
    cursor.close();
  }
  return allParksList;
}
```

Chapter 5

The preceding method states that it will accept GET requests (the @GET annotation) and will return data in the JSON format (the @Produces annotation). The body of the method gets the database collection where the park information is stored, and then performs a find() query to retrieve all of the stadiums. The code then iterates over each result and populates an MLBPark model object with the data provided by the query. Once all of the results have been parsed, the results are returned by the method in the JSON format.

The last method we need to add to our class is the findParksWithin() method that will allow the requester to pass in coordinates that we need to search for baseball stadiums that fall within the provided locations:

```
@GET
@Produces("application/json")
@Path("within")
public List<MLBPark> findParksWithin(@QueryParam("lat1") float lat1,
@QueryParam("lon1") float lon1, @QueryParam("lat2") float lat2,
@QueryParam("lon2") float lon2) {

  ArrayList<MLBPark> allParksList = new ArrayList<MLBPark>();
  DBCollection mlbParks = this.getMLBParksCollection();

  // make the query object
  BasicDBObject spatialQuery = new BasicDBObject();
  ArrayList<double[]> boxList = new ArrayList<double[]>();
  boxList.add(new double[] { new Float(lon2), new Float(lat2) });
  boxList.add(new double[] { new Float(lon1), new Float(lat1) });

  BasicDBObject boxQuery = new BasicDBObject();
  boxQuery.put("$box", boxList);

  spatialQuery.put("coordinates", new BasicDBObject("$within", boxQuery));
  System.out.println("Using spatial query: " + spatialQuery.toString());

  DBCursor cursor = mlbParks.find(spatialQuery);
  try {
    while (cursor.hasNext()) {
      allParksList.add(this.populateParkInformation(cursor.next()));
    }
  }
```

```
    finally {
      cursor.close();
    }

    return allParksList;
  }
```

Lastly, we need to add a closing curly brace to end our class:

```
}
```

Once you have performed these code changes, add the source file and commit your changes to your local repository:

```
$ git add .
$ git commit -am "Adding REST web services"
```

Verifying the REST web services

At this point, we should have everything created and committed to our local repository and should be ready to deploy the REST services to our running OpenShift gear. To ensure that you have all of the changes committed to your local repository, change the root directory of the application and issue the following command:

```
$ git status
```

Make sure that you do not have any untracked changes on your local filesystem. If you do have untracked changes, add the files and commit the changes.

Guess what? We are finally ready to deploy the application and test the web services that we created. To deploy your `mlbparks` application to your OpenShift gear, enter the following command:

```
$ git push
```

The `git push` command might take a few minutes to complete as Maven needs to download all the dependencies that are specified in the `pom.xml` file. This only happens the first time a build is performed or if new dependencies are added that are not available in the cache.

Once the application has been deployed, open your favorite web browser and point to `http://mlbparks-yourDomainName.rhcloud.com/ws/parks`.

If the application is successfully deployed, you should see a listing of all baseball stadiums and teams as depicted in the following screenshot:

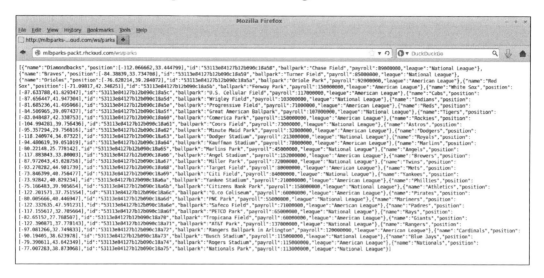

Creating the user interface

The final piece of our application involves creating a user interface that interacts with the web services that we have developed previously in this chapter, and then presents the information to the user in a cohesive and usable manner. Developing the user-facing parts of an application is where the real joy of programming is for me. I love being able to take all of the backend services and data and then present the results in a new and fascinating way. For this example, we are going to create a web-based frontend, but given that the application services we developed previously in this chapter are accessible via HTTP requests, the possibilities are limitless as to how you can present the information to the user. If you have experience developing mobile or thick client applications, I suggest that you develop a frontend using these mediums as well.

As you can recall, the requirements for the application state that the application should display a map of the United States with a pin on the map representing the location of each major league baseball stadium. The user should be able to zoom in and out on the map, and the map should automatically update the baseball stadiums based on the visible area on the users' screen. When the user clicks on a stadium, the information about the team should be displayed to the user. To fully understand how to develop the frontend portion of the application, we are going to satisfy each requirement in small increments and slowly build upon each step to fully develop the frontend application.

Creating the map using Leaflet and OpenStreetMap

In order to create the map for our application, we are going to use two projects: Leaflet and OpenStreetMap.

The description provided on the official project page for Leaflet superbly describes the features and benefits of the project. The official page (http://leafletjs.com/) states that Leaflet is a modern open source JavaScript library for mobile-friendly, interactive maps. Vladimir Agafonkin and a team of dedicated contributors developed it. Weighing in at just about 33 KB of JavaScript, it has all the features most developers will ever need for online maps.

Leaflet is designed with simplicity, performance, and usability in mind. It works efficiently across all major desktop and mobile platforms out of the box, taking advantage of HTML5 and CSS3 on modern browsers while still being accessible on older ones. It can be extended with a huge amount of plugins, has a beautiful, easy-to-use, well-documented API, and a simple code base that is readable and easy to understand.

OpenStreetMap is a collaborative project that provides free and open map data that can be integrated with applications. We will be using the data provided by OpenStreetMap in conjunction with Leaflet in order to produce a map that is visible to users.

 For more information on OpenStreetMap and to learn how you can contribute to the project, visit the official page of the project at http://www.openstreetmap.org/.

The first thing we want to do is remove the existing index.html file that is created by the OpenShift Online template for JBoss EAP applications. The existing index file presents a "getting started" page that looks like the following screenshot:

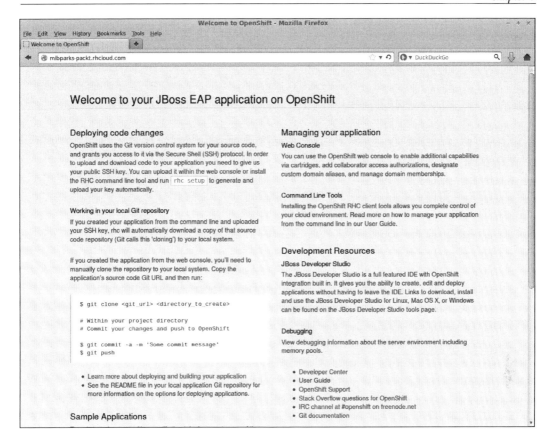

To remove this file, switch to the `mlbparks/src/main/webapp` directory and issue the following commands:

```
$ git rm index.html
$ git commit -am "Remove existing index file"
```

Now that we have removed the existing index file, it's time to create a new one. Open your favorite text editor and create a file named `index.html` under the `mlbparks/src/main/webapp` directory. The first bit of information we want to add to the source file is some basic CSS that specifies the look and feel of the UI components as well as adding dependencies to pull in remote JavaScript resources for both Leaflet and jQuery. Add the following lines of code to the top of the `index.html` file:

```
<!doctype html>
<html lang="en">
<head>
<!-- Set the title of the application that will be displayed on the
browser window -->
```

```html
<title>Map of MLB Parks</title>

<!-- Specifiy to load the correct remote stylesheet for Leaflet
depending on the browser -->
<link rel="stylesheet"
  href="http://cdn.leafletjs.com/leaflet-0.5.1/leaflet.css" />
  <!--[if lte IE 8]>
    <link rel="stylesheet" href="http://cdn.leafletjs.com/
leaflet-0.5.1/leaflet.ie.css" />
  <![endif]-->

<!-- Load in the remote JS for JQuery -->
<script src="http://code.jquery.com/jquery-2.0.0.min.js"></script>

<!-- Load in the remote JS for Leaflet -->
<script src="http://cdn.leafletjs.com/leaflet-0.5.1/leaflet.js"></script>

<!-- Specify that we will be using the OSWALD font provided by Google
-->
<link href='http://fonts.googleapis.com/css?family=oswald'
  rel='stylesheet' type='text/css'>

<!-- Set the initial parameters for the viewport-->
<meta name="viewport" content="width=device-width, initial-scale=1.0,
maximum-scale=1.0, user-scalable=no" />

<!-- Create custom CSS styles for our display-->
<style type="text/css">
body {
  padding: 0;
  margin: 0;
}
html,body,#map {
  height: 100%;
  font-family: 'oswald';
}
.leaflet-container .leaflet-control-zoom {
  margin-left: 13px;
  margin-top: 70px;
}
#map {
  z-index: 1;
```

```
}
#title {
  z-index: 2;
  position: absolute;
  left: 10px;
}
</style>
</head>
```

With the preceding code snippet, as described in the HTML comments, we have created our HTML head section that included the dependencies for external JavaScript libraries as well as created a few custom styles for our interface. The next thing we need to do is start creating our map by implementing the `<body>` section of the HTML code. Add the following directly underneath the closing `</head>` tag from the previous section:

```
<body>
  <h1 id="title">MLB Stadiums</h1>
```

The preceding code will create the body section of the HTML file and create a label that will be displayed according to the `#title` CSS style that we created in the `<head>` portion of the HTML document.

The next thing we want to do is create an attribution on the map that lets our users know that we are using the Leaflet project for the mapping API and OpenStreetMap for the data that powers the map that will be displayed to the user. Add the following lines of code to your `index.html` file directly under the h1 title tag:

```
<div id="map"></div>
  <script>
    Number.prototype.toCurrencyString = function() { return "$"
+ Math.floor(this).toLocaleString() + (this % 1).toFixed(2).
toLocaleString().replace(/^0/,''); }
    center = new L.LatLng(39.82, -98.57);
    zoom = 5;
    var map = L.map('map').setView(center, zoom);
    var markerLayerGroup = L.layerGroup().addTo(map);
    L.tileLayer('http://{s}.tile.openstreetmap.org/{z}/{x}/{y}.png', {
      maxZoom: 18,
      attribution: 'Map data &copy; <a href="http://openstreetmap.org">OpenStreetMap</a> contributors, <a href="http://creativecommons.org/licenses/by-sa/2.0/">CC-BY-SA</a>'
    }).addTo(map);
```

Creating and Deploying Java EE Applications

What did we just do? We started by creating a `<div>` element that will contain the actual map that is displayed to the user. After creating the `<div>` element, we created a function called `toCurrencyString()` that will format numbers to a currency representation, which will be displayed when a user views details about a stadium. We then set the starting center point of the map to the latitude and longitude of `39.82` and `-98.57`, respectively. If you are not familiar with these coordinates, don't worry; this is simply the location of the middle of the United States. To not introduce bias in which stadium is displayed first, I couldn't think of a better way to start the application than by being stadium-agnostic. If you do have a favorite MLB team, you can certainly change these coordinates to the city of your favorite team.

After we set the center point of the map, we defined the default zoom level the user will experience when loading the web page. We then added the attribution tile and set the maximum level we want the users to be able to zoom in to.

The last thing we need to do before we can test that our map is displayed correctly is close the open `<script>`, `<body>`, and `<html>` tags. Add the following code to the very bottom of the `index.html` file:

```
</script>
</body>
</html>
```

Once you have added the closing tags, save your changes to the file, and then deploy the application using the following commands:

```
$ git add .
$ git commit -am "Adding map to the application"
$ git push
```

If there are no code errors, the deployment should be completed successfully, as indicated by the following output displayed on your screen:

```
remote: Preparing build for deployment
remote: Deployment id is 02e426b5
remote: Activating deployment
remote: Starting MongoDB cartridge
remote: Deploying jbosseap cartridge
remote: Starting jbosseap cartridge
remote: Found 127.7.150.129:8080 listening port
remote: Found 127.7.150.129:9999 listening port
remote: /var/lib/openshift/5311180f500446f54a0003bb/jbosseap/standalone/
deployments /var/lib/openshift/5311180f500446f54a0003bb/jbosseap
```

Chapter 5

```
remote: /var/lib/openshift/5311180f500446f54a0003bb/jbosseap
remote: Artifacts deployed: ./ROOT.war
remote: -----------------------
remote: Git Post-Receive Result: success
remote: Activation status: success
remote: Deployment completed with status: success
```

Verifying that the map was deployed and is responsive

In the previous section, we created and deployed the basics of a mapping application using the Leaflet and OpenStreetMap projects. To verify that the map was created correctly and is getting displayed to the user via the web application, open your favorite browser and point to the URL of your application. If everything works as it should, you will see the following map including the title in the top-left corner of the map as well as the attributions of the projects we have used. Your browser should look like the following screenshot:

Creating and Deploying Java EE Applications

If you recall from the requirements, the application should also be responsive in nature so that it can be viewed just as easily on a mobile device.

> A responsive web design means that your application's user interface should be able to adapt to different devices and resolutions without hindering the user experience.

To verify that our application is indeed responsive, pull out your smartphone and load the URL of your application in the browser of your mobile device. As you can see in the following images, the Leaflet library we are using for our mapping capabilities implements responsive web design, gets displayed correctly on these mobile devices, and gets updated based on the orientation of the device (portrait or landscape):

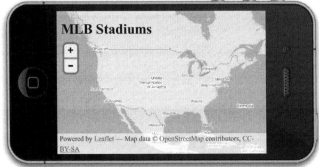

Getting the stadiums from our REST services

Now that we have verified that our map is deployed and is functioning correctly, we are ready to add the stadium information as pins on the map. The first step in order to accomplish this is to create a function that will perform the REST call to our backend services that we created previously in this chapter. Open up the `index.html` file and add the following code snippet before the closing `</script>` tag at the bottom of the file:

```
function getPins(e){
bounds = map.getBounds();
  url = "ws/parks/within?lat1=" + bounds.getNorthEast().lat + "&lon1="
+ bounds.getNorthEast().lng + "&lat2=" + bounds.getSouthWest().lat +
"&lon2=" + bounds.getSouthWest().lng;
  $.get(url, pinTheMap, "json")
}
```

The preceding code snippet might look complicated but it is really quite simple. The first thing we do is define a function called `getPins()` that will contain the logic for making the call to our REST service that we have already deployed as part of our application.

After our function is defined, we get the area of the map that is currently visible on the screen and assign it to the `bounds` variable. We then create a URL for the endpoint we are calling and pass in the correct latitude and longitude for the viewable area.

Finally, we create the REST call, passing in the URL of the endpoint as well as the callback function (`pinTheMap`) that we will get processed once we receive a response from the service.

Adding the stadiums to the map

In the previous section, we stated that we wanted to call a function named `pinTheMap` when a response is received from the web service. In this section, we are going to add this function to our `index.html` file directly after the `getPins()` function. Open the `index.html` file again and add the following code snippet directly after the `getPins()` function but before the closing `</script>` tag at the bottom of the file:

```
function pinTheMap(data){
  //clear the current pins
  map.removeLayer(markerLayerGroup);

  //add the new pins
```

```
    var markerArray = new Array(data.length)
    for (var i = 0; i < data.length; i++){
       park = data[i];
       var popupInformation = "<b>" + park.name + "</b></br>" + park.
ballpark + "</br>";
       popupInformation += "<b>Team Payroll: </b>" + park.payroll.
toCurrencyString() + "</br>";
       popupInformation += "<b>League: </b>" + park.league + "</br>";
       markerArray[i] = L.marker([park.position[1], park.position[0]]).
bindPopup(popupInformation);
    }

    markerLayerGroup = L.layerGroup(markerArray).addTo(map);
}
```

The preceding function takes a data parameter that contains all of the baseball stadiums' information for the viewable map area that is displayed on the screen. The first thing the function does is clear any other pins (markers) on the map, as we are going to replace them with the information passed in via the data variable. After the existing pins are removed, the function iterates over each element in the array of stadiums and creates a string that contains all of the information we want to display about the stadium and the associated baseball team. We then add this string to an array called `makerArray` and finally, we add this information to the map.

Automatically updating the map

The final bit of code that we need to add will provide the functionality that updates the map if the user changes the zoom level or drags the map around to display a new section of the United States. Open the `index.html` file again and add the following code directly after the `pinTheMap()` function but before the closing `</script>` tag and the bottom of the file:

```
map.on('dragend', getPins);
map.on('zoomend', getPins);
map.whenReady(getPins);
```

Testing the application

Congratulations! You have just completed an application that includes a dynamic map of the world that will also display all of the baseball stadiums in use by MLB. To verify that everything is working correctly, deploy your changes using the following commands:

```
$ git commit -am "Adding stadiums to map"
$ git push
```

Once your application has been deployed, open your web browser and play around with the application. The application you have just developed and deployed should match the images at the beginning of this chapter.

Taking the easy way out

Don't hate me for telling you this at the very end of the chapter, but there is an easy way out if you couldn't get all the source code typed in or copied over just right. OpenShift allows you to create applications from existing Git repositories with a single command. To try this out, delete your existing `mlbparks` application and enter in the following command to create an application, add MongoDB, download the `mlbparks` application source code, import the dataset, and deploy the code:

```
$ rhc app create mlbparks jbosseap-6 mongodb-2.4 --from-code https://
github.com/gshipley/mlbparks.git --timeout 3600
```

> It is important to remember that when you delete an application gear on OpenShift, the local copy of the source code remains intact. For this reason, you will need to delete the *mlbparks* directory on your local machine or the preceding command will fail if you executed it where an *mlbparks* directory already exists.

Summary

In this chapter, we learned how to create a Java-EE-based application using the JBoss EAP application server. As part of the development process, we learned how to use the MongoDB NoSQL database as well as how to import data into the database. After importing the data, we created a spatial index that allowed us to perform geospatial queries to find all stadiums within a given latitude and longitude. Lastly, we learned how to create a frontend for the application by taking advantage of two popular open projects, which are Leaflet and OpenStreetMap. Using these two projects allowed us to quickly create a responsive application that behaves in the same way regardless of the device the user accesses the application from.

In the next chapter, we are going to continue to learn how to build and deploy a Java applications to the OpenShift platform by converting this application to the Spring Framework.

6
Creating and Deploying Spring Framework Java Applications

In this chapter, we are going to learn how to use OpenShift in order to create and deploy Java applications that utilize the popular Spring Framework. To illustrate how to do this, we are going to convert the `mlbparks` application that we wrote in *Chapter 5*, *Creating and Deploying Java EE Applications*, so that it uses the Spring Framework instead of Java EE. First, we are going to cover the history of the framework, and then we will learn how to create Tomcat-based applications on the OpenShift platform. After we have created our application, we will embed the MongoDB NoSQL database and then begin our application coding. We will then learn how to deploy our application from either the source code or binary `.war` files.

An overview of the Spring Framework

In the beginning, there was EJB, and EJB was bad. Why would I say that? I spent the early part of my career as a Java fan and I believed that Java could do no wrong. I labored for weeks, months, and even years creating EJBs for highly scalable enterprise class applications. Even though I fully understood the specification, I felt that creating these JavaBeans was overly complex and required a lot of arcane interfaces and coding structure that didn't make sense to me. Having worked with a lot of other Java developers at the time, I realized that many of my fellow developers in the industry shared this same opinion. While you could accomplish fantastic results with the early EJB implementations, our friends were coding circles around us in more simple-to-use languages. Of course, the argument we would always make for sticking with EJB and Java normally included loaded terms such as scalable and enterprise grade.

At that time, I was on a team of two Java developers inside of a larger team of developers consisting of PHP and Perl developers. I was so adamant about the merits of Java that my team implemented weekly coding challenges to see how quickly we could solve programming problems in our respective languages. We would be timed on the length of the implementation and then on the execution speed of the code. Given that the size of challenges was broken up into small chucks, we would normally spend 10 minutes or less on the actual implementation to solve the problem. This was a great experience for me, as I developed strong friendships with other developers that continue to exist today even though 15 years have passed. More importantly, I began to see merits in other languages, except Perl, of course!

As I have gained more experience in my career and learned to open my mind to see the value in other languages, I have learned an important lesson: a language is just a tool, and you can accomplish great things regardless of your programming language weapon. To develop great applications, you need to understand how to architect software and put all the moving pieces together in an extensible manner. If you are a hardcore Java enthusiast, I probably just committed the cardinal sin by speaking ill of your language. Don't get me wrong; I love Java today and use it for many projects. However, let's be honest with each other; the early version of web programming in Java was really bad and not a joy to program in.

Where was I? Oh, sorry, we are supposed to be talking about the Spring Framework. As I said previously, the early implementation of EJB left a bad taste in a lot of Java developers' mouths. We wanted something simple and quick that still allowed us to create enterprise-grade applications. We were tired of EJB and wanted to get back to the roots of Java. Enter the Spring Framework!

The Spring Framework was a radical departure from the traditional way of developing software using the Java programming language. The biggest selling point of Spring was its ability to develop applications using only POJO(s). POJO breathed new life into the language and dramatically reduced the complexity of programming. It also introduced an inversion of control and had tight integration with the Hibernate ORM project. Many felt that using Spring alongside Hibernate was a marriage made in heaven and would stand the test of time.

The first 1.0 GA version of Spring was released in March, 2004, and I am happy to report that this framework is still innovative and is still a very popular framework. The framework was originally created by Rod Johnson but has gone through several ownership changes over the years. Recently, VMWare spun the Spring Framework out to its own company, which is called Pivotal.

Spring Framework version	Release date
1.0	March, 2004
2.0	October, 2006
3.0	December, 2009
4.0	December, 2013

The Spring Framework consists of the following core modules:

Module name	Description
IoC	Inversion of the Control container
AOP	Aspect-oriented programming
Data access	Provides API(s) to communicate with data stores
Transactions	Provides API(s) to wrap code inside of transactions with the rollback capability
MVC	The model view controller framework that creates applications
Remote access	API(s) to create objects that can be accessed over the network
Authentication	API(s) for authentication and authorization
Messaging	API(s) for the implementation of message-driven Java code

On top of the core modules, several subprojects exist to provide API(s) that work with social networks, Big Data, and even to help develop mobile applications. For a complete list of Spring components, you can visit the official project site at `http://www.spring.io`.

Creating a Spring application

Now that we have a good understanding of why Spring was created and the modules available as part of the distribution, let's explore how to create and deploy applications on the OpenShift platform. For the sample application, called `springmlb`, we are going to convert the application we created in the previous chapter to utilize this framework. Just to recap, the requirements for the application are as follows:

- A single map that a user can zoom in and out
- As the user moves the map around, the map must be updated with all baseball stadiums that are located in the shown area

- The location of the stadiums must be searchable based on map coordinates that are passed to the REST API
- The data should be transferred in the JSON format
- The web application must be responsive so that it is displayed correctly regardless of the resolution of the browser
- When a stadium is listed on the map, the user should be able to click on the stadium to view details about the associated team

The final state application will look like the following screenshot:

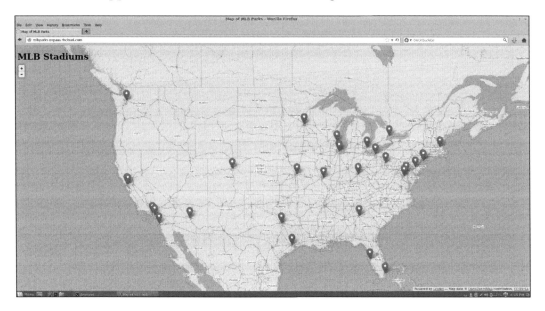

Now that we have our requirements and know what the end result will look like, let's start creating the application.

Taking the easy way out

For the remainder of this chapter, we are going to build a Spring-based application using the source code included as part of this chapter. If typing in the source code is not your cup of tea, there are several options available to you.

The first option is to clone the Git repository that is available on GitHub. Head over to the project page at https://github.com/gshipley/springmlb for instructions.

The second option is to chain the RHC command arguments together to create the application, embed the database, and download the source code—all with one command. Keep in mind that after running the RHC command, you will still need to import the JSON documents into the database, as outlined in this chapter. If you want to take this approach, enter the following command:

```
$ rhc app create springmlb tomcat7 mongodb-2.4 --from-code https://github.com/gshipley/springmlb.git
```

When the preceding command is finished, all you need to do is import the data. Magic indeed!

Creating a Tomcat gear on OpenShift

You decided to do all of the coding yourself? Awesome; let's get to work.

If you are familiar with Spring, chances are that you are deploying your applications on the popular Tomcat servlet container. While Spring-based applications will certainly work and perform well on the JBoss suite of application servers, I have found that developers typically deploy their Spring applications on top of Tomcat. For this reason, we are going to learn how to create Tomcat-based gears on the OpenShift platform.

The first thing we need to do is create a gear that will hold our application code. In order to do this, enter the following command in your terminal prompt:

```
$ rhc app create springmlb tomcat
```

After entering the preceding command, you'll most certainly see the following error message:

```
Short Name     Full name
==========     =========
jbossews-1.0   Tomcat 6 (JBoss EWS 1.0)
jbossews-2.0   Tomcat 7 (JBoss EWS 2.0)
```

There are multiple cartridges that match `Tomcat`. Please provide the short name of the correct cart.

This is because OpenShift supports multiple versions of the Tomcat servlet container and the platform did not know which version you wanted to use for your deployment. For the application that we are going to create, let's select the Tomcat 7 servlet container for our `springmlb` application with the following command:

```
$ rhc app create springmlb tomcat7
```

> If you received an error message stating that you have reached your maximum number of gears, you will need to delete an application that you are no longer using. The free tier for OpenShift Online only allows users to create a limited number of running applications without paying for the service. I would suggest that now might be a good time to review the affordable pricing plans available for the service and consider upgrading to a pay-as-go account.

If the preceding command is executed successfully, your application gear is created and the default template application is cloned to your local filesystem under the `springmlb` directory.

> If you want to use a newer version of Tomcat than what is provided by default, such as an alpha version, we will cover how to do this later in the book when learning about creating **Do-It-Yourself** (**DIY**) application gears.

Adding the MongoDB NoSQL database to our application

As we learned in *Chapter 2, Creating and Managing Applications*, OpenShift provides several add-on cartridges that allow developers to extend the functionality of a gear. The steps required to add a database and import data are exactly the same as what we did in *Chapter 5, Creating and Deploying Java EE Applications*, where we imported all of the stadium information.

To embed the MongoDB database into our existing `springmlb` OpenShift gear, run the following command:

```
$ rhc cartridge add mongodb-2.4 -a springmlb
```

Once the command is executed and the database has been added to your application, you will see the following information on the screen that contains the username and password for the database:

```
Adding mongodb-2.4 to application 'springmlb' ... done
mongodb-2.4 (MongoDB 2.4)
-------------------------
  Gears:          Located with jbossews-2.0
  Connection URL: mongodb://$OPENSHIFT_MONGODB_DB_HOST:$OPENSHIFT_MONGODB_DB_PORT/
```

```
Database Name:      springmlb
Password:           JEf8CTqJSG9_
Username:           admin
```

MongoDB 2.4 database added. Please make note of these credentials:

```
Root User:       admin
Root Password:   JEf8CTqJSG9_
Database Name:   springmlb
```

Connection URL: mongodb://$OPENSHIFT_MONGODB_DB_HOST:$OPENSHIFT_MONGODB_DB_PORT/

To get started, SSH to your OpenShift gear for the springmlb application by issuing the following command in your terminal prompt:

`$ rhc app ssh springmlb`

Once you are connected to the remote gear, you need to download the JSON file and store it in the /tmp directory of your gear. To complete these steps, use the following commands on your remote gear:

`$ cd /tmp`

`$ wget https://raw.github.com/gshipley/springmlb/master/mlbparks.json`

Once the file has completed downloading, take a quick look at the contents using your favorite text editor in order to get familiar with the structure of the document. When you are comfortable with the data that we are going to import into the database, execute the following command on the remote gear in order to populate MongoDB with the JSON documents:

```
$ mongoimport --jsonArray -d $OPENSHIFT_APP_NAME -c teams --type
json --file /tmp/mlbparks.json  -h $OPENSHIFT_MONGODB_DB_HOST --port
$OPENSHIFT_MONGODB_DB_PORT -u $OPENSHIFT_MONGODB_DB_USERNAME  -p
$OPENSHIFT_MONGODB_DB_PASSWORD
```

If the command was executed successfully, you should see the following output on the screen:

```
connected to: 127.7.150.130:27017
Fri Feb 28 20:57:24.125 check 9 30
Fri Feb 28 20:57:24.126 imported 30 objects
```

Creating and Deploying Spring Framework Java Applications

To verify that the data was loaded properly, use the following command that will print out the number of documents in the `teams` collections of the `springmlb` database:

```
$ mongo -quiet $OPENSHIFT_MONGODB_DB_HOST:$OPENSHIFT_MONGODB_DB_
PORT/$OPENSHIFT_APP_NAME -u  $OPENSHIFT_MONGODB_DB_USERNAME -p
$OPENSHIFT_MONGODB_DB_PASSWORD --eval "db.teams.count()"
```

The result should be **30**.

Lastly, we need to create a `2d` index on the `teams` collection to ensure that we can perform spatial queries on the data.

To add the `2d` index to the `teams` collection, enter the following command on the remote gear:

```
$ mongo $OPENSHIFT_MONGODB_DB_HOST:$OPENSHIFT_MONGODB_DB_PORT/$OPENSHIFT_
APP_NAME --eval 'db.teams.ensureIndex( { coordinates : "2d" } );'
```

Adding Spring support to the application

As we have learned previously in this book, OpenShift makes use of the Maven build system for Java-based projects. Because of this, we can simply add the dependencies for the Spring Framework to our `pom.xml` file that is included in the default template. To accomplish this, open up the `pom.xml` file in the application's root directory with your favorite text editor or IDE. The first thing we want to do is remove the dependencies for PostgreSQL and MySQL by removing the following lines from the `<dependencies>` section of the file:

```
<dependency>
<groupId>org.postgresql</groupId>
  <artifactId>postgresql</artifactId>
  <version>9.2-1003-jdbc4</version>
</dependency>
<dependency>
  <groupId>mysql</groupId>
  <artifactId>mysql-connector-java</artifactId>
  <version>5.1.25</version>
</dependency>
```

Once we have removed these unneeded dependencies, we can add support for the Spring Framework by adding the following code in the `<dependencies>` section of the `pom.xml` file:

```
<dependency>
<groupId>org.springframework</groupId>
```

```
      <artifactId>spring-webmvc</artifactId>
      <version>4.0.2.RELEASE</version>
    </dependency>
    <dependency>
      <groupId>javax.servlet</groupId>
      <artifactId>javax.servlet-api</artifactId>
      <version>3.1.0</version>
      <scope>provided</scope>
    </dependency>
    <dependency>
      <groupId>com.fasterxml.jackson.core</groupId>
      <artifactId>jackson-databind</artifactId>
      <version>2.3.1</version>
    </dependency>
    <dependency>
      <groupId>org.springframework.data</groupId>
      <artifactId>spring-data-mongodb</artifactId>
      <version>1.3.4.RELEASE</version>
    </dependency>
```

We also need to add a configuration item in the file to specify that we do not want the build to fail if we are missing a `web.xml` file in our project. For this, add the following line of code directly after the `<configuration>` opening tag under the `<build>` section of the file:

```
<failOnMissingWebXml>false</failOnMissingWebXml>
```

Once you have added the preceding XML code, save your changes to the file.

Adding a configuration to the application

Now that we have our application skeleton created and have added support for the Spring Framework and associated dependencies, the next thing we want to do is set up the connection information for our MongoDB database in our Java source code. In order to do this, create a new directory under your application's root folder, called `src/main/java/org/springapp/config`. Once this directory has been created, create a new source code file named `ApplicationConfig.java` and add the following code snippet:

```
package org.springapp.config;

import org.springframework.context.annotation.Bean;
import org.springframework.context.annotation.Configuration;
import org.springframework.data.authentication.UserCredentials;
```

```
import org.springframework.data.mongodb.MongoDbFactory;
import org.springframework.data.mongodb.core.MongoTemplate;
import org.springframework.data.mongodb.core.SimpleMongoDbFactory;

import com.mongodb.Mongo;

@Configuration
public class ApplicationConfig {

  @Bean
  public MongoTemplate mongoTemplate() throws Exception {
    String openshiftMongoDbHost = System.getenv("OPENSHIFT_MONGODB_DB_HOST");
    if(openshiftMongoDbHost == null){
      return new MongoTemplate(new Mongo(), "springmlb");
    }
    int openshiftMongoDbPort = Integer.parseInt(System.getenv("OPENSHIFT_MONGODB_DB_PORT"));
    String username = System.getenv("OPENSHIFT_MONGODB_DB_USERNAME");
    String password = System.getenv("OPENSHIFT_MONGODB_DB_PASSWORD");
    Mongo mongo = new Mongo(openshiftMongoDbHost, openshiftMongoDbPort);
    UserCredentials userCredentials = new UserCredentials(username, password);
    String databaseName = System.getenv("OPENSHIFT_APP_NAME");
    MongoDbFactory mongoDbFactory = new SimpleMongoDbFactory(mongo, databaseName, userCredentials);
    MongoTemplate mongoTemplate = new MongoTemplate(mongoDbFactory);
    return mongoTemplate;
  }
}
```

The preceding code snippet specifies the connection information in order to connect to the MongoDB database that we embedded previously in this chapter.

Note that we are connecting to the database by utilizing the environment variables for the username, password, host, and so on that are created by the OpenShift platform.

Now that we have written our Java code that specifies our database connection information, the next step is to create a `WebMvcConfig` class that extends the `WebMvcConfigurerAdpater` class, which ships as part of the Spring Framework. This allows us to create a JSON view for our REST endpoint. Create a new file called `WebMvcConfig.java` and place it in the `src/main/java/org/springapp/config` directory. Once you have created the new file, add the following source code:

```
package org.springapp.config;

import org.springapp.rest.MLBParkResource;
import org.springframework.context.annotation.Bean;
import org.springframework.context.annotation.ComponentScan;
import org.springframework.context.annotation.Configuration;
import org.springframework.web.servlet.config.annotation.EnableWebMvc;
import org.springframework.web.servlet.config.annotation.
WebMvcConfigurerAdapter;
import org.springframework.web.servlet.view.json.
MappingJackson2JsonView;

@EnableWebMvc
@ComponentScan(basePackageClasses = MLBParkResource.class)
@Configuration
public class WebMvcConfig extends WebMvcConfigurerAdapter {

  @Bean
  public MappingJackson2JsonView jsonView() {
    MappingJackson2JsonView jsonView = new MappingJackson2JsonView();
    jsonView.setPrefixJson(true);
    return jsonView;
  }
}
```

The last configuration item that we need to add to our application is the `SpringAppWebApplicationInitializer` class that implements the `WebApplicationInitializer` interface, which is a standard interface for the Spring Framework. Create this file under the `src/main/java/org/springapp/config` directory and add the following source code:

```
package org.springapp.config;

import javax.servlet.ServletContext;
import javax.servlet.ServletException;
```

```
import javax.servlet.ServletRegistration.Dynamic;

import org.springframework.web.WebApplicationInitializer;
import org.springframework.web.context.support.
AnnotationConfigWebApplicationContext;
import org.springframework.web.servlet.DispatcherServlet;

public class SpringAppWebApplicationInitializer implements
WebApplicationInitializer {

  @Override
  public void onStartup(ServletContext servletContext) throws
ServletException {
     AnnotationConfigWebApplicationContext webApplicationContext = new
AnnotationConfigWebApplicationContext();
     webApplicationContext.register(ApplicationConfig.class,
WebMvcConfig.class);

     Dynamic dynamc = servletContext.addServlet("dispatcherServlet",
new DispatcherServlet(webApplicationContext));
     dynamc.addMapping("/api/v1/*");
     dynamc.setLoadOnStartup(1);
  }
}
```

The preceding source code loads our configuration and specifies the default URL mapping of /api/v1 for the REST web services that we are going to create.

Adding the domain model to the application

At this point in the development process, we should have accomplished the following tasks:

- Created a new application gear to hold our source code
- Added the MongoDB NoSQL database to our OpenShift gear
- Added configuration items to our Java source code

Now, it is time to add our domain model that represents the baseball stadium object. Create a new file named MLBPark.java and place it in the src/main/java/org/springapp/domain directory. Once the new Java file has been created, add the following lines of code:

```
package org.springapp.domain;

import org.springframework.data.annotation.Id;
```

```java
import org.springframework.data.mongodb.core.index.Indexed;
import org.springframework.data.mongodb.core.mapping.Document;

@Document(collection="teams")
public class MLBPark {

  @Id
  private String id;

  private String name;
  @Indexed
  private double[] coordinates;
  private String ballpark;
  private long payroll;
  private String league;
  public String getId() {
    return id;
  }
  public void setId(String id) {
    this.id = id;
  }
  public String getName() {
    return name;
  }
  public void setName(String name) {
    this.name = name;
  }
  public double[] getCoordinates() {
    return coordinates;
  }
  public void setCoordinates(double[] coordinates) {
    this.coordinates = coordinates;
  }
  public String getBallpark() {
    return ballpark;
  }
  public void setBallpark(String ballpark) {
    this.ballpark = ballpark;
  }
  public long getPayroll() {
    return payroll;
  }
  public void setPayroll(long payroll) {
```

```
      this.payroll = payroll;
  }
  public String getLeague() {
    return league;
  }
  public void setLeague(String league) {
    this.league = league;
  }
}
```

Adding the REST endpoint to the application

The final piece of Java code that we need to add is the actual logic for the REST web service that will be available at the /api/v1/parks URL. The class will contain the following two methods:

- `getAllParks()`: This method will return a JSON document that contains all the baseball stadiums that we imported previously in this chapter
- `findParksWithin()`: This method will return baseball stadiums within the supplied latitude and longitude

Create a new source file named MLBParkResource.java, and place the file in the src/main/java/org/springapp/rest directory. Once the file has been created, add the following code snippet:

```
package org.springapp.rest;

import java.util.List;

import org.springapp.domain.MLBPark;
import org.springframework.beans.factory.annotation.Autowired;
import org.springframework.data.mongodb.core.MongoTemplate;
import org.springframework.data.mongodb.core.geo.Box;
import org.springframework.data.mongodb.core.geo.Point;
import org.springframework.data.mongodb.core.query.Criteria;
import org.springframework.data.mongodb.core.query.Query;
import org.springframework.http.MediaType;
import org.springframework.stereotype.Controller;
import org.springframework.web.bind.annotation.RequestMapping;
import org.springframework.web.bind.annotation.RequestMethod;
import org.springframework.web.bind.annotation.RequestParam;
```

```
import org.springframework.web.bind.annotation.ResponseBody;

@Controller
@RequestMapping("/parks")
public class MLBParkResource {

  @Autowired
  private MongoTemplate mongoTemplate;

  @RequestMapping(method = RequestMethod.GET, produces = MediaType.
APPLICATION_JSON_VALUE)
    public @ResponseBody List<MLBPark> getAllParks() {
      return mongoTemplate.findAll(MLBPark.class);
    }
  @RequestMapping(value="within", method = RequestMethod.GET, produces
= MediaType.APPLICATION_JSON_VALUE)
    public @ResponseBody List<MLBPark> findParksWithin(@
RequestParam("lat1") float lat1, @RequestParam("lon1") float lon1, @
RequestParam("lat2") float lat2, @RequestParam("lon2") float lon2) {
      Query query = Query.query(Criteria.where("coordinates").within(new
Box(new Point(lon2,lat2), new Point(lon1,lat1))));
      return mongoTemplate.find(query , MLBPark.class);
    }
}
```

Deploying the application

At this point, we have all the pieces of the puzzle in order to deploy our application and to verify that the REST web service is behaving correctly. To deploy the code, we need to add all of the new source files that we created to our local repository, commit the changes, and finally, push the new code to our OpenShift gear. Change to the root directory of your application and execute the following commands:

```
$ git add .
$ git commit -am "Adding configuration and REST endpoint"
$ git push
```

Once you push the changes, the build process will begin. The first time a Java application is built using the Maven build system, it can take a few minutes as all of the new dependencies are downloaded to your gear. On subsequent builds, the process will be faster as the dependencies are cached in the local Maven repository.

Once your application has been deployed, try it out by visiting the link for the application in your web browser at `http://springmlb-packt.rhcloud.com/api/v1/parks`.

> Ensure that you replace the example namespace, which is `packt`, with the correct one for your OpenShift account.

If everything has been deployed correctly, you should see the following screenshot:

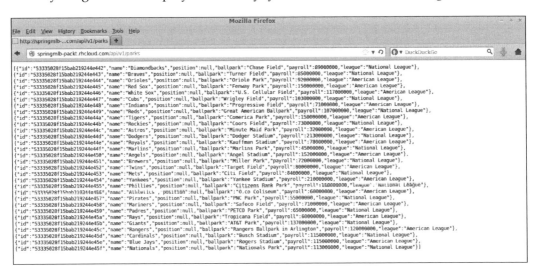

Congratulations! You just wrote and deployed a Spring application complete with MongoDB, REST-based web services, and geospatial capabilities.

Adding the web frontend

If you recall from *Chapter 5*, *Creating and Deploying Java EE Applications*, we are using the Leaflet and OpenStreetMap projects in order to create our frontend. Since we covered these technologies in the previous chapter, we will not be covering the HTML source file in this chapter in depth. Instead, I will list the instructions for removing the default `index.html` file that is part of the gear template and provide the source code for the new file that will communicate with our REST web service.

The first thing we want to do is remove the existing `index.html` file that is created by the OpenShift Online template for Tomcat-based applications. The existing index file presents a getting started page that looks like the following screenshot:

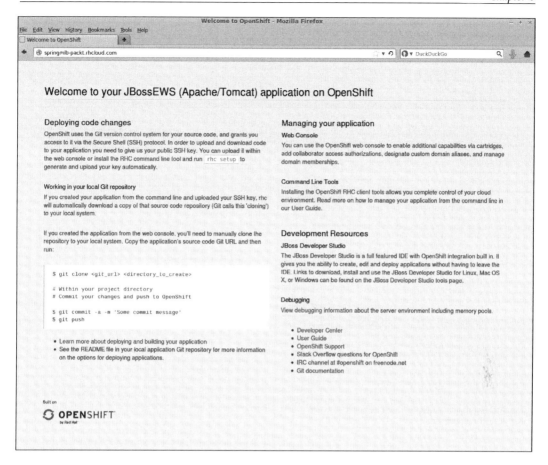

To remove this file, switch to the `springmlb/src/main/webapp` directory and issue the following commands:

```
$ git rm index.html
$ git commit -am "Remove existing index file"
```

Now that we have removed the existing index file, it's time to create a new one. Open your favorite text editor and create a file named `index.html` under the `springmlb/src/main/webapp` directory. Once the file has been created, add the following source code:

```
<!doctype html>
<html lang="en">
<head>
  <title>Map of MLB Parks</title>
```

```
    <link rel="stylesheet" href="http://cdn.leafletjs.com/leaflet-0.5.1/
leaflet.css" />
    <!--[if lte IE 8]>
      <link rel="stylesheet" href="http://cdn.leafletjs.com/
leaflet-0.5.1/leaflet.ie.css" />
    <![endif]-->
    <script src="http://code.jquery.com/jquery-2.0.0.min.js"></script>
    <meta name="viewport" content="width=device-width, initial-
scale=1.0, maximum-scale=1.0, user-scalable=no" />    <style type="text/
css">
  body {
    padding: 0;
    margin: 0;
  }
  html, body, #map {
    height: 100%;
    font-family: 'oswald';
  }
  .leaflet-container .leaflet-control-zoom {
    margin-left: 13px;
    margin-top: 70px;
  }

  #map { z-index: 1;}
  #title { z-index: 2; position: absolute; left: 10px; }
  </style>

</head>
```

The preceding code snippet creates the `<HEAD>` element of the HTML file and specifies the JavaScript dependencies that we need for both the Leaflet and JQuery projects. We also define some custom CSS styles that we will use while creating the layout of the HTML page. We are now ready to create the `<BODY>` section of the HTML file. Open the `index.html` file again and add the following code directly after the closing `</HEAD>` tag:

```
<body>
  <h1 id="title">MLB Stadiums</h1>
  <div id="map"></div>
  <script src="http://cdn.leafletjs.com/leaflet-0.5.1/leaflet.js"></
script>
  <script>
    center = new L.LatLng(39.82, -98.57);
    zoom = 5;
```

```
    var map = L.map('map').setView(center, zoom);
    var markerLayerGroup = L.layerGroup().addTo(map);
    L.tileLayer('http://{s}.tile.openstreetmap.org/{z}/{x}/{y}.png', {
      maxZoom: 18,
      attribution: 'Map data &copy; <a href="http://openstreetmap.
org">OpenStreetMap</a> contributors, <a href="http://creativecommons.
org/licenses/by-sa/2.0/">CC-BY-SA</a>'
    }).addTo(map);
```

In the preceding code snippet, we defined the center of the map that the user will see when opening the web page. The center is set to the `39.92` and `-98.57` coordinates, which is the center of the United States. We also created our `attribution` tag that will be displayed on the bottom right-hand corner of the map.

It is now time for us to create a couple of functions to get the locations of the stadiums by calling our REST API and then placing the pins or markers on the map in order to display the location of each stadium. Open the `index.html` file and add the following lines of code to the bottom of the file:

```
    function getPins(e){
       bounds = map.getBounds();
       url = "api/v1/parks/within?lat1=" + bounds.getNorthEast().
lat + "&lon1=" + bounds.getNorthEast().lng + "&lat2=" + bounds.
getSouthWest().lat + "&lon2=" + bounds.getSouthWest().lng;
       $.get(url, pinTheMap, "json")
    }

    Number.prototype.toCurrencyString = function() { return "$"
+ Math.floor(this).toLocaleString() + (this % 1).toFixed(2).
toLocaleString().replace(/^0/,''); }

    function pinTheMap(data){
       //clear the current pins
       map.removeLayer(markerLayerGroup);

       //add the new pins
       var markerArray = new Array(data.length)
       for (var i = 0; i < data.length; i++){
          park = data[i];
          var popupInformation = "<b>" + park.name + "</b></br>" + park.
ballpark + "</br>";
          popupInformation += "<b>Team Payroll: </b>" + park.payroll.
toCurrencyString() + "</br>";
          popupInformation += "<b>League: </b>" + park.league + "</br>";
```

```
            markerArray[i] = L.marker([park. coordinates [1], park.
coordinates [0]]).bindPopup(popupInformation);
        }


        markerLayerGroup = L.layerGroup(markerArray).addTo(map);


    }

    map.on('dragend', getPins);
    map.on('zoomend', getPins);
    map.whenReady(getPins)

  </script>
 </body>
 </html>
```

Once the code has been added, save your changes, and then deploy the application again with the following commands:

```
$ git add index.html
$ git commit -am "adding UI"
$ git push
```

Once the code has been deployed, point your web browser to the URL of your application, and you should see the finished application as shown in the following screenshot:

Chapter 6

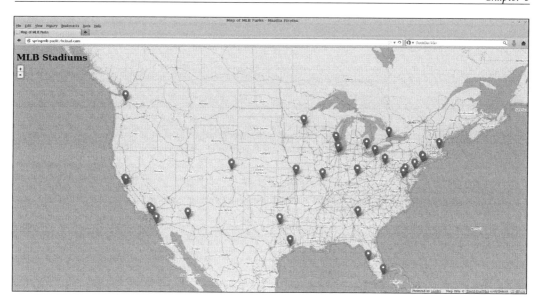

Having fun with the web UI

Fantastic! At this point, our first iteration of the application is complete and functional, but it's time to make a few tweaks to the user interface. One of the great benefits of using projects such as Leaflet and OpenStreetMap is being able to switch out the tiles that are displayed to the user. For instance, suppose we are tired of the same look and feel of our application and want to spice it up a bit by showing the terrain view. In order to accomplish this, let's switch out the tiling system in the `index.html` file. The existing line that specifies the tiles is as follows:

```
L.tileLayer('http://{s}.tile.openstreetmap.org/{z}/{x}/{y}.png', {
```

Change the preceding line of code to the following line of code:

```
L.tileLayer('http://{s}.tile.stamen.com/terrain/{z}/{x}/{y}.png', {
```

Creating and Deploying Spring Framework Java Applications

Save and commit your change and then push the code to your OpenShift server. When the deployment is complete, you should see the following new map available:

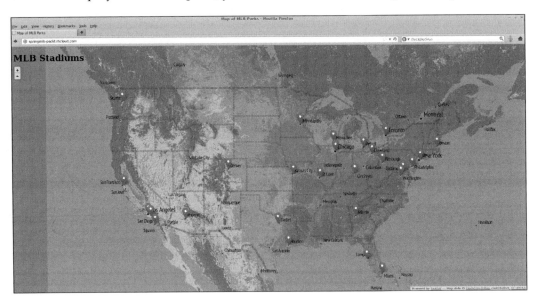

Pretty fancy, isn't it? Why stop there; let's try out a watercolor view with the following code change:

```
L.tileLayer('http://{s}.tile.stamen.com/watercolor/{z}/{x}/{y}.png', {
```

The map now looks like the following image:

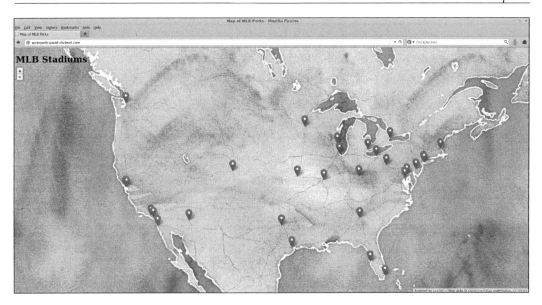

 The preceding map tiles are made available by Stamen Design and are licensed under Creative Commons. For more information on using these tile sets and attribution, head over to http://maps.stamen.com/.

Summary

In this chapter, we learned how to create a Spring-Framework-based application using the Tomcat 7 servlet container. Along the journey, we tackled tasks such as using environment variables to configure the MongoDB database and how to create REST-based web services. We also explored how to change the tile sets that are displayed to the user when interacting with the application.

In the next chapter, we are going to learn how to use a continuous integration environment by adding support for the popular Jenkins project to our baseball parks application.

7
Adding a Continuous Integration Environment to Applications

In this chapter, we are going to learn how to add a continuous integration environment to the `mlbparks` application that we wrote as part of *Chapter 5, Creating and Deploying Java EE Applications*. For this chapter, we are going to use the popular Jenkins build system, which is a fully supported cartridge on the OpenShift Online platform. We will start by creating a Jenkins server and then add the Jenkins client to our existing application. At the end of this chapter, any code changes we make to the `mlbparks` application will be compiled by our Jenkins server instead of being built on the OpenShift application gear where the `mlbparks` application resides.

What is continuous integration?

Continuous integration (**CI**) is not a new concept in the software development industry, but it might be new to you. For this reason, I am going to cover the high-level basics of what it is and why you would want to use it while developing applications that you deploy to the OpenShift platform.

The implementation of a CI server gained popularity with the rush of development teams practicing the Agile/Scrum methodology of development. In this type of environment, developers work in iterations or sprints and the team should have a shippable software project at the end of each cycle. Granted, not all features will be implemented, but the idea is that after a sprint, the code that has been written should be tested, should be able to be demoed, and should be able to be released if the team chooses. Because of the amount of work that each team member puts in while working on a specific feature independently of the rest of the team, many saw a challenge in merging all of the code together at the end of a sprint without breaking other code or having extensive merge conflicts.

Adding a Continuous Integration Environment to Applications

The CI movement was used to alleviate and ease the pain of massive merges at the end of a sprint cycle by encouraging developers to write unit tests and commit their code to the integration environment frequently. Once the code has been committed to the CI environment, the unit tests will run and a full build will be performed. If any compilation issues or test failures surfaced during the build, the team will be notified and the developer will be able to resolve the errors quickly—after being publicly shamed for breaking the build, of course!

In the OpenShift world, another use case for a CI server is to allow for greater uptime of your application. As you have learned throughout this book, when you push code changes to your OpenShift gear, the build occurs on the remote gear. Once the build is finished, the code is deployed to the application server. The OpenShift deployment process performs the following steps:

- The developer makes code modifications
- The developer adds and commits all changes to the local Git repository
- The developer pushes the changes up to the remote OpenShift gear
- The prebuild action hooks are executed, if they exist
- The application server on the remote OpenShift gear is stopped
- The new code is built on the remote OpenShift gear
- The deployment of new application code is performed on the OpenShift gear
- The application server is restarted on the remote OpenShift gear

This might look good on the surface and will suffice for the majority of applications, but there are a couple of gotchas that developers might not be aware of. First of all, the application server is stopped and does not serve requests while the application code is being compiled. Depending on the size of your application code base, this could mean a significant amount of downtime while your application is being built. Second, and most importantly, if the application fails to get built due to compilation failures, the application server will not be restarted and your application will be in outage until you resolve the build errors. Once the build errors have been corrected, the developer then needs to start the build process all over again.

Implementing the Jenkins CI environment as an OpenShift cartridge can help alleviate these two problem areas. Once the Jenkins server has been added to your application, all builds will be performed on a separate builder gear and then deployed once the compilation is successful. The new workflow while using the Jenkins CI cartridge is as follows:

- The developer makes code modifications
- The developer adds and commits all changes to the local Git repository

- The developer pushes code to the remote repository with a `git push` command
- OpenShift is aware that you have Jenkins CI enabled and triggers a build on the CI server
- Jenkins runs all tests and performs a build by creating a separate builder gear that only lives for the life of the build process
- The application server is stopped
- The code is deployed
- The application server is started

Using a CI environment, such as Jenkins, with your OpenShift application ensures that your OpenShift gear is only stopped while performing a deployment of code that has been successfully compiled and has passed all tests. Furthermore, you can enable hot deployment so that your application server is not stopped during a deployment.

Summarizing this, a few of the benefits of leveraging the Jenkins CI environment for your application include the ability to have archived build information, no application downtime while the code is being built, failed builds not getting deployed to your OpenShift gear, and more resources being available in order to build your application as each build spins up a new gear for a short-lived period of time.

Adding support for a Jenkins server

Now that we understand a few of the advantages of using a CI environment for your OpenShift applications, let's get started by adding the Jenkins server to our `mlbparks` application that we created in *Chapter 5, Creating and Deploying Java EE Applications*.

To get started with adding CI support to the application, the first thing we need to do is create an application gear that contains the Jenkins software. The Jenkins cartridge is a top-level web cartridge on the OpenShift platform and is available just like any other runtime. In order to create our server, issue the following command:

```
$ rhc app create ciserver jenkins
```

After entering the preceding command, the OpenShift platform will spin up a new gear and deploy the Jenkins server software. You should see the following output once the process is complete:

```
Using jenkins-1 (Jenkins Server) for 'jenkins'
Application Options
-------------------
```

```
Domain:     packt
Cartridges: jenkins-1
Gear Size:  default
Scaling:    no

Creating application 'ciserver' ... done
  Jenkins created successfully.  Please make note of these credentials:
   User: admin
   Password: eXUWlFGnIsiq
Note:  You can change your password at: https://ciserver-packt.rhcloud.
com/me/configure

Waiting for your DNS name to be available ... done

Cloning into 'ciserver'...
Your application 'ciserver' is now available.
  URL:        http://ciserver-packt.rhcloud.com/
  SSH to:     535ed9225004467d8d000852@ciserver-packt.rhcloud.com
  Git remote: ssh://535ed9225004467d8d000852@ciserver-packt.rhcloud.
com/~/git/ciserver.git/
  Cloned to:  /home/gshipley/code/ciserver
Run 'rhc show-app ciserver' for more details about your app.
```

> Make a note of the username and password, as this information will be required in order to log in to the server.

Verifying that the Jenkins server is up and running

At this point, we should have a Jenkins server deployed and running on the OpenShift service. To test this out, go to `http://ciserver-yourDomainName.rhcloud.com`.

 Ensure that you replace `yourDomainName` in the preceding URL with the domain name of your account that you created previously in this book.

Upon entering the preceding URL, you will be presented with the Jenkins authentication page. Provide the username and password that were displayed on the screen when you created the server and click on the **log in** button, as depicted in the following screenshot:

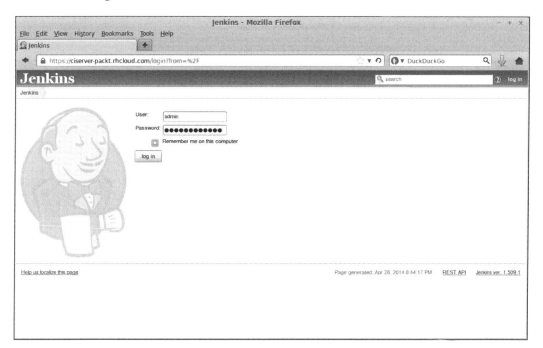

If the authentication was successful, you should see the main Jenkins dashboard, as shown in the following screenshot:

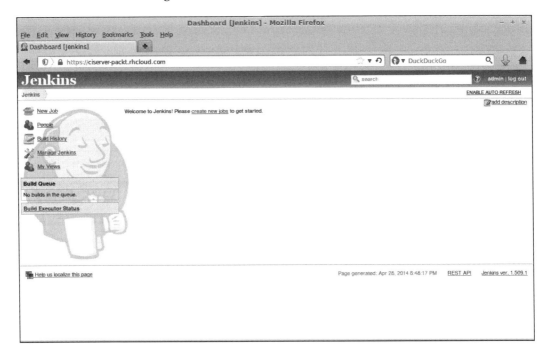

Congratulations; you now have a Jenkins server running on your OpenShift account!

Embedding Jenkins into an existing application

Now that we have a Jenkins server set up and running, we can add support to our `mlbparks` application, which will allow all future builds to get compiled on builder gears created by the Jenkins server. To embed the Jenkins support cartridge in your application, use the following command:

```
$ rhc cartridge add jenkins-client -a mlbparks
```

Once you enter the preceding command, you should see the following output, which provides the status of the operation:

```
Using jenkins-client-1 (Jenkins Client) for 'jenkins-client'
Adding jenkins-client-1 to application 'mlbparks' ... done

jenkins-client-1 (Jenkins Client)
---------------------------------
  Gears:   Located with jbosseap-6, mongodb-2.4
  Job URL: https://ciserver-packt.rhcloud.com/job/mlbparks-build/

Associated with job 'mlbparks-build' in Jenkins server.
```

Verify that the Jenkins client was added to your application by running the following command:

```
$ rhc app show mlbparks
```

You should see the following information indicating that Jenkins has been enabled for the `mlbparks` application:

```
mlbparks @ http://mlbparks-packt.rhcloud.com/ (uuid: 5311180f500446f54a0003bb)
-----------------------------------------------------------------------------
  Domain:     packt
  Created:    Feb 28  4:13 PM
  Gears:      1 (defaults to small)
  Git URL:    ssh://5311180f500446f54a0003bb@mlbparks-packt.rhcloud.com/~/git/mlbparks.git/
  SSH:        5311180f500446f54a0003bb@mlbparks-packt.rhcloud.com
  Deployment: auto (on git push)

  jbosseap-6 (JBoss Enterprise Application Platform 6)
  ----------------------------------------------------
    Gears: Located with mongodb-2.4, jenkins-client-1


  mongodb-2.4 (MongoDB 2.4)
  -------------------------
```

```
    Gears:              Located with jbosseap-6, jenkins-client-1
    Connection URL: mongodb://$OPENSHIFT_MONGODB_DB_HOST:$OPENSHIFT_
MONGODB_DB_PORT/
    Database Name:      mlbparks
    Password:           q_6eZ22-fraN
    Username:           admin

  jenkins-client-1 (Jenkins Client)
  ----------------------------------
    Gears:    Located with jbosseap-6, mongodb-2.4
    Job URL:  https://ciserver-packt.rhcloud.com/job/mlbparks-build/
```

The Jenkins client has now been embedded into the `mlbparks` application. This will ensure that all future builds will be performed on builder gears created by the continuous integration server instead of the OpenShift gear that contains the JBoss application server.

Using the Jenkins web console

Now that we have our Jenkins CI server up and running as well as the client added to the application, it's time to take a look at the Jenkins web console in order to understand the workflow that is followed when a developer pushes new source code to the remote Git repository.

Open your web browser and go to the main Jenkins dashboard where you will see a new item labeled **mlbparks-build**, as shown in the following screenshot:

Chapter 7

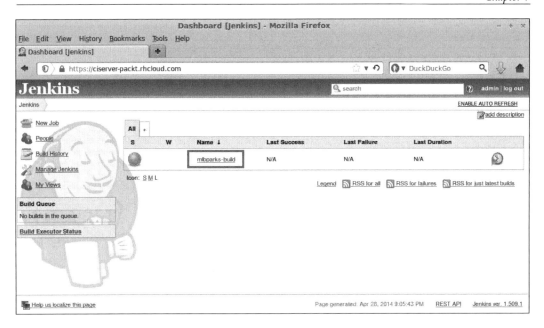

In order to view details about the build configuration, click on the **mlbparks-build** item and then select **Configure** on the next page. This will display configuration items for the build that will happen when the new code is pushed to the remote `mlbparks` Git repository. This should look similar to the following screenshot:

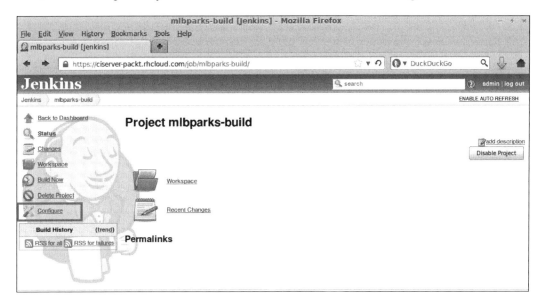

[155]

A few interesting configuration items are displayed on this page, which will allow you to fine-tune how your builds for the specified application are performed. Let's look at each section that might be of interest.

The first interesting configuration is concerned with the builder. The following configuration states that Jenkins should create a builder with a small size gear using the JBoss EAP cartridge and that the Jenkins master will wait for 5 minutes for the slave to come online, as shown in the following screenshot:

Application UUID	5311180f500446f54a0003bb
Builder Size	small
Builder Timeout	300000
Builder Type	redhat-jbosseap-6

If you have a large application that takes a considerable amount of time to compile, you might consider moving the builder size to a medium or large size gear.

> Gear sizes for OpenShift Online come in three flavors: small, medium, and large. Small gears consist of 512 MB of memory, medium gears contain 1 GB of memory, and large gears can consume up to 2 GB of memory. To get access to larger gear sizes, you must upgrade your account to a paid offering on the platform.

The next configuration item of interest is the **Source Code Management** section. It specifies the URL of the Git repository to be used, the branch to be used, and so on. This section is important if you want to use Jenkins to build a project that exists outside of OpenShift Online. This will be useful for developers who have an existing repository that they would like to build from.

A couple of common use cases for this are a repository that is hosted internally behind the company's firewall or a private repository that is hosted on GitHub. As you can see in the following screenshot, the default location is the Git repository that is hosted on your application's gear:

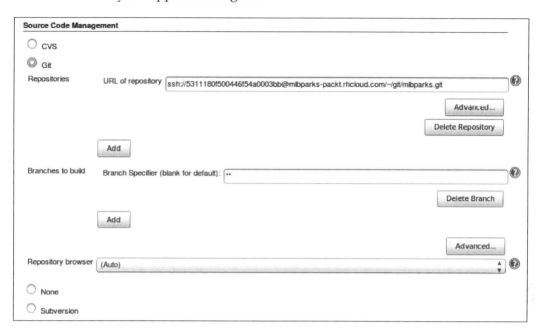

The last configuration item that is interesting is under the **Build** section. In this section, you can specify a shell script for building the project. If you want a glimpse under the hood of how OpenShift deploys a new build to an existing server, this section of code should have your mouth watering.

By default, the shell script that is executed is as shown in the following screenshot:

Building code with Jenkins

Now that you have the Jenkins client embedded into your `mlbparks` application gear, any future `git push` commands will send the code to the Jenkins server for compilation. To test this out, let's make a small code change to our `mlbparks` application by editing the `index.html` file found under the `/src/main/webapp` directory. Open the file and find the following line of code:

```
<h1 id="title">MLB Stadiums</h1>
```

Once you have found the preceding line of code, change the line of code as follows:

```
<h1 id="title">MLB Stadiums with CI</h1>
```

In order to see our new build server in action, we need to commit the change to our local repository and then push the change to our remote Git repository. For this, enter the following commands:

```
$ git commit -am "Changing index message"
$ git push
```

You should notice a slightly different workflow than what you are used to seeing when performing a build on the application server gear. If everything went smoothly, you will see the following output:

```
Counting objects: 11, done.
Compressing objects: 100% (5/5), done.
Writing objects: 100% (6/6), 463 bytes | 0 bytes/s, done.
Total 6 (delta 4), reused 0 (delta 0)
remote: Executing Jenkins build.
remote:
remote: You can track your build at https://ciserver-packt.rhcloud.com/job/mlbparks-build
remote:
remote: Waiting for build to schedule..................................................................Done
remote: Waiting for job to complete........................................................................................Done
remote: SUCCESS
remote: New build has been deployed.
remote: ------------------------
remote: Git Post-Receive Result: success
remote: Deployment completed with status: success
To ssh://5311180f500446f54a0003bb@mlbparks-packt.rhcloud.com/~/git/mlbparks.git/
   d4b77ea..d6d9ae9  master -> master
```

Awesome! We just performed a build using the Jenkins CI server, and then automatically deployed the binary artifact to our JBoss EAP server. Don't believe me? Load the `mlbparks` application in your browser and notice that the title for the map has changed, as shown in the following screenshot:

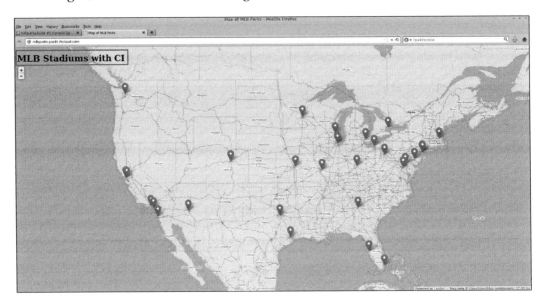

You might have noticed that the build using the Jenkins server took a bit longer than building the code on the application server gear. This is because there is some overhead involved with dynamically creating a new builder gear on the OpenShift platform and then having to perform a full Maven build without an available cache of .jar files. Even though the build might have taken a bit longer, the benefits of using a CI environment far outweigh the additional time required for building. While the build is being performed, you can authenticate to the Jenkins web console and view the status of the build as well as view the console output from the builder gear.

Troubleshooting the build

What happens if the build didn't get completed? This is a common problem that I see when talking to users who are using OpenShift Online and integrating with the Jenkins CI server. 99 times out of 100, it is because they have run out of free resources on the service. This is an important concept to understand if your build failed as it is most likely due to this problem. At the current time, the free tier for OpenShift Online generously allows users to create up to three gears before requiring the user to upgrade their account with more access.

If you remember from earlier in this chapter, the Jenkins CI server creates a dynamic gear on the fly for all builds with a profile that is specified in the build configuration items. Even though this builder gear is short lived, it still counts against your gear ratio on the platform. What this means is that in order for you to utilize the Jenkins build server, you can only have two running gears when performing a build. As an example, the `mlbparks` application will consume the following gears:

- One gear for the core JBoss EAP server that serves application requests. This is the `http://mlbparks-yourUsername.rhcloud.com` gear.
- One gear for the Jenkins server. This is the `http://ciserver-yourUsername.rhcloud.com` gear.
- One gear that will be created dynamically in order to perform builds, and then will be destroyed after the build is complete.

Manually triggering a build

One of the great things about integrating your application with the Jenkins CI environment is the ability to start a new build without having to modify or push your source code. To initiate a new build, log in to the Jenkins dashboard and select the **mlbparks** builder. Once you are on this page, simply click on the **Build Now** button that is located on the left-hand side of the screen, as shown in the following screenshot:

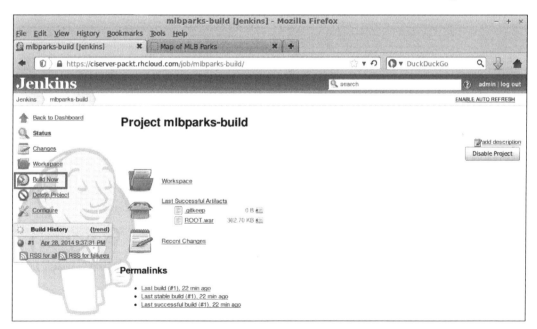

Once you click on the **Build Now** button, a new build will be scheduled on the server and will be reflected under the **Build History** section of the dashboard:

For more information about the current build, you can click on **build** under the **Build History** section in order to view the details, including the console output, as shown in the following screenshot:

Summary

In this chapter, we learned how to implement the popular Jenkins continuous integration environment with our applications that have been deployed on the OpenShift Online platform. We started by creating a Jenkins server, and then moved to embedding the Jenkins client to an existing application, `mlbparks`, that we created in *Chapter 5, Creating and Deploying Java EE Applications*. After we embedded the client, we explored some configuration items that can be modified in order to gain more performance from our builds. Lastly, we performed builds using the new CI environment using the `git push` command as well as manually starting a build while using the web console of the Jenkins server.

In the next chapter, we are going to take team development a bit further by exploring how to create multiple domains for an OpenShift account and how to add additional developers with restricted access rights to an application in that domain.

8
Using OpenShift for Team Development

In this chapter, we are going to explore how to use the OpenShift Online platform to manage a team of developers that might be working on the same application or deploying applications under the same account. Learning how to utilize the access controls and permission system that are built into OpenShift will provide the account owner, who might be paying the bills, the authority to grant specific rights to an individual developer. The current access permissions that can be assigned by the account owner are view, edit, and administer.

The view permission level only allows the user to view the details of an application for the domain, such as the name, the add-on cartridges, the number of gears, the amount of storage, and so on. A user with the view access role will not be able to clone the Git repository, SSH to the gear, stop or start the application, or embed add-on cartridges. This role is simply for viewing information about the running applications under the domain.

The edit permission level will allow the user to perform all functions on the domain, such as adding cartridges, creating new applications, deleting applications, viewing and changing the source code, and triggering new deployments. However, this role does not grant you the permission to modify, add, or delete users from the domain access list.

The administer permission level allows you to give full control of the domain to another user. Caution should be observed when granting this permission level, as the added user will be able to modify any setting for the specified domain.

Setting up multiple domains

OpenShift Online allows a user to create multiple domains that are associated with their account. Keep in mind that domain in this context does not refer to the domain name of the application, but a unique identifier for grouping your applications. You can think of an OpenShift domain as a filing cabinet into which you can organize your applications by placing them in the correct cabinet. To understand the impact the domain has on your application, let's examine the URL for an application that is hosted on OpenShift. The standard naming convention for an application URL is `http://appname-domainname.rhcloud.com`.

As you can see in the preceding example, the domain that you choose will become a part of the URL for the application. Given this, it is important to choose a domain that accurately reflects what you are trying to accomplish with the domain.

A common use case for team development is to have a domain for different environments that your application will go through before reaching production. These domains can be named `dev`, `qa`, `stage`, and `production`. You can create additional domains for your account by using the command line or the web console.

> Adding multiple domains to an OpenShift account is only available if you are on a paid plan to use the service. For more information on the available pay-as-you-go offerings, visit `http://www.openshift.com/pricing`.

Adding a new domain with the command line

To add a new domain to your application using the command line, you can use the RHC client tools that we have been using throughout this book. For example, to create a new domain under your account called `packtdev`, issue the following command:

```
$ rhc domain create packtdev
```

If the domain was created as requested, you should see the following output on the screen:

```
Creating domain 'packtdev' ... done
You may now create an application using the rhc create-app command.
```

You might have seen an error message while executing the preceding command. The most common error message is as follows:

```
Creating domain 'packtdev' ... You may not have more than 1 domain.
```

[166]

If you received the preceding message, remember that in order to create additional domains, you need to be on one of the paid offerings for `OpenShift.com`.

The other common error message that users might see is the following:

```
Creating domain 'packtdev' ... Namespace 'packtdev' is already in use.
Please choose another.
```

This error message indicates that another user has already created a domain with the name that you are trying to use. Each domain that is created on the OpenShift platform must be unique across all users of the system.

Once your domain has been created, you can view a list of all domains associated with your account using the following command:

```
$ rhc domain list
```

Adding a new domain with the web console

The OpenShift web console provides a user interface to interact with and manage the domains associated with your account. In order to create a new domain using the web console, log in to the platform by opening up a web browser and going to `http://www.openshift.com`. Once you have authenticated to the web console, you will see the main dashboard as depicted in the following screenshot:

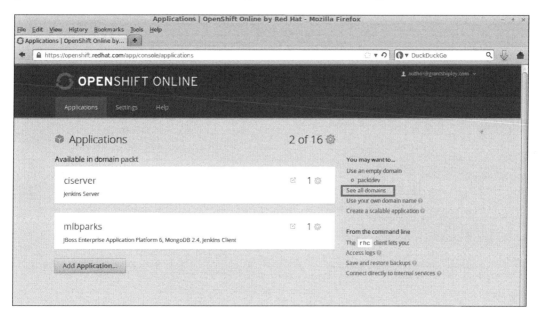

Click on the **See all domains** link on the right-hand side of the screen, as shown in the preceding screenshot. This will take you to the area of the console where you can manage the domains associated with your account. In order to create a new domain, click on the **Add Domain...** button that is underneath your existing domains.

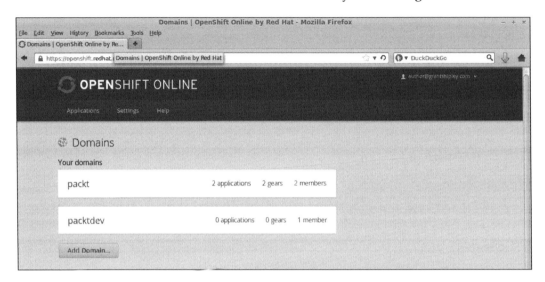

After clicking on the **Add Domain...** button, you will be presented with a screen where you can provide the name of the domain that you want to add to your account. Enter the name and then click on the **Create** button, as shown in the following screenshot:

Once the domain has been added, you will be presented with the settings page that will allow you to modify the configuration for your account. We will cover this settings page in more detail in *Chapter 9, Using the OpenShift Web Console*. For the time being, go back to the domain list for your account to verify that the new item was successfully added. If everything went smoothly, you should see the new domain listed as shown in the following screenshot:

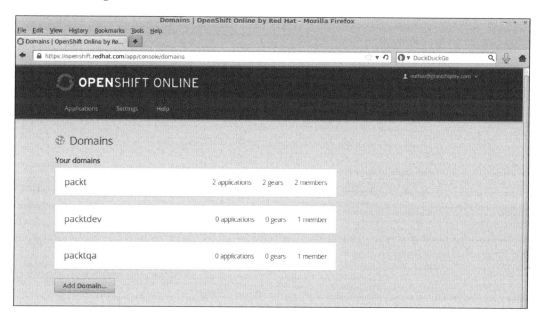

Adding members to a domain

Now that we understand the different roles that can be assigned to a user for a specific domain, it's time to learn how to add new members that will contribute to the projects. The OpenShift platform allows you to add additional members to your domain as long as the user you are adding has an existing account on the platform. If you don't know any other users of the OpenShift platform and just want to try some of these examples out, feel free to use the user account that I have created for the examples in this book, which is `author@grantshipley.com`.

You can add members to your domain using either the web console or the command-line utilities. We will start by learning how to manage members by leveraging the command line and then learn how to perform the same functions via the web console.

Managing members with the command line

In order to add members to a domain using the command line, we will take advantage of the RHC command-line tools that we have used throughout the examples in this book. The first thing we want to do is list the existing members of our domain. To accomplish this task, open up your terminal window and type in the following command, making sure to replace `yourDomainName` with the correct name of the domain that you want to list the membership for:

```
$ rhc member list -n yourDomainName
```

> When performing actions that involve managing members, you must specify the domain you want to perform the action on by using the `-n` argument.

Since we haven't added any members to our domain yet, the only user with membership should be you. For example, my username is `author@grantshipley.com`, so the output when I run the command is as follows:

```
Login                    Role
----------------------   -------------
author@grantshipley.com  admin (owner)
```

In order to add a new member to the domain, you simply use the `member add` arguments as follows:

```
$ rhc member add authordev@grantshipley.com -n yourDomainName
```

Upon the execution of the preceding command, you should see the following message, which indicates that the operation was successful:

```
Adding 1 editor to domain ... done
```

To verify that the new member was added, execute the following command:

```
$ rhc member list -n yourDomainName
```

You should see the following output, which confirms that the new member was added:

```
Login                          Role
---------------------------    ------------
author@grantshipley.com        admin (owner)
authordev@grantshipley.com edit
```

Modifying a member's role in a domain

An interesting thing that you might have noticed is that we did not specify the role that we wanted to be applied to the member. In the case where a role is not specified, the OpenShift platform will default the membership to the edit role. Let's imagine that we made a mistake and actually wanted to add the new member under the view-only role. In order to change a role for a member, you can simply execute the `rhc member add` command again while also specifying the role to be applied to the member. For example, to update the role for the `author+dev@grantshipley.com` member, we can simply issue the following command:

```
$ rhc member add author+dev@grantshipley.com -n yourDomainName --role view
```

You should see the following output, thus confirming the operation was successful:

```
Adding 1 viewer to domain ... done
```

> To view the available roles and the associated access rights for each one, you can use the `rhc member help` command.

To verify that the new member was added, execute the following command:

```
$ rhc member list -n yourDomainName
```

You should see the following output, thus confirming that the new member was added:

```
Login                          Role
---------------------------    -------------
author@grantshipley.com        admin (owner)
authordev@grantshipley.com     view
```

Deleting a member from a domain

The time will come when someone you have granted a membership role decides to stop working on the application, moves to a new development team, or perhaps leaves the company. When this happens, it is important that you are able to remove their access to the domain and all associated applications. Performing this management task is an easy and straightforward process by utilizing the `rhc member remove` command, as shown in the following example:

```
$ rhc member remove authordev@grantshipley.com -n yourDomainName
```

Once the command has been executed, you should see the following confirmation:

```
Removing 1 member from domain ... done
```

Managing members with the web console

The OpenShift Online web console provides the membership management functionality directly in your browser. In order to access this functionality, log in to your OpenShift account and then navigate to the domain management screen as shown in the following screenshot:

Chapter 8

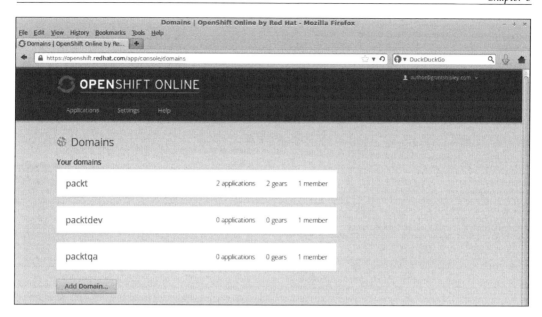

On this page, you can see the number of applications that belong to the domain, the total number of gears consumed by all of the applications, as well as the number of members who have access to the domain. In order to manage the membership for a particular domain, simply click on the domain that you want to manage, and you will be presented with the following screenshot:

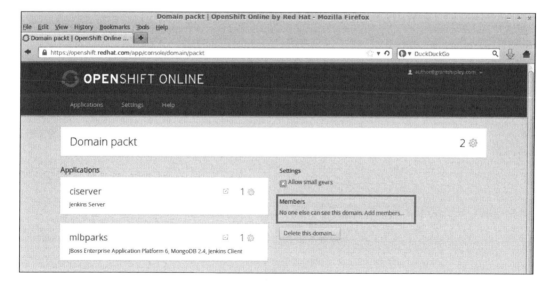

Using OpenShift for Team Development

On this screen, you can see all the applications that you have deployed as well as the number of gears that each application is consuming. On the right-hand side of the screen, you will see the **Members** section that will list all the current members with permissions for the domain. In order to add a new member to the domain, simply click on the **Add members...** link. After clicking on this link, a dialog will be presented where you can enter the username of the member you want to add as well as the corresponding role that should be assigned to the member, as shown in the following screenshot:

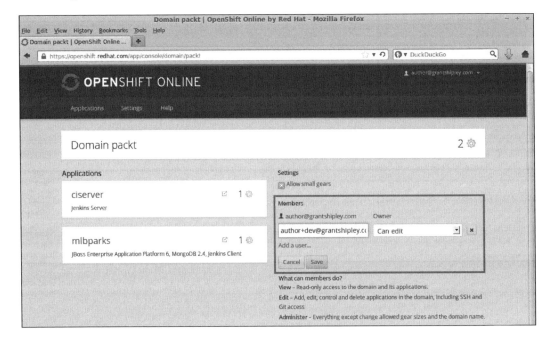

Once you have added the username and role for the new member, click on the **Save** button. After the operation is complete, you will see a message indicating that the addition of the member was successful.

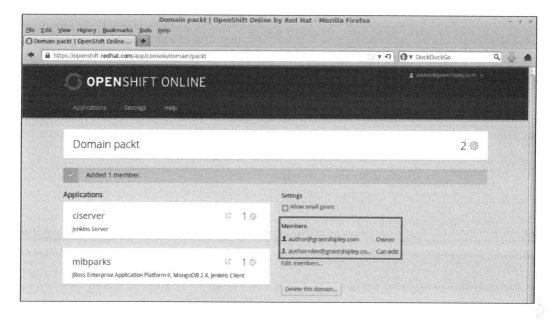

Modifying a member's role and deleting a member

In order to modify the permissions or role that a member has for a domain, you can simply click on the **Edit members...** link, and a dropdown that allows you to select the new role list will be presented. Highlight the new role and click on the **Save** button, as shown in the following screenshot:

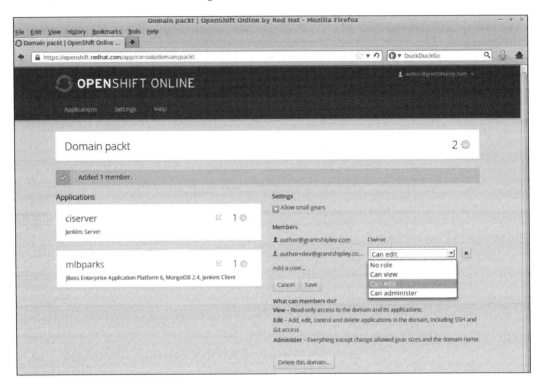

In order to delete a member from a domain, you can click on the **x** button that is displayed next to the users role, and then click on the **Save** button.

Promoting code between environments

One of the most common questions that I get asked about the OpenShift Online platform by larger organizations and development teams is how to perform code promotion between different environments.

Organizations want to allow developers to have full control over the development environment where they can create gears on demand in order to take advantage of the speed with which they can develop the software.

Chapter 8

The QA team wants full access to the QA environment as well as to be the only ones who can provision servers and deploy stable builds from the development environment. Once the QA team has deployed the application to their environment, they don't want pesky developers to be able to log in to the gears and modify configuration settings or code that might invalidate their test cases.

In the production environment, the system administrators and release engineers need full control over the environment while locking out both the development and quality assurance teams.

Fortunately, using the information you have learned in this chapter, you should have the tools and knowledge required to accomplish this common scenario by creating additional domains and assigning proper membership and roles to each domain.

For this scenario to work properly, you will need to create three domains: dev, qa, and production. Once the domains have been created, you can then begin assigning access permissions to each member in the corresponding team that needs access to that environment. The following diagram shows how you can configure your account for this scenario:

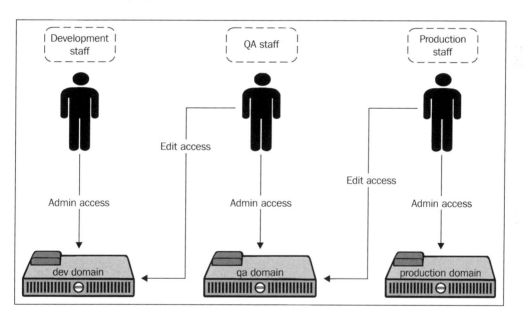

Using OpenShift for Team Development

To fully understand this concept, let's look at each team in a bit more detail:

- **Development staff**: This has full admin access to the dev domain. It will allow the member of the operations team to add additional team members, provision gears, create applications, embed cartridges, clone repositories, and push code to the continuous integration environment. This team has no access to the qa or production domains.

- **QA staff**: This has full admin access to the qa domain. It will allow the member of the operations team to add additional team members, provision gears, create applications, embed cartridges, clone repositories, and deploy code. This has edit access to the dev domain. Having this edit access is essential in order to be able to create a copy of the final build that is deployed to the development environment.

- **Production staff**: This has full admin access to the production domain. It will allow the member of the operations team to add additional team members, provision gears, create applications, embed cartridges, clone repositories, and deploy code. This has edit access to the qa domain. Having this edit access is essential in order to be able to create a copy of the final build that has passed all tests in the QA environment.

Promoting the code

The developers have been hard at work and have deployed the final version of the application to their development environment. It is now time to hand this build over to the QA team so that they can run their test suite and validate the release. Since the QA team has edit permissions on the development domain and admin permissions on the QA domain, they will be able to simply clone the existing deployment, including all the runtimes, databases, data in the database, and any additional add-on cartridges. Luckily, this can be accomplished with a single command that is provided as part of the RHC tool suite. For example, if the application was named mlbparks, the QA team can simply enter the following command:

```
$ rhc app create devmlb -n qaDomainName --from-app devDomainName/mlbparks
```

> Keep in mind that if the application you are cloning from the development domain has a dependency on a Jenkins server, the QA domain must also have a Jenkins server available for use.

Once the preceding command has been executed, you will see the following output:

```
Application Options
-------------------
Domain:      qaDomainName
Cartridges:  jbosseap-6 (addtl. costs may apply), mongodb-2.4, jenkins-client-1
From app:    mlbparks
Gear Size:   Copied from 'mlbparks'
Scaling:     no (copied from 'mlbparks')
Creating application 'devmlb' ... done
  MongoDB 2.4 database added.  Please make note of these credentials:
   Root User:      admin
   Root Password: B8spTFvYFAK6
   Database Name: devmlb
Connection URL: mongodb://$OPENSHIFT_MONGODB_DB_HOST:$OPENSHIFT_MONGODB_DB_PORT/
Associated with job 'devmlb-build' in Jenkins server.
Waiting for your DNS name to be available ... done
Setting deployment configuration ... done
Pulling down a snapshot of application 'mlbparks' to
/var/folders/jd/bdhxtn214mgfpmy72dyyy4140000gn/T/mlbparks_temp_clone.tar.gz ...
done
Restoring from snapshot /var/folders/jd/bdhxtn214mgfpmy72dyyy4140000gn/T/mlbparks_temp_clone.tar.gz to
application 'devmlb' ...

Cloning into 'devmlb'...
```

Wait, what? Did that really just happen? Indeed, it did. We just cloned an existing application that was created by a team member in another domain to our own environment. Not only did we clone the application code, but we also cloned all of the add-on cartridges and any data that was populated in the database. Pretty powerful stuff!

Adding access using SSH keys

So far in this chapter, we have discussed the concept of using the built-in membership management system in order to allow additional users access to your domain. Another option, although not recommended, is that you simply add the user's SSH key to which you want to grant access to your OpenShift account. The easiest way to accomplish this is to make the user send you their public SSH key and upload it via the web console. For this, log in to the OpenShift console and click on the **Settings** tab at the top of the screen.

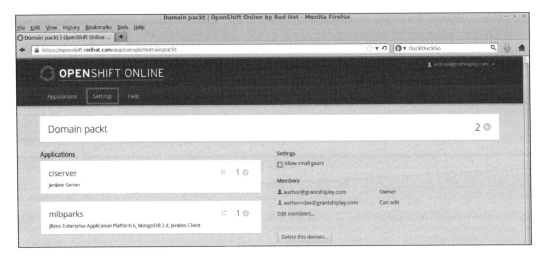

Once you are on the **Settings** page, you will see all of the SSH keys that are associated with your account. To add a new key, click on the button labeled **Add a new key...** and paste the contents of the user's public key into the text area.

Chapter 8

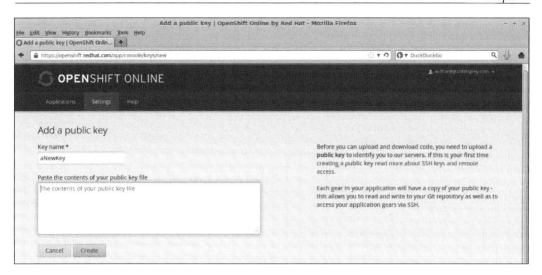

Once you have added the user's key, they will be able to clone the Git repository that resides on the remote OpenShift gear as well as push code changes to the server.

 The user will not be able to perform operations on the application—such as adding cartridges or restarting the server—as these operations require the RHC command-line tools as well as an authorization token that can only be obtained by knowing the username and password for the account.

You can also add an SSH key to your account using the following command:

`$ rhc sshkey add <name> <path to SSH key file>`

To remove a key, issue the following command:

`$ rhc sshkey remove <name>`

[181]

Summary

In this chapter, we learned how to create and manage additional domains for your OpenShift account. We also learned how to add new members to a domain and specify the access role that is associated with each member. The available access roles are view, edit, and administer. We also learned how to utilize the membership system in order to promote code from one environment to another by cloning the existing deployed application. Finally, we learned how to add SSH keys to your account that will provide access to other developers in order to clone your Git repository as well as push new code to your OpenShift gear.

In the next chapter, we are going to focus on the OpenShift web console and learn how to manage your account and application from the browser. We will also learn how to add a custom domain name to your application so that you can use any URL that you own to access your application.

9
Using the OpenShift Web Console

In this chapter, we are going to focus on and learn how to interact with the OpenShift platform by using the web console that is available to all users of the system. We are going to start by learning how to create applications. After we learn how to create applications, we are going to explore how to embed add-on cartridges, and then learn how to manage applications deployed to the platform. Finally, we are going to learn how to create and apply a custom domain name for an application.

Creating applications

Previously in this book, we created several applications using the command-line tools that are provided by the platform. There will often be times when you want to quickly spin up an application, such as the Drupal CMS system, without having to use the command line. A popular use of the web console is to browse available community cartridges and application stacks, as all of these are integrated into the web console. This can save you a lot of time by being able to view a list of approved projects that you can get started with versus having to search Google to find what you are looking for.

To get started with creating an application with the web console, the first thing you need to do is log in to the platform by opening up your favorite browser and visiting `http://www.openshift.com`.

Once the site is loaded, click on the **LOG IN** button on the right-hand side of the page and provide your authentication details.

Using the OpenShift Web Console

> Your authentication details are the username and password that you created in *Chapter 1, Creating Your First OpenShift Application*.

After you are successfully authenticated to the platform, you will be presented with the application dashboard. In order to create a new application on the platform, click on the **Add Application...** button as shown in the following screenshot:

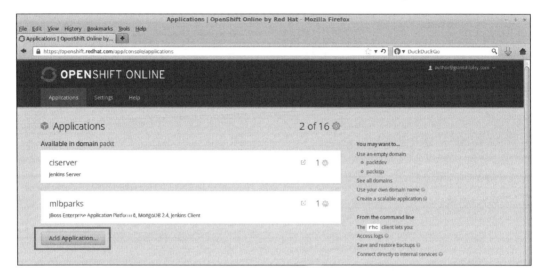

After clicking on this button, the system will display the first step of the create application wizard where you can choose the runtime or application stack that you want to use for your gear. This page is broken up into several areas:

- **Featured applications area**: This section of the page will display any currently highlighted application stacks that are available for you to use. This is normally populated with new and exciting cartridges that may have been contributed by the community.

- **Instant applications area**: These applications are preconfigured code repositories that normally consist of a full application stack for popular applications and frameworks. A good example is the WordPress instant application that includes the PHP runtime, a MySQL database, and the WordPress source code—all ready to use. Instant applications are also commonly referred to as quickstarts.

- **Language-specific areas**: These areas are dedicated to specific runtimes and applications that are tagged for a specific language. The sections are broken down into areas such as Java, Python, and PHP.

- **Code anything area**: This area is set aside for developers who want to create an application based on an existing custom cartridge that they have a URL for. Developers also have the ability to create a DIY application, which will be covered in *Chapter 13, Using the Do-It-Yourself Cartridge*.

Each of these areas will display a list of choices that the user can choose from when creating a new application. An example of one of these sections is shown in the following screenshot, which displays the area focused on PHP-based applications:

Each item listed in the preceding screenshot contains a logo for the specific application type on the left-hand side of the item and then the title for the choice. On the right-hand side of the selection is a list of images that will help you understand information on the cartridge you will be installing. The shield, as shown in the **PHP 5.3** selection in the preceding screenshot, lets the user know that this cartridge will receive automatic security updates from the OpenShift team. The icon to the right of the shield in the **PHP 5.3** example is a symbol that represents a cartridge. Furthermore, the icon displayed to the right of the **CakePHP** choice informs the user that this is a quickstart.

> When choosing a cartridge, it is important to understand the difference between those that receive automatic security updates and those that don't. For cartridges that receive automatic updates, the OpenShift team will routinely patch cartridges that power your application to ensure that any security errata is applied. This allows the developer to have one less thing to worry about. On the other hand, if automatic security updates are not provided for the chosen cartridge, the developer is responsible for updating and applying any security errata to the gear.

If you want to search for a particular application type, you can use the search box at the top of the screen or browse all of the selections based on the tag associated with the item, as indicated in the following screenshot:

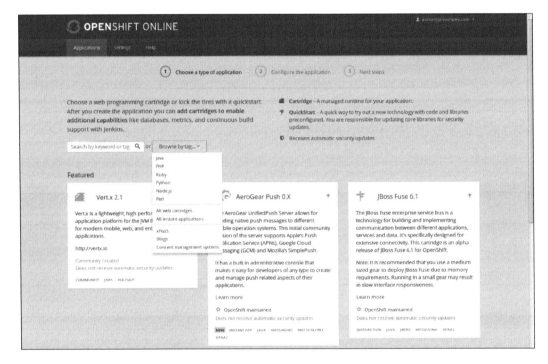

Using instant applications

To learn how to create OpenShift gears based on an instant application, we are going to utilize the search box at the top of this page. Scroll to the top and enter `codeigniter`, and then press the *Enter* key on your keyboard or click on the magnifying glass on the right-hand side of the search box. Once the search is complete, the CodeIgniter quickstart will be displayed on the screen.

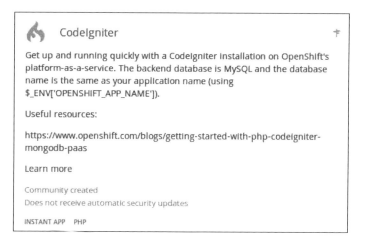

If you want to dig a little bit deeper to understand all of the components that will be installed on your gear as well as where the source code will initially be cloned from, you can click on the **Learn more** link:

Using the OpenShift Web Console

As we can see from the preceding screenshot, this instant application will install the PHP runtime, a MySQL database, and then clone the source for the CodeIgniter framework from the listed GitHub repository.

> CodeIgniter is a popular Model-View-Controller framework that is written for the PHP language. It has a small footprint and was designed for developers who want a simple toolkit to create robust and full-featured PHP applications. For more information on this framework, visit the official project page at `http://ellislab.com/codeigniter`.

Now, click on the **Deploy Now** button at the top of the screen to be presented with the second step of the application creation wizard.

[188]

This step of the application's creation process has the following sections:

- **Based On**: This will display information on the quickstart or instant application template that will be used to create your gear. This area also contains information to let you know whether the cartridge will be automatically updated with security errata.

- **Public URL**: This allows you to specify the name of the application that will be appended to your OpenShift domain in order to create the full URL of the application. If you have multiple domains associated with your account, a drop-down list will be provided in order to allow you to select the domain under which you want the application to be created.

- **Source Code**: This area contains the optional GitHub repository that your application will clone upon creation. For a quickstart or instant application, this field will be automatically filled in with the correct repository. If you are creating an application from scratch, you can leave this field blank.

- **Gears**: This allows you to specify the size of the gear that the application will reside in. If you are on the free plan, the only option available will be a small gear. However, paid users have the option to select additional gear sizes with more available memory and disk space.

- **Cartridges**: This specifies the runtime cartridge that will be used for your application. If you are creating an application based on a quickstart or instant application, this area will also contain any add-on cartridges that are required for the application to be deployed.

- **Scaling**: This allows you to specify whether you want your application to automatically scale up to additional gears based on the amount of HTTP traffic that the gear is handling. This will be explained in more detail in *Chapter 12, Scaling Applications*.

For this example, change the name of the application from `php` to `codeigniter`, and then click on the **Create Application** button at the bottom of the screen.

After the gear has been created, you will see a confirmation screen that displays some vital information. This information will include the connection information for the MySQL database and the command that clones your newly created application's remote Git repository.

 While the authentication and connection information is provided for databases added to your application, it is important to remember that the recommended way of connecting is through the use of environment variables.

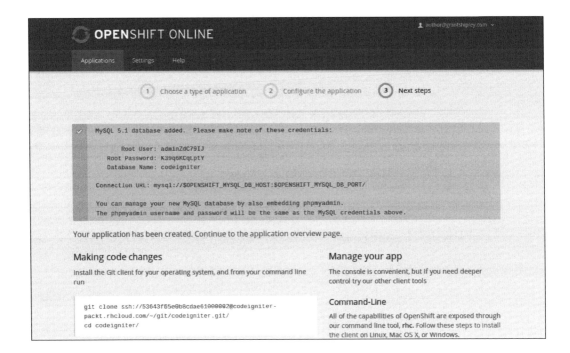

Verify that your application has been created by visiting the site with your web browser. If everything is working correctly, you should see the following screenshot:

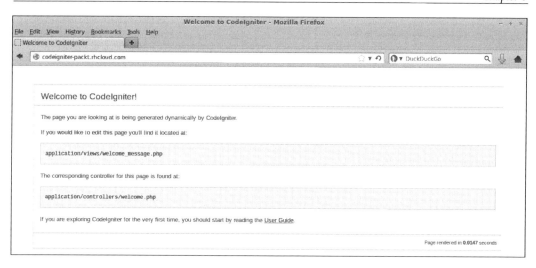

Modifying the source code

Now that we have our application gear created, let's examine how to make modifications to the source code. If you recall from *Chapter 2, Creating and Managing Applications*, when an application is created using the command-line tools, part of the process is to clone the remote Git repository to your local machine. When creating applications using the web console, this step is not performed. In order to push new code changes to your OpenShift gear, you will need to clone the repository for your application. This can be performed in one of two ways. You can either use the RHC command-line tools or use the Git command to clone the repository.

First, let's learn how to clone the repository using the Git command that is installed on your operating system. Open a command line and navigate to the directory where you want the source code to be located. Once you are in this directory, issue the following command:

```
$ git clone <git_remote_url>
```

 Ensure that you replace `<git_remote_url>` with the correct URL that was provided to you on the confirmation screen when you created the application. The URL for your Git repository is also available via the `rhc app show` command.

This will create a directory on your local filesystem named `codeigniter`. Switch to this newly created directory and edit the `welcome_message.php` file that is located under the `php/application/view` directory. Change `<h1>Welcome to CodeIgniter!</h1>` to `<h1>Welcome to CodeIgniter on OpenShift!</h1>`.

Once you have modified and saved this file, you can push the changes up to the OpenShift gear using the same process that you are already familiar with, namely the `commit` and `push` commands:

```
$ git commit -am "Change welcome message"
$ git push
```

After the modified code has been deployed, verify that the change was successful by opening your application in a web browser. If everything went as expected, you should see the updated text as shown in the following screenshot:

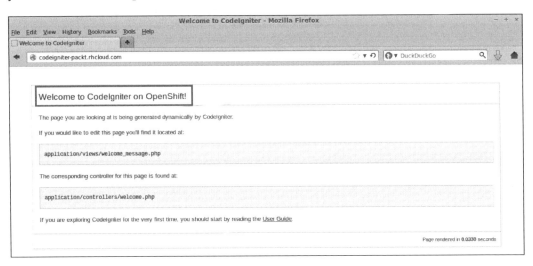

As you can see, once you have cloned the application's repository to your local machine, the workflow for changing the source code is the same, regardless of what tool you used to create the application.

Now that we know how to clone an application using the Git command, let's explore how to perform the same function with the RHC client tools. You might be wondering why you would want to use the RHC command-line tools to clone an OpenShift repository instead of using the Git command proper. Using the RHC tools provides a lot of convenience to the developer in that the developer does not need to know the URL of the Git repository. The developer only needs to know the name of the application that he/she wants to clone locally. Furthermore, for the RHC context-aware commands to work properly, you will need to use the RHC tools to clone the repository, as this adds additional metadata to the `.git/config` file. To clone the `codeigniter` application that we created using the RHC command-line tools, enter the following command:

```
$ rhc git-clone codeigniter
```

> The metadata that is added to the `.git/config` file as part of the clone using the RHC command-line tools contains the `app-id`, `app-name`, and `domain-name` of the application.

Managing applications

The OpenShift web console allows you to perform many, but not all, administration tasks for your application that the command-line tools allow. This includes adding cartridges, restarting your application, adding custom domain names, managing SSH keys, and deleting an entire application.

Using the OpenShift Web Console

Adding cartridges

Most applications that are created on the OpenShift platform will rely on add-on cartridges to extend the functionality of the application. The most common use case of an add-on cartridge is the addition of a database cartridge to an application. During this section, we are going to learn how to embed add-on cartridges using the web console.

Now that you are familiar with how to create applications using the web console, create a new gear named `cartadd` and then navigate to the application's overview page, as shown in the following screenshot:

On this page, you can see all of the current cartridges associated with the application as well as have the ability to add additional ones. To view a list of all of the available cartridges for the runtime that you have chosen for your gear, click on the **Or, see the entire list of cartridges you can add** link. This will take you to a page that details all of the available cartridges.

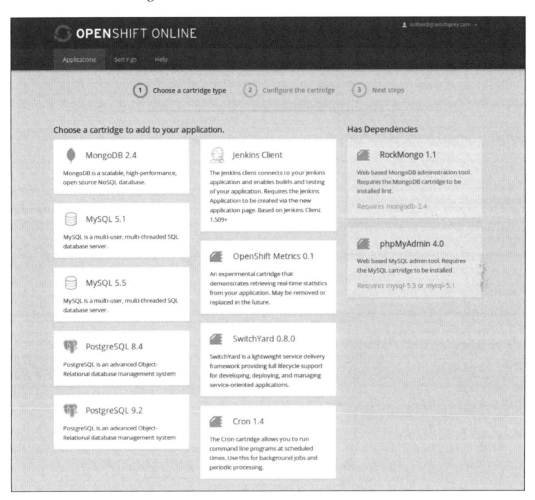

Using the OpenShift Web Console

Let's install the MongoDB 2.4 cartridge by clicking on the box for that selection. Once you click on the add-on cartridge that you want to embed in your gear, you will be shown a confirmation page that displays information about the cartridge. To confirm that you want to embed this cartridge, click on the **Add Cartridge** button at the bottom of the screen.

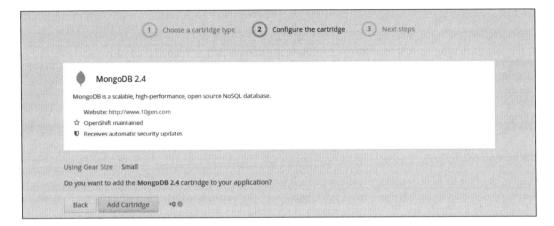

Once the cartridge has been added to your gear, you will see a confirmation screen that will provide you with the details that you will need in order to authenticate to the database.

> If a particular add-on cartridge that you want to use is not listed on the **Add Cartridge** page, you can search GitHub for community-based cartridges, such as Redis, that you can install and use on the platform.

Restarting an application

In order to restart an application from the web console, browse to the application's overview page of the gear you want to restart by clicking on the application name from the OpenShift dashboard. Once you are on the application's page, restarting the gear is as simple as clicking on the **Restart** button in the top-right corner of the page. For example, if you wanted to restart the `cartadd` application that we created in the previous section of this chapter, you can click on the button highlighted in the following screenshot:

Chapter 9

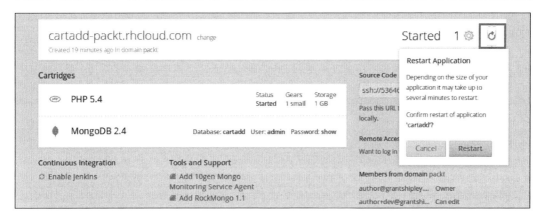

Once the application has been restarted, you will receive a confirmation message on the application's overview page.

 There is currently no way to stop or restart a specific cartridge, such as MongoDB, via the web console. If you only want to restart a specific cartridge instead of the entire gear, you will need to use the RHC command-line tools.

Adding a custom domain name and SSL certificate

OpenShift Online supports the use of custom domain names for an application so that a user does not have to use the automatically generated one that is based on the application name and domain for the users' account. For example, suppose that we want to use `http://www.example.com` domain name for the `cartadd` application that we created in a previous section of this chapter. The first thing you need to do before you set up a custom domain name is buy the domain name from a domain registration provider.

Once the domain name has been purchased, you have to add a CNAME record for the custom domain name with the DNS provider for your domain. Once you have created the CNAME record, you can let OpenShift Online know about the CNAME using the web console.

 For more information on what a CNAME record is, it is suggested that you visit `http://en.wikipedia.org/wiki/CNAME_record`.

To add a custom alias to the `cartadd` application, browse the application's overview page and click on the **change** link next to your application's name.

In the following page, you can specify the custom domain name for your application. Go ahead and add a custom domain name of `www.example.com`, as shown in the following screenshot:

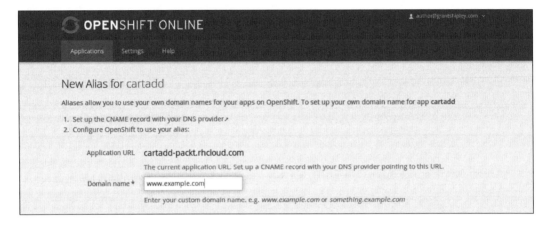

When adding a custom domain name for your application, you also have the option to add a custom SSL certificate for the domain name that you are adding. For this, you will need to first purchase an SSL certificate from a provider, and then upload the certificate, certificate chain, private key, and pass key.

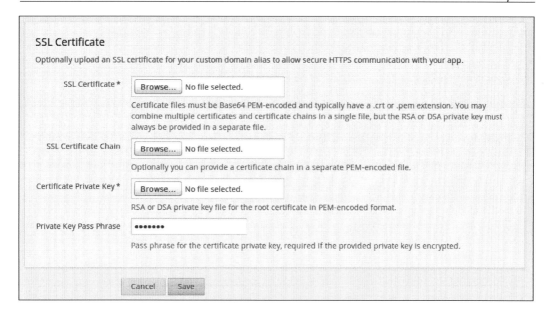

 Adding a custom SSL certificate is only available on one of the many pay-as-you-go plans offered by the OpenShift platform.

Once you have added the custom domain and optionally added a custom SSL certificate, you should see the new domain name listed on the application's overview page.

 If you point your web browser to `http://www.example.com`, you will notice that your application is not displayed. This is because the domain name has not been set up with a DNS registry. In order to verify that this vhost was added to your application gear, you can add an entry in your `/etc/hosts` or equivalent file for your operating system.

Creating a URL for application cloning

A great feature of OpenShift that is not widely known is its ability to create a URL that will populate the application creation fields on the web console in order to allow someone to clone your application with a single click. This is a very powerful feature if you want to share the application code among a group of developers, as it eliminates the headache of a new developer having to set up an environment. As an example, we are going to create a single click URL for the mlbparks application that we wrote as part of *Chapter 5, Creating and Deploying Java EE Applications*. The URL is broken down into the following parts:

- The main domain name for the OpenShift Online service that creates custom applications (https://openshift.redhat.com/app/console/application_types/custom).

- The cartridges that will be used for the application passed in as an array since more than one cartridge might be needed for the application. For instance, the mlbparks application requires the JBoss EAP cartridge as well as the MongoDB cartridge:

    cartridges[]=jbosseap-6&cartridges[]=mongodb-2.4

- The initial Git repository for the application. For the mlbparks application, we are going to use the GitHub repository that contains the source code from *Chapter 5, Creating and Deploying Java EE Applications* (initial_git_url=https%3A%2F%2Fgithub.com/gshipley/mlbparks.git).

- The last argument, which is name=mlbparks, is the default name that will be populated when the user clicks on the URL.

The complete URL that incorporates all of the preceding arguments to perform this magic is https://openshift.redhat.com/app/console/application_types/custom?cartridges[]=jbosseap-6&cartridges[]=mongodb-2.4&initial_git_url=https%3A%2F%2Fgithub.com/gshipley/mlbparks.git&name=mlbparks.

> For an even better experience when sharing these custom URLs, you might consider using a URL shortening service that makes it even easier for a new user to get started deploying your application.

Deleting an application

The OpenShift web console makes it extremely easy to delete an application that you no longer need. This is important if you want to free up a gear for use by another application. To learn how to perform this task, let's delete the `cartadd` application that we created earlier in this chapter.

Navigate to the application's overview page for the `cartadd` application and click on the **Delete this application...** button that is in the bottom right-hand corner of the page.

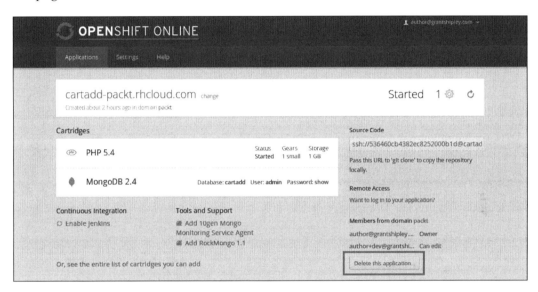

Once you click on the **Delete this application...** button, you will be presented with a confirmation screen that ensures that you really want the system to perform this action. If you are sure you want to remove the application, click on the **Delete** button.

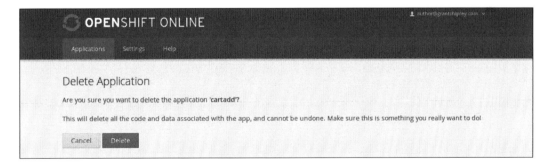

Once the delete operation is complete, you will be returned to the application dashboard, and a confirmation message will be displayed letting you know that the action was a success.

Summary

In this chapter, we learned how to use the OpenShift web console to create applications, and how to embed add-on cartridges to extend the functionality of the newly created gear. After this, we explored how to manage an existing application by adding a custom domain and SSL certificate. We also learned how to create a reusable URL that enables you to share your application with others by allowing them to create a clone of the gear with a single URL. Lastly, we learned how to delete applications with the web console when they are no longer in use.

In the next chapter, we are going to learn how to debug applications that are running on a remote OpenShift gear. We will learn how to enable remote debugging inside of the Eclipse IDE, and then, how to set break points to step through the application code.

10
Debugging Applications

If you are a software developer, you know that being able to debug application code is critical when developing and troubleshooting applications. In this chapter, we are going to learn how to use port forwarding to connect to remote databases. After this, we are going to explore how to use remote debugging to debug the application code by setting breakpoints from within the Eclipse and IntelliJ IDEs. Finally, we are going to learn how to leverage OpenShift Online partners to enhance the capabilities of our application to add support for log viewing and monitoring.

Using port forwarding

As we have learned previously in this book, you can embed add-on cartridges to your application gears, such as MySQL and MongoDB. However, connections to these remote data stores are restricted to requests that come from the local gear where the cartridge resides. This is great for security but a poor experience if you want to remotely connect to a database in order to import data or to view, edit, or create the schema of the database. Fortunately, the RHC command-line tools come equipped with a feature that allows you to connect to the remote database using port forwarding. Don't be alarmed if you don't understand the details of how port forwarding works as the client tools automate the process.

> Port forwarding translates connections created on one host to another by utilizing the available SSH connection. This allows users to connect to remote daemons on a private network by treating them as locally running services as long as the local machine has access to the remote private network.

Debugging Applications

To illustrate how port forwarding works on the OpenShift platform, we are going to forward the MongoDB database that we created in *Chapter 5, Creating and Deploying Java EE Applications*, so that we can connect to it locally. The first thing we want to do is run the port forwarding command on our local machine with the following command:

```
$ rhc port-forward -a mlbparks
```

Once you enter the preceding command, you will see the following output:

```
Checking available ports ... done
Forwarding ports ...

To connect to a service running on OpenShift, use the Local address

Service Local                OpenShift
------- ---------------      --------------------
java    127.0.0.1:3528    => 127.7.150.129:3528
java    127.0.0.1:4447    => 127.7.150.129:4447
java    127.0.0.1:5445    => 127.7.150.129:5445
java    127.0.0.1:8080    => 127.7.150.129:8080
java    127.0.0.1:9990    => 127.7.150.129:9990
java    127.0.0.1:9999    => 127.7.150.129:9999
mongodb 127.0.0.1:27017   => 127.7.150.130:27017

Press CTRL-C to terminate port forwarding
```

 Port forwarding will remain active until you stop the process by pressing *Ctrl* + *C* on your keyboard.

In the preceding output, we can see that several ports on the remote server are now available on the local machine. For instance, MongoDB is running at the remote IP address of `127.7.150.130` on port `27017` but is now available locally by connecting to `127.0.0.1`, or localhost, using port `27017`. A developer will connect locally and all the traffic will be forwarded via an encrypted SSH connection to the remote OpenShift gear, as shown in the following diagram:

Chapter 10

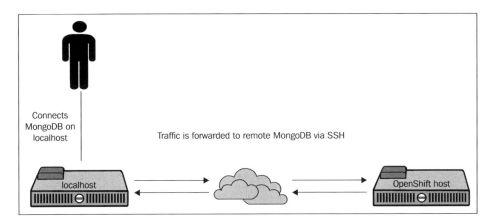

Connecting to MongoDB

Now that we have our NoSQL database available on the local machine, we can connect to it just as if it were running locally. In order to be able to communicate with MongoDB, you will need to have the MongoDB client installed on your local machine.

> The instructions for installing the client on Ubuntu are listed in the following section, but you will need to consult the official MongoDB documentation for instructions on how to install the client for your operating system.

To install the client tools on an Ubuntu-based operating system, open a terminal window and enter the following command:

```
$ sudo apt-get install mongodb-clients
```

In order to connect to the remote MongoDB database, you will need to know the username and password to authenticate to the data store. You can find this information by showing information about the MongoDB cartridge that you added to the mlbparks application with the following command:

```
$ rhc cartridge show mongodb -a mlbparks
```

This will display all of the relevant details that you need in order to connect to the database, including the username and password, as shown in the following output:

```
Using mongodb-2.4 (MongoDB 2.4) for 'mongodb'
mongodb-2.4 (MongoDB 2.4)
-------------------------
```

Debugging Applications

```
Gears:              Located with jbosseap-6, jenkins-client-1
Connection URL: mongodb://$OPENSHIFT_MONGODB_DB_HOST:$OPENSHIFT_
MONGODB_DB_PORT/
Database Name:      mlbparks
Password:           q_6eZ22-fraN
Username:           admin
```

In the preceding output, the username is `admin` and the password is `q_6eZ22-fraN`.

> Be sure to use the proper username and password for your cartridge installation and not the one displayed as an example in this book.

Now that we have the authentication information and the `mongo` client installed, we can connect using the following command on our local machine:

```
$ mongo 127.0.0.1:27017/mlbparks -u admin -p q_6eZ22-fraN
```

This will present you with the MongoDB shell. To verify that you are indeed connected to the remote MongoDB database, issue a command to get the count of baseball teams in the database:

```
$ db.teams.count()
```

> If you want to see the JavaScript source code that MongoDB is running to execute the query, you can leave off the parenthesis of any command to view the source of the command.

If everything went correctly, the result should be **30**.

You can also use your favorite database management software to connect to and manage your database. For example, let's examine how to use the popular UMongo package to connect to our remote MongoDB instance.

> UMongo is written in Java and is therefore available for the three big operating systems: Windows, Mac OS X, and Linux. To download this software package, head over to the official download site at http://www.edgytech.com/umongo.

Chapter 10

Once you have downloaded the UMongo tool, start the program and select **File** and then **Connect** to create a new connection. Once the connection dialog is displayed, click on the edit icon to modify the current connection.

After clicking on the edit connection icon, you will be presented with a dialog that will allow you to enter the connection and authentication information for the database. Remember to use the correct username and password for your database and ensure that you specify the `127.0.0.1` IP address and the corresponding port.

Debugging Applications

Once you have connected to the database, you can run queries and use the tool just as if the database was running locally. This is illustrated in the following screenshot where I ran a query to list all of the documents in the `teams` collections:

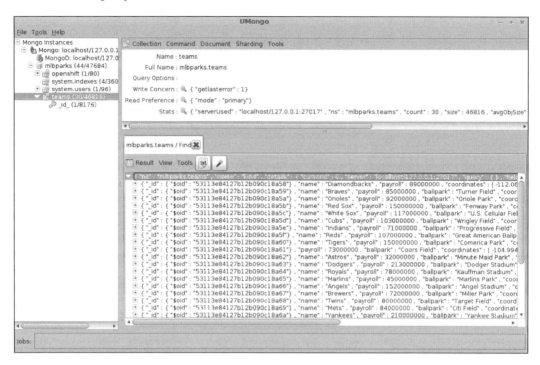

Once you are finished with your work on the remote database, remember to close the port forwarding connection by pressing *Ctrl* + *C* in the terminal window where the connection is established.

Using Eclipse for Java debugging

As a developer, being able to set breakpoints and step through code is crucial to the development process when trying to debug or troubleshoot your application code. OpenShift supports this functionality by allowing Java developers to enable remote debugging by setting a marker that alerts the platform that you want to enable this feature. Don't worry if you don't understand the marker system at this point, as we cover it in detail as part of *Chapter 11, Using the Marker and Action Hook System*. For the purposes of this chapter, we are going to create a new marker and add it to our application using the Git revision control system.

Chapter 10

Open your terminal prompt and go to the directory where your `mlbparks` application is cloned on your local machine. Once you are in your application's directory, run the following command to create a blank file named `enable_jpda` in the `.openshift/markers` directory of your application:

```
$ touch .openshift/markers/enable_jpda
```

If you are not familiar with JPDA, you can find more information at `http://en.wikipedia.org/wiki/Java_Platform_Debugger_Architecture`.

Once you have created this empty file, add the file to your repository, commit the change, and then push the marker to your OpenShift gear:

```
$ git add .
$ git commit -am "enable remote debugging"
$ git push
```

You can also create this marker directly inside of Eclipse by right-clicking on your **mlbparks** project, selecting **OpenShift**, and then selecting **Configure Markers...**.

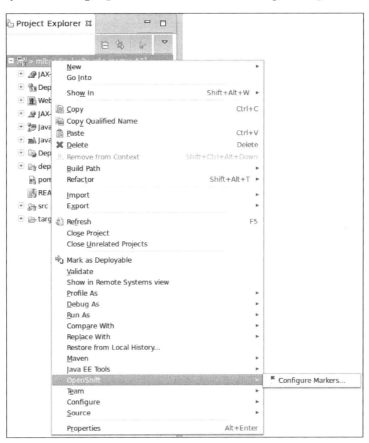

Debugging Applications

Once you select **Configure Markers...**, a dialog will be presented where you can select to enable JPDA, as shown in the following screenshot:

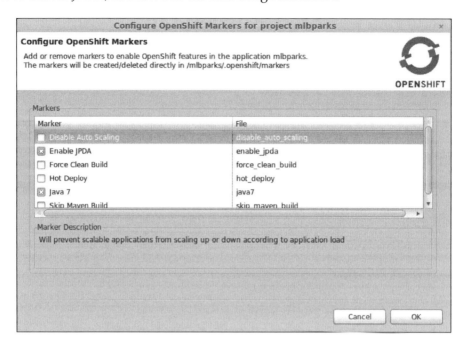

Once JPDA has been enabled and the marker has been pushed to the OpenShift gear, the next step is to enable port forwarding for our application. This will allow us to connect to the debug port (8787) on the remote machine as if it were a local running server. You can start port forwarding using the command-line method we learned in the previous section of this chapter, or you can use the IDE to start the forwarding. To enable port forwarding from within the Eclipse IDE, go to the **OpenShift Explorer** view and find the **mlbparks** application. Right-click on the application and select **Port forwarding...** from the menu, as shown in the following screenshot:

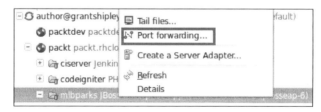

Chapter 10

The IDE will verify that the SSH authentication is configured with the remote OpenShift gear, and then it will present a dialog that shows you the current status of each port. At this point, you can start forwarding by clicking on the **Start All** button on the right-hand side of the dialog.

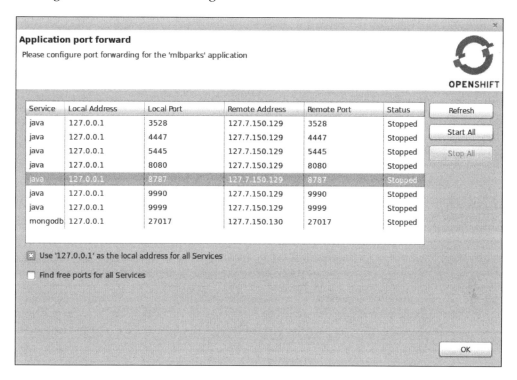

Once the forwarding has started, you can click on the **OK** button to hide the dialog window.

Debugging Applications

The next step is to create a debug configuration that contains the information required to connect to our remote JBoss EAP server running on OpenShift. For this, click on the **Run** menu item at the top of the Eclipse IDE. After clicking on **Run**, select **Debug Configurations**, and then select **Remote Java Application** in the available options. Once this item has been selected, click on the new button in the top-left corner in order to create a new configuration. You can then provide the connection information that was displayed when you started port forwarding.

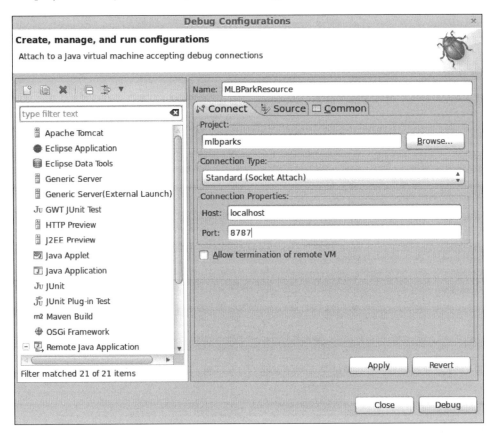

Chapter 10

After the connection information has been entered, click on the **Apply** button, and then click on **Debug** to establish a remote debug session.

The last thing we need to do in order to debug our application is to set a breakpoint in our application code. Open the `MLBParkResource.java` file located under the `src/main/java/org/openshift/mlbparks/rest` directory and set a breakpoint in the following line in the `findParksWithin` method:

```
ArrayList<MLBPark> allParksList = new ArrayList<MLBPark>();
```

The IDE will display an icon next to the line on the left-hand side in order to let you know that a breakpoint has been added.

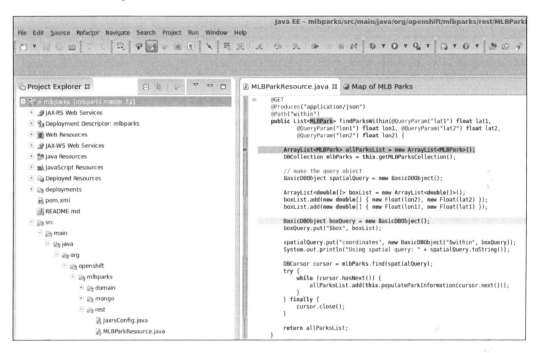

[213]

Debugging Applications

Open a web browser and enter the URL for your application, and you will see that the application breaks at the specified location and allows you to step through the code by using the debug perspective that is part of the Eclipse IDE.

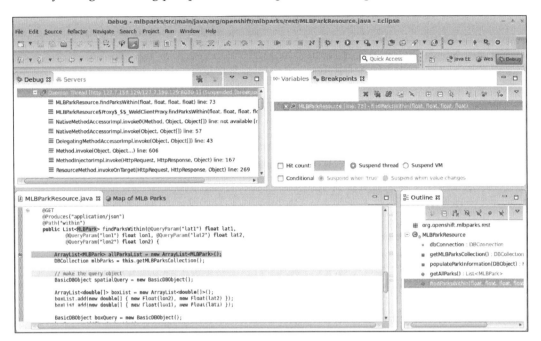

 If the application did not break at the specified breakpoint, ensure that you have port forwarding enabled and are running the application in the debug mode.

Using IntelliJ for Java debugging

In the previous section, we learned how to use Eclipse for the remote debugging of Java applications. In this section, we are going to show you how to use the popular IntelliJ IDE to perform the same action. As you will learn in this section, IntelliJ provides a cleaner experience as the port forwarding requirement is handled under the covers by the IDE when you click on the **Debug** button. Installing the IDE is out of the scope of this book, so I will assume that you have already downloaded and installed the software.

Chapter 10

If this is the first time that you are using IntelliJ to connect to your OpenShift account, you will need to configure your credentials. Open the **Settings** pane and browse to the **Clouds** section. Once this section is displayed, click on the plus sign at the top of the dialog and select **OpenShift**. Enter your authorization information and click on the **Test connection** button.

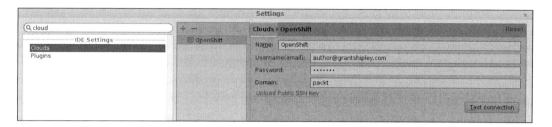

If the connection was a success, exit the **Settings** pane, select **Check out from Version Control**, and choose **git** as the version control system to be used.

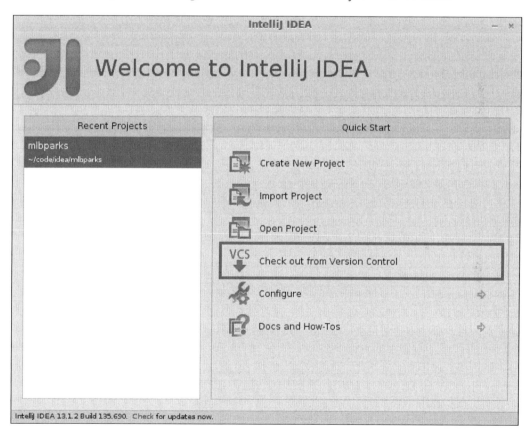

Debugging Applications

Once you select **git**, you will need to provide the URL for the Git repository of your `mlbparks` application. Input the required information in the dialog and click on the **Clone** button.

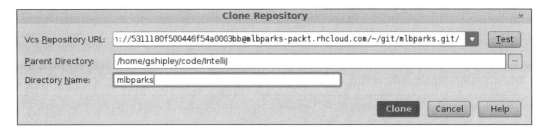

The next thing we need to do is configure a deployment for the `mlbparks` application that we just cloned and created a project for. You can do this by clicking on the **Run** menu item from the IDE menu and selecting **Edit Configurations** from the drop-down list. This will open up a new dialog where you need to click on the green **+** button to add a new configuration. Finally, select **OpenShift Deployment** to create a new OpenShift deployment.

In the dialog box that is presented to you, name the deployment OpenShift and then click on the **OK** button.

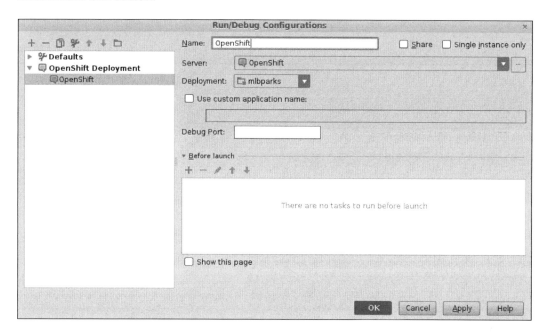

To begin debugging your application, simply select **Run** and then select **Debug OpenShift** from the IDE menu.

>
> To speed up application deployments for the mlbparks application, you might want to consider removing the Jenkins client from the application with the following command:
>
> $ rhc cartridge remove jenkins -a mlparks

Once your application has been deployed, you should see the console window from within the IDE that lets you know that the port forwarding for the debug port has been enabled by displaying the following text:

```
Connected to the target VM, address: '127.0.0.1:8787', transport: 'socket'
```

Debugging Applications

To verify that the IDE is able to connect to the remote port for debugging, open the `MLBParkResource.java` file located under the `src/main/java/org/openshift/mlbparks/rest` directory and set a breakpoint in the following line in the `findParksWithin` method:

```
ArrayList<MLBPark> allParksList = new ArrayList<MLBPark>();
```

The IDE will confirm that a breakpoint has been set on the line by highlighting the line, as shown in the following screenshot:

Open your browser and point to the URL of your application to confirm that the IDE breaks at the requested line.

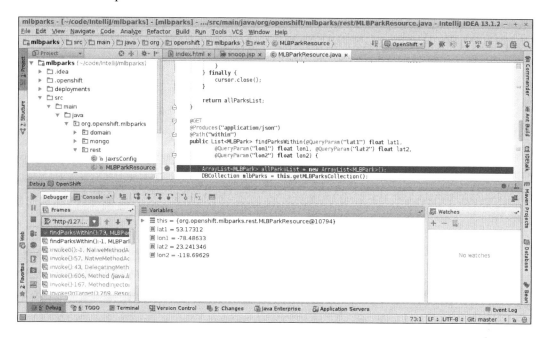

Congratulations! You now know how to configure the popular IntelliJ IDE in order to work with OpenShift deployed projects, including the ability to set breakpoints and step through the application code.

Using logfiles for debugging

The OpenShift Online platform has a great partner ecosystem where you can embed various functionality to enhance your applications. In this section, we are going to learn how to utilize the Logentries integration with existing OpenShift applications in order to get a view of the system performance and logs.

The first thing you need to do is sign up for a free Logentries account by visiting their website at `https://logentries.com/`. Once you have created an account, you will need to make a note of your account key, which is provided under the **Profile** tab of your account details.

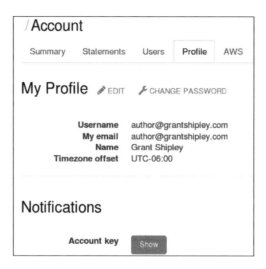

Once you have your account key, the next step is to add the Logentries source code to your `mlbparks` application. Switch to the root directory of your application and enter the following command to add the Logentries remote GitHub repository where the OpenShift integration resides:

```
$ git remote add upstream -m master https://github.com/logentries/le_openshift.git
```

Once you have added the repository, you can merge the changes with the following `pull` command:

```
$ git pull -s recursive -X theirs upstream master
```

This will create a new directory under your application's home folder named `logentries`. Switch to this directory, edit the `le_config.ini` file, and enter the account key for your Logentries account.

Once you have added your key, add and commit the changes and then push the code to your OpenShift gear:

```
$ git add .
$ git commit -am "adding logentries support"
$ git push
```

Once your application has been deployed, head back over to the Logentries site, and you will notice that it is already reporting CPU, disk, network, and memory statistics.

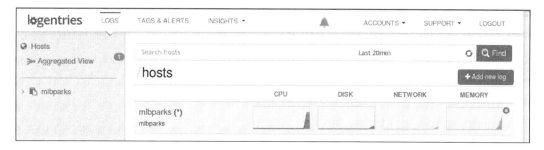

To view logfiles, click on the `mlbparks` host to view all of the logs that Logentries is following. If a logfile that you want to watch is not listed in the console, this simply means that it is not being followed by default. To specify additional logfiles to be followed, SSH to your `mlbparks` gear and switch to the directory where your logfile is located. For instance, if we wanted to add the JBoss EAP and MongoDB logfiles, we will execute the following command:

```
$ rhc app ssh mlbparks
```

Once you're connected to the remote gear, run the following commands:

```
$ cd $OPENSHIFT_LOG_DIR
$ ${OPENSHIFT_REPO_DIR}logentries/le follow jbosseap.log
$ ${OPENSHIFT_REPO_DIR}logentries/le follow mongodb.log
$ ${OPENSHIFT_REPO_DIR}logentries/le monitordaemon
```

Debugging Applications

Once you have followed the JBoss EAP and MongoDB logs, refresh your Logentries dashboard to see the change reflected.

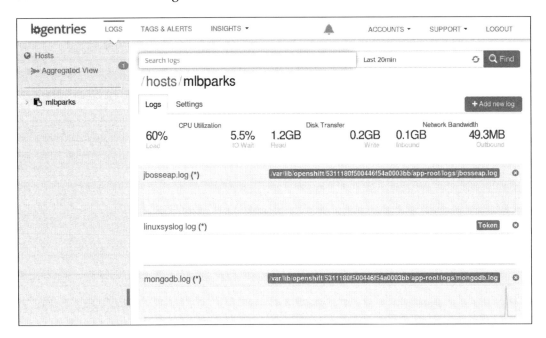

If you want to trigger an event that will show up in the MongoDB log, you can restart the MongoDB cartridge with the following command:

```
$ rhc cartridge restart mongodb -a mlbparks
```

Once you have restarted MongoDB, click on the MongoDB log in the Logentries dashboard to view the events that were sent to the server.

Chapter 10

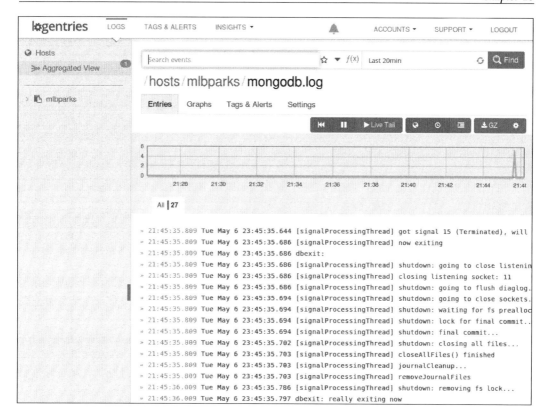

 Logentries is just one of many partners of the OpenShift Online platform. For a complete list of partners and the integrations they provide, visit the official OpenShift partner page at http://www.openshift.com/partners.

Summary

In this chapter, we learned how to use port forwarding to connect to databases that reside in the remote OpenShift gear. We also learned how to enable Java debugging using the `enable_jpda` marker. Once JPDA was enabled, we explored how to configure the Eclipse and IntelliJ IDEs to set breakpoints and step through the application code that is running on the OpenShift gear. Finally, we learned how to view and monitor logfiles and system performance by integrating with Logentries, which is an OpenShift Online partner.

In the next chapter, we are going to explore the OpenShift marker system as well as application hooks that will allow you to customize your application to perform actions at specific points in the development life cycle.

11
Using the Marker and Action Hook System

In this chapter, we are going to learn how to use the marker and action hook systems that are part of OpenShift Online. Using the action hook system, we can customize the application by providing hooks that will be executed at defined points during the deployment life cycle. The marker system allows us to enable hot deployment, remote debugging, and the version of the Java SDK to be used to build and run applications.

An overview of the marker system

The marker system is provided as a convenient way for developers to notify the OpenShift platform that they want to change a particular behavior. In this chapter, we are going to look at the `hot_deploy`, `enable_jpda`, and `disable_auto_scaling` markers.

The hot_deploy marker

As you have noticed when deploying code to the OpenShift Online platform, the system performs several steps after a `git push` command is executed. The platform stops all running services on the remote gear, builds the code, deploys the code, and lastly, restarts all of the services. This is inconvenient and time consuming, especially for languages that are interpreted, such as PHP, where a restart of the application server is not required. In fact, even modern versions of Java application servers support hot deploying application code without requiring a full restart of the server.

In the following table, I have displayed the application runtime and depicted whether the hot deploy marker is available for use with the runtime:

Application runtime	Supports hot deploy
Tomcat/JBoss EWS	Yes
JBoss AS / EAP	Yes
PHP	Yes
Perl	Yes
Ruby	Yes
Python	Yes
Node.js	Yes
Jenkins	No
HAProxy	No
Zend Server (PHP)	Yes
DIY	No

JBoss-specific markers

OpenShift supports several markers that are specific to JBoss-based applications that will allow developers to control and manage some of the runtime features associated with their application. The available markers for the JBoss Application Server are as follows:

- `enable_jpda`: Setting this marker will enable the remote debugging of applications by enabling the **Java Platform Debugger Architecture (JPDA)** socket.

> If you are not familiar with JPDA, you can find more information at `http://en.wikipedia.org/wiki/Java_Platform_Debugger_Architecture`.

- `skip_maven_build`: Setting this marker will skip a Maven build when a new application's code is pushed to the remote gear.
- `force_clean_build`: This marker performs a full build using Maven, including clearing the Maven dependency cache and downloading all dependencies specified in the `pom.xml` file.
- `hot_deploy`: This marker will deploy the newly built `.war` or `.ear` files without restarting the application server.

- `java7`: This marker will enable Java 7 to run your application and application server. If this marker is not set, the base version of Java will be used, which is Java 6 at the time of writing this book.

Creating and using markers

In order to use a marker, you simply create a file with the given name in the `.openshift/markers` directory, which is located in the root directory of your application. In order to illustrate this, let's create a new Java-based application and enable some of the available markers.

The first thing we need to do is create a new application named `markertest`, and then specify that we want to use the JBoss EAP application server:

```
$ rhc app create markertest jbosseap
```

Once you enter the preceding command, you should see the following output on your screen, indicating that the operation was successful:

```
Using jbosseap-6 (JBoss Enterprise Application Platform 6) for 'jbosseap'
Application Options
-------------------
Domain:     packt
Cartridges: jbosseap-6 (addtl. costs may apply)
Gear Size:  default
Scaling:    no

Creating application 'markertest' ... done


Waiting for your DNS name to be available ... done
Cloning into 'markertest'...
Your application 'markertest' is now available.

  URL:        http://markertest-packt.rhcloud.com/
  SSH to:     538266264382ecae6000009c@markertest-packt.rhcloud.com
  Git remote: ssh://538266264382ecae6000009c@markertest-packt.rhcloud.com/~/git/markertest.git/
  Cloned to:  /Users/gshipley/code/packt/markertest


Run 'rhc show-app markertest' for more details about your app.
```

Using the hot_deploy marker

Now that our application has been created, the first thing we want to do is enable hot deployment. In order to do this, we simply need to create an empty file named `hot_deploy` and place it in the `.openshift/markers` directory of our application. For this, you can enter the following commands:

```
$ cd markertest
$ touch .openshift/markers/hot_deploy
```

Now that we have our hot deploy marker file created, we simply need to add it to our application repository and then push the changes to our remote gear as follows:

```
$ git add .
$ git commit -am "Adding hot_deploy marker"
$ git push
```

Now that we have hot deployment enabled, all future deployments will occur without having to restart the JBoss Application Server. Let's test this out by creating a new JSP file and deploying the changes. Create a new file called `date.jsp` and place it under the `/src/main/webapp` directory of your application. Once you have created this file, add the following line of code and save the changes:

```
<%= new java.util.Date() %>
```

Now, we need to add, commit, and push the changes to our remote OpenShift gear:

```
$ git add .
$ git commit -am "Adding test file"
$ git push
```

Once you push the new code to your gear, you should see the following output, which indicates that hot deployment has been enabled for your application:

`remote: Not stopping cartridge jbosseap because hot deploy is enabled`

The code will then be built and deployed. Once the code has been deployed, you will see the following message, indicating that the application server does not need to be started:

`remote: Not starting cartridge jbosseap because hot deploy is enabled`

Using the force_clean_build marker

Using the `force_clean_build` marker is similar to using the `hot_deploy` marker. You simply need to create an empty file in the `.openshift/markers` directory named `force_clean_build`, and when you push the code, the system will download all of the dependencies again. Run the following commands to create and use this marker:

```
$ touch .openshift/markers/force_clean_build
$ git add .
$ git commit -am "adding a marker to perform a clean build"
$ git push
```

Once you push the change to your remote OpenShift gear, you will notice that Maven downloads all the dependencies listed in the `pom.xml` file.

> Keep in mind that your application will continue to perform a clean build each time you push the new code until you remove the `force_clean_build` marker.

To remove the marker, you can simply remove the file from your repository and push the changes to your gear as follows:

```
$ git rm .openshift/markers/force_clean_build
$ git commit -am "removing clean build marker file"
$ git push
```

You will now see that your application is built using the Maven system. However, the existing dependencies that have been downloaded will be used.

An overview of the action hook system

The OpenShift Online platform provides a system that allows developers an entry point into the application build and deployment life cycle called action hooks. These action hooks reside in the application's home directory under the `.openshift/action_hooks` directory. One of the great things about action hooks is that they can be written in any language, with the only requirement being that they be executable by the gears' operating system. This opens up a whole world of possibilities in order to plug into the build and deploy life cycle of your application.

> Action hooks are scripts that can be written in virtually any programming language that is executable on the remote operating system, including Bash, Ruby, Python, Perl, and so on.

You might be wondering when you would want to use action hooks in your code. One of the common use cases for which I implement action hooks is clearing and rebuilding my application's database. This ensures that each time I deploy a new version of the application that I am developing, I start with a fresh set of data in the database.

Another example of when action hooks can be implemented is to alert the developer when their application server is stopped or restarted. Logging this information via an action hook will allow the developer to analyze how much time is spent during this part of the life cycle.

There are two groupings of action hooks in the OpenShift platform. The first grouping is called `build` action hooks and is performed after the developer issues a `git push` command. This grouping of action hooks allows the developer to plug directly into the build and deployment life cycle of their application.

The available action hooks for the build and deployment life cycle are as follows:

- `pre_build`: This action hook is executed directly before the application is built. For example, the `pre_build` action hook will be executed before Maven for Java-based projects.
- `build`: The `build` action hook is executed during the compilation, or build phase, of the application.
- `deploy`: This action hook is executed as part of the deploy process for an application.
- `post_deploy`: This action hook is executed directly after the application has completed the deploy phase of the life cycle.

The second grouping of action hooks allows the developer to have an entry point into the cartridge life cycle of an application. For example, a user can add an action hook that is executed every time the MySQL database is restarted in order to refresh the data in the database to its original state. The following action hooks are available in order to plug into the cartridge life cycle:

- Cartridge start control action:
    - `pre_start`
    - `pre_start_{cartridgeName}`
    - `post_start`
    - `post_start_{cartridgeName}`

- Cartridge stop control action:
    - `pre_stop`
    - `pre_stop_{cartridgeName}`
    - `post_stop`
    - `post_stop_{cartridgeName}`
- Cartridge reload control action:
    - `pre_reload`
    - `pre_reload_{cartridgeName}`
    - `post_reload`
    - `post_reload_{cartridgeName}`
- Cartridge restart control action:
    - `pre_restart`
    - `pre_restart_{cartridgeName}`
    - `post_restart`
    - `post_restart_{cartridgeName}`
- Cartridge tidy control action:
    - `pre_tidy`
    - `pre_tidy_{cartridgeName}`
    - `post_tidy`
    - `post_tidy_{cartridgeName}`

Creating and using action hooks

Now that we have a good understanding of what action hooks are useful for, and the available ones that we can use, let's see how they work by integrating them into an application. Create an application called `action` using the PHP-5.4 runtime with the following command:

```
$ rhc app create action php-5.4
```

Once the application has been created and the source code has been cloned to your local computer, switch to the `.openshift` directory of your application with the help of the following command:

```
$ cd action/.openshift
```

Using the Marker and Action Hook System

Once you are in the directory, list all of the contents with the help of the following command:

```
$ ls -l
```

You should see the following output:

```
drwxr-xr-x   3 gshipley   staff    102 May 26 10:04 action_hooks
drwxr-xr-x   8 gshipley   staff    272 May 26 10:04 cron
drwxr-xr-x   3 gshipley   staff    102 May 26 10:04 markers
-rw-r--r--   1 gshipley   staff      0 May 26 10:04 pear.txt
```

As you can see in the preceding output, we have an `action_hooks` directory. This is where all the scripts that you create should be located. Switch to the `action_hooks` directory with the following command:

```
$ cd action_hooks
```

Inside of this directory, you will notice a `README.md` file that ships as part of the application template. This file will provide documentation on the available action hooks by providing a link to the official OpenShift Online user guide.

Creating the deploy action hook

As an example of creating an action hook, we are going to create a simple hook that will echo a message every time the application is deployed. In order to do this, create a new file in the `action/.openshift/action_hooks` directory named `deploy` with the following contents:

```
#!/bin/bash

echo " ***** Starting the deploy action hook ***** "
```

Once you have saved this file, you need to modify the script so that it is executable. For this, we can use the `chmod` command:

```
$ chmod +x deploy
```

To verify that the script is now executable, enter the following command:

```
$ ./deploy
```

You should see the following output:

```
***** Starting the deploy action hook *****
```

Now that we have our `deploy` action hook created, we need to add, commit, and push the file to our remote gear. For this, run the following commands:

```
$ git add deploy
$ git commit -am "adding deploy action_hook"
$ git push
```

Pay close attention to the output that is displayed on your screen while the `git push` command is being executed. As part of the push process, the application code is deployed and all associated action hooks are executed, including the one we just added. The output from the command is as follows:

```
Counting objects: 8, done.
Delta compression using up to 8 threads.
Compressing objects: 100% (5/5), done.
Writing objects: 100% (5/5), 577 bytes | 0 bytes/s, done.
Total 5 (delta 0), reused 0 (delta 0)
remote: Stopping PHP 5.4 cartridge (Apache+mod_php)
remote: Waiting for stop to finish
remote: Waiting for stop to finish
remote: Building git ref 'master', commit 58c7b6b
remote: Checking .openshift/pear.txt for PEAR dependency...
remote: Preparing build for deployment
remote: Deployment id is 7491a262
remote: Activating deployment
remote:   ***** Starting the deploy action hook *****
remote: Starting PHP 5.4 cartridge (Apache+mod_php)
remote: Application directory "/" selected as DocumentRoot
remote: -------------------------
remote: Git Post-Receive Result: success
remote: Activation status: success
remote: Deployment completed with status: success
To ssh://538373ac4382ec3af10001a1@action-packt.rhcloud.com/~/git/action.git/
   dcaf5db..58c7b6b  master -> master
```

If you notice, the output includes the following line, indicating that our `deploy` script is being executed as part of the life cycle:

```
remote:   ***** Starting the deploy action hook *****
```

Now that we know that our `deploy` action hook is being executed, we can begin to do more interesting things such as adding a database and refreshing the contents each time the application is deployed. To start, let's embed a MySQL database into our application:

```
$ rhc cartridge add mysql-5.5 -a action
```

Once the database has been added to the application, create a new file named `schema.sql` in the root directory of the `action` application. Insert the following lines of code into the file and save the changes:

```sql
DROP TABLE IF EXISTS `users`;
CREATE TABLE `users` (
  `user_id` int(11) NOT NULL AUTO_INCREMENT,
  `username` varchar(200) DEFAULT NULL,
  PRIMARY KEY (`user_id`)
) ENGINE=InnoDB AUTO_INCREMENT=2 DEFAULT CHARSET=utf8;
LOCK TABLES `users` WRITE;
INSERT INTO `users` VALUES (1,'gshipley');
UNLOCK TABLES;
```

Ensure that this file is located in the root directory of the `action` application. The code in the `schema.sql` file is SQL commands that perform the following SQL operations:

- Drop the `users` table if it exists
- Create a table named `users` and define the columns for the table
- Insert a row into the `users` table

Now that we have a DDL file that will delete and create the schema, we want to modify our `deploy` action hook to perform the SQL commands during the deployment phase. To do this, open the `.openshift/action_hooks/deploy` file and enter the following lines of code, replacing what is already there:

```bash
#!/bin/bash

echo " ***** REFRESHING THE DATABASE ***** "
/usr/bin/mysql -u "$OPENSHIFT_MYSQL_DB_USERNAME"
--password="$OPENSHIFT_MYSQL_DB_PASSWORD" --host="$OPENSHIFT_MYSQL_DB_HOST" $OPENSHIFT_APP_NAME < $OPENSHIFT_REPO_DIR/schema.sql
echo " ***** REFRESH COMPLETE ***** "
```

Let's examine each line of the `deploy` script in detail to ensure that we fully understand it:

- `#!/bin/bash`: This line simply defines that the information contained in the file is a script for the Bash Linux shell.
- `echo " ***** REFRESHING THE DATABASE ***** "`: This line informs the user that we are going to refresh the database. This is what is printed on the terminal when the action hook is being executed.
- `/usr/bin/mysql -u "$OPENSHIFT_MYSQL_DB_USERNAME" --password="$OPENSHIFT_MYSQL_DB_PASSWORD" --host="$OPENSHIFT_MYSQL_DB_HOST" $OPENSHIFT_APP_NAME < $OPENSHIFT_REPO_DIR/schema.sql`: This is where we connect to the MySQL database and run the SQL commands that we defined in our `schema.sql` file. This line is further broken down as follows:
    - `/usr/bin/mysql`: This is the path of the `mysql` executable on the remote OpenShift gear.
    - `-u "$OPENSHIFT_MYSQL_DB_USERNAME"`: This specifies the username that will be used to authenticate to the database. Note that instead of hardcoding the username, we are using the environment variable for our application to ensure that this script is portable across deployments.
    - `--password="$OPENSHIFT_MYSQL_DB_PASSWORD"`: This is the password for the user that we are authenticating with. Again, we are using the environment variable instead of hardcoding the password.
    - `--host="$OPENSHIFT_MYSQL_DB_HOST"`: When connecting to MySQL, we need to specify the host that we are connecting to. Remember that in OpenShift Online, a MySQL database has its own internal private IP address and does not use `127.0.0.1`. For this reason, we have to specify the location of the server.
    - `$OPENSHIFT_APP_NAME`: We specify the application name by itself in order to alert MySQL of the database we want to connect to. Since a default database is created based on the name of the application, using the `$OPENSHIFT_APP_NAME` environment will provide the database with the correct information.
    - `< $OPENSHIFT_REPO_DIR/schema.sql`: This is the last section of the command and will simply redirect the contents of the `schema.sql` file into the database. When this happens, the SQL commands inside of the file are executed against the database.

Testing the deploy action hook

Now that our schema file and action hook have been created, it's time to test them out. Add all the new files to your repository, and then commit and push them to your application as follows:

```
$ git add .
$ git commit -am "Adding deploy action hook to refresh database"
$ git push
```

During the deployment, you will notice the following section of output that is presented on the terminal screen:

```
remote: Preparing build for deployment
remote: Deployment id is cc259719
remote: Activating deployment
remote: Starting MySQL 5.5 cartridge
remote:   ***** REFRESHING THE DATABASE *****
remote:   ***** REFRESH COMPLETE *****
```

This indicates that the refresh was successful. Let's test this out by logging in to our remote gear and looking at the contents of the MySQL database. First, we need to SSH in with the following command:

```
$ rhc app ssh action
```

Once you have been authenticated to the remote server, you will be presented with a terminal prompt. To connect to MySQL, simply enter the following command:

```
$ mysql
```

> When running the `mysql` command while connected to the remote gear, the OpenShift platform will automatically authenticate you to the database without having to provide any credentials.

From the MySQL shell, enter the following commands:

```
mysql> use action;
mysql> select * from users;
```

You should see the following output:

```
+---------+----------+
| user_id | username |
+---------+----------+
|       1 | gshipley |
+---------+----------+
1 row in set (0.00 sec)
```

Insert an additional row into the database with the following command:

`mysql> insert into users values (null, 'reader');`

Verify that the new user was added by running the `select` statement again. Now that we have a new user created in the database, let's make a change to the code and deploy the application again. Create a new file called `hello.php` in the root directory of the application and add the following code:

```
<?php

echo "Learning how the deploy action_hook works"
```

Once you have saved the file, add, commit, and push the changes to your remote gear:

```
$ git add hello.php
$ git commit -am "adding new file"
$ git push
```

During the deployment phase of the life cycle, you will see the following lines in the remote server:

```
remote: Stopping MySQL 5.5 cartridge
remote: Stopping PHP 5.4 cartridge (Apache+mod_php)
remote: Waiting for stop to finish
remote: Waiting for stop to finish
remote: Building git ref 'master', commit 1211b7a
remote: Checking .openshift/pear.txt for PEAR dependency...
remote: Preparing build for deployment
remote: Deployment id is a2ed0fcf
remote: Activating deployment
```

```
remote: Starting MySQL 5.5 cartridge
remote:  ***** REFRESHING THE DATABASE *****
remote:  ***** REFRESH COMPLETE *****
remote: Starting PHP 5.4 cartridge (Apache+mod_php)
remote: Application directory "/" selected as DocumentRoot
remote: ------------------------
remote: Git Post-Receive Result: success
remote: Activation status: success
remote: Deployment completed with status: success
```

You will notice that the database was refreshed, as indicated by the following two lines of output:

```
remote:  ***** REFRESHING THE DATABASE *****
remote:  ***** REFRESH COMPLETE *****
```

To verify that the database was indeed refreshed, SSH to your application and execute the `mysql` command again:

```
$ rhc app ssh action
$ mysql
```

From the MySQL shell, enter the following commands:

```
mysql> use action;
mysql> select * from users;
```

You should see the following output:

```
+---------+----------+
| user_id | username |
+---------+----------+
|       1 | gshipley |
+---------+----------+
1 row in set (0.00 sec)
```

Pretty awesome, huh? From now on, every time we deploy a new change to our application, we can be assured that we are starting with a fresh set of data in the databases.

What would be even better is if we could refresh our database with a simple reload command:

`$ rhc cartridge reload mysql-5.1`

Good news, you can do this by creating an action hook named post_reload_{cartridgeName}. For example, you can copy the deploy action hook to a new file with the following command:

`$ mv .openshift/action_hooks/deploy .openshift/action_hooks/post_reload_mysql-5.1`

After you add the new file and push your changes, the script will get executed every time you issue a reload command to the MySQL cartridge.

Summary

In this chapter, we learned about the marker and action hook functionality that is provided as part of the OpenShift Online platform. We started by creating marker files in order to enable hot deployment, and then created a marker to force a clean build of our application code. After this, we learned how to use the marker system, examined the action hook system, and learned how to create a deploy action hook that refreshes the contents of the database after each new deployment. The action hook system is a powerful feature that will allow you to customize the workflow of your application by providing an entry point into the OpenShift system.

In the next chapter, we are going to learn about application scaling and how automatic and manual scaling works. We will also learn how to customize the scaling algorithm in order to allow us to scale based on metrics that are provided by the developer.

12
Scaling Applications

One of the great things about using **Platform as a Service (PaaS)**, such as OpenShift Online, is the ability to leverage application scaling to satisfy the demands of your users for fast response times. Having an application that can handle all incoming traffic, even under the heaviest of loads, is critical for production quality applications. We all dream of a time when an application we have written is under such heavy usage that adding additional servers to handle the capacity is a requirement. Unless you are extremely familiar with system administration, setting up a clustered environment is not an easy task. In this chapter, we will learn how to leverage the provided scaling functionality inside of OpenShift so that our minds can be at ease with regards to satisfying high demand for our applications. We will also examine how to set scaling limits to ensure that we always stay under budget for our deployments.

Why scaling matters

One of the common use cases for OpenShift Online is developing a backend for mobile applications. If you are not familiar with writing mobile applications, don't worry. Follow along with me, as this use case is applicable to other types of applications as well.

Imagine that you have spent thousands of hours developing a mobile application with a backend hosted on a private server. The application is a calorie counter that looks up food data and information via a REST API call. You developed the application using a backend, as it wasn't feasible to store all of the food information on each device. Having a backend that provides the data also allows you to update the database without requiring each user of the application to update to a new version.

Scaling Applications

Sales have been slow during the initial rollout of your application, so one backend server is more than adequate to handle all of the requests that users of your application are performing. You wake up one morning and find out that your application is listed as a featured application on the app store. Suddenly, the number of users of your application has exploded and your backend server is not able to keep up with the number of requests. Users of your application become frustrated and leave a negative review while also deleting the application because the experience was slow and unresponsive. At the most critical time for your application, your backend server could not handle the increased amount of traffic, and you weren't able to add additional servers fast enough to keep up with the increased traffic before your users became frustrated. You think to yourself that you should have just started with additional servers, but you didn't want to spend the additional money to maintain servers when one was enough to handle all of the current traffic. Enter OpenShift and automatic scaling.

Vertical and horizontal scaling

There are two types of scaling that IT people are familiar with: vertical scaling and horizontal scaling.

You can think of vertical scaling as providing a single huge monolithic server that has large amounts of RAM and CPUs on a single server. This huge server is typically the only server that handles requests for your application. If the server is not able to handle the number of incoming requests in a timely manner, the solution is to throw more memory or CPUs into the server. For instance, traditional relational databases typically reside on a single server that holds all of the data. Of course, this data can be replicated for failovers, but generally, all requests go through a single server.

Horizontal scaling, on the other hand, is a new way of approaching the scalability problems that we see today with web-based applications. Horizontal scaling means having lots of smaller-sized servers working together to handle all of the requests of a user instead of having a single large server. To illustrate the differences between vertical and horizontal scaling, take a look at the following diagram:

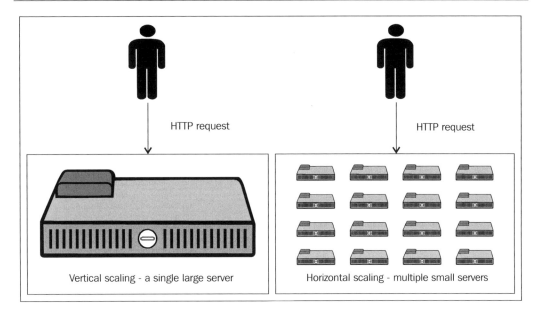

An easy way to envision how horizontal scaling works is to imagine eating a bag of potato chips. While eating these chips, you accidentally drop one on the ground but decide not to pick it up. You then go about your business and leave the chip where it fell. Not long after dropping the chip on the ground, an army of ants approaches the chip. These ants break the chip into thousands of tiny pieces and each ant takes a single fragment of the chip back to their home. Instead of a single ant trying to take the whole chip back to the colony, they all worked together as a team to accomplish the goal. This is how horizontal scaling works.

Using automatic scaling

One of the unique features of OpenShift Online is the ability to automatically scale your application based on the amount of traffic that your application is receiving. The platform monitors the number of concurrent HTTP requests and will add additional gears to your application if the demand is not being met. The platform will then monitor your gears and determine when it is safe to begin scaling back when demand is being met.

> At the time of writing this book, if you have more than 16 concurrent connections, the platform will add an additional gear. For the current configuration limit of the number of concurrent connections, see the official OpenShift Online documentation.

Scaling Applications

To understand how scaling works on OpenShift, let's examine what happens when you create an application that is not scaled. For instance, suppose that we created an application named `notscaled` that uses the PHP-5.4 runtime and a MySQL database. We will create this application with the following command:

```
$ rhc app create notscaled php-5.4 mysql-5.5
```

When issuing the preceding command, a single gear will be created for you on the OpenShift Online platform. This single gear contains both the PHP runtime and the MySQL database, as depicted in the following diagram:

Creating a scaled application with the command line

By default, all applications that are created on the platform are not scaled, which means that a single gear contains all of the application code and cartridges. In order to create a scaled application, you need to pass the `-s` flag to an application when creating it. For example, to create a scalable application with the PHP-5.4 runtime and a MySQL database, we will enter the following command:

```
$ rhc app create scaledapp php-5.4 mysql-5.5 -s
```

When creating a scaled application on OpenShift, the gear creation process differs slightly in that a load balancer is added to the equation and the database resides on its own distinct gear. A good way to think of a scaled application is not a single gear but a gear group that belongs to the application. For example, given the preceding command, our application would look like the following diagram from a conceptual viewpoint:

Chapter 12

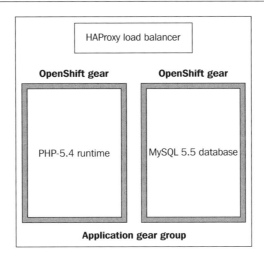

You can verify that MySQL and PHP are indeed running on separate gears by issuing the following command to view the details for your application:

```
$ rhc app show scaledapp
```

You will see the following output:

```
scaledapp @ http://scaledapp-packt.rhcloud.com/ (uuid:
5383e2c8500446265e000271)
---------------------------------------------------------------------------
  Domain:     packt
  Created:    5:56 PM
  Gears:      2 (defaults to small)
  Git URL:    ssh://5383e2c8500446265e000271@scaledapp-packt.rhcloud.
com/~/git/scaledapp.git/
  SSH:        5383e2c8500446265e000271@scaledapp-packt.rhcloud.com
  Deployment: auto (on git push)

  mysql-5.5 (MySQL 5.5)
  --------------------
    Gears:          1 small
    Connection URL: mysql://$OPENSHIFT_MYSQL_DB_HOST:$OPENSHIFT_MYSQL_DB_
PORT/
    Database Name:  scaledapp
```

```
    Password:          3D2Lq4R-4jgs
    Username:          adminFshVG51


 haproxy-1.4 (Web Load Balancer)
 -------------------------------
    Gears: Located with php-5.4

 php-5.4 (PHP 5.4)
 -----------------
    Scaling: x1 (minimum: 1, maximum: available) on small gears
```

In the preceding output, we can see that we are consuming two gears for our application: one for the PHP-5.4 runtime and an additional gear for the MySQL database. You might be wondering why the application isn't consuming three gears, one for each of the following:

- HAProxy
- PHP-5.4
- MySQL

This is because when creating a scaled application on OpenShift, HAProxy and the runtime are initially collocated on the same gear. These two items will remain on the same gear until three additional runtime gears are added. At this time, the PHP-5.4 runtime will be disabled on the head gear that is collocated with HAProxy, which enables HAProxy to perform better under increased load.

Creating a scaled application with the web console

Creating a scaled application with the web console is a very straightforward process. Simply log in to the web console by visiting `http://www.openshift.com`.

In order to create a scaled application with the web console, you will need to perform the following steps:

1. Authenticate to the OpenShift platform.
2. Click on the **Add Application** button at the bottom of the application dashboard.

3. Select to create a new application based on the PHP-5.4 runtime.
4. Name the application `webscaled`.
5. Scroll to the bottom of the screen and select to scale the application based on the web traffic.

The preceding steps are illustrated in the following screenshot:

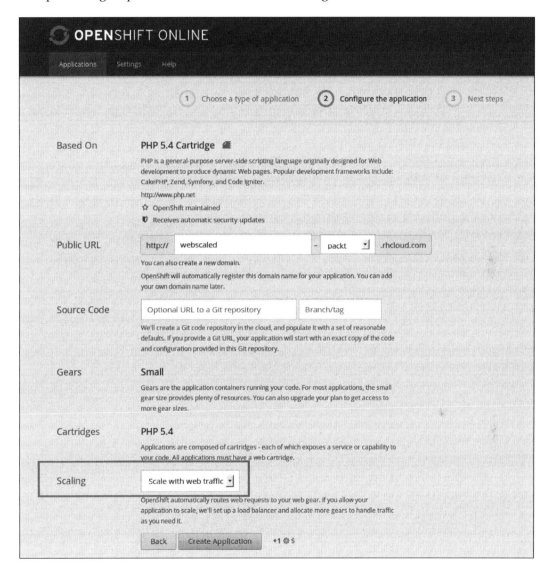

Scaling Applications

Click on the **Create Application** button to begin the gear-creation process. Once the application has been created, click on the link titled **continue to the application overview page**. Once you are on this screen, add the MySQL database by clicking on the link highlighted in the following screenshot:

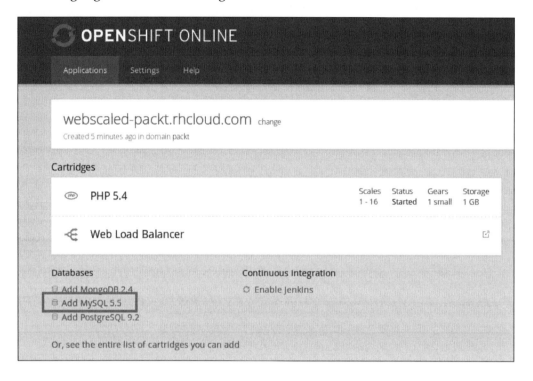

Once the MySQL database has been added to your application, you will see that the application is consuming two gears, as shown in the following screenshot:

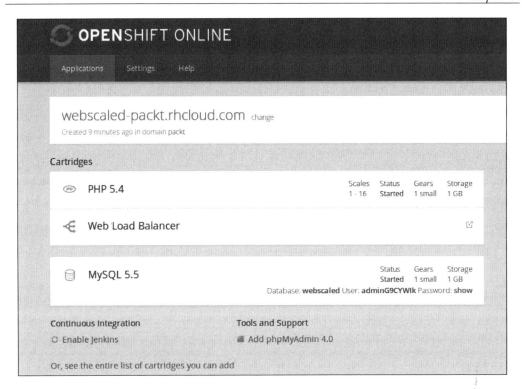

That's all there is to it. OpenShift Online will now automatically scale your application when extra capacity is needed. This is truly a set-it-and-forget-it type of mentality.

Using manual scaling

While automatic scaling is great for unplanned traffic spikes, manual scaling is a better alternative when you know that you are going to have an increased demand for your application. Let's explore this further using the same example that we used previously in this chapter where we had a mobile backend that is hosted on OpenShift Online. Suppose that we get an e-mail from Apple or Google letting us know that our application is going to be featured in three days. Given that we know about the potential for increased demand in advance, we would want to go ahead and manually add a couple of gears to our gear group in order to ensure that our customers have a great user experience.

Scaling Applications

The first thing we need to do to manually scale is disable automatic scaling for our application. We can achieve this using a marker, as discussed in *Chapter 11, Using the Marker and Action Hook System*. To create this marker, open a terminal window and enter the following command, ensuring that you are in the application's root directory:

```
$ touch .openshift/markers/disable_auto_scaling
$ git add .
$ git commit -am "Disable automatic scaling for our application"
$ git push
```

Once you have disabled automatic scaling, I have found that restarting the application will ensure that HAProxy does not automatically scale down the manually added gears:

```
$ rhc app stop -a scaledapp
$ rhc app start -a scaledapp
```

Now that automatic scaling has been disabled, we can manually add additional gears using the RHC command-line tools:

```
$ rhc app-scale-up -a scaledapp
```

Once you enter the preceding command, a new gear will be created on the OpenShift Online platform and will be added to your application gear group. Once the gear has been added, the application code will be copied from the head gear to the newly created gear using the `rsync` Linux utility. Once the application code has been copied over, the platform will add the new gear to the HAProxy load balancer. Once the command is complete, you will see the following output on your screen:

```
RESULT:
scaledapp scaled up
```

To verify that an additional gear has been added to your gear group, issue the following command:

```
$ rhc app show -a scaledapp
```

At this point, you should see that your application is using three gears, as shown in the following output:

```
scaledapp @ http://scaledapp-packt.rhcloud.com/ (uuid: 5383e2c8500446265e000271)
---------------------------------------------------------------------
  Domain:     packt
  Created:    5:56 PM
```

Chapter 12

```
Gears:      3 (defaults to small)
Git URL:    ssh://5383e2c8500446265e000271@scaledapp-packt.rhcloud.com/~/git/scaledapp.git/
SSH:        5383e2c8500446265e000271@scaledapp-packt.rhcloud.com
Deployment: auto (on git push)
```

Go ahead and add a couple of additional gears to clearly understand how gear creation works. For example, if we had added five additional gears to our application, we would see the following output on the command line:

```
scaledapp @ http://scaledapp-packt.rhcloud.com/ (uuid: 5383e2c8500446265e000271)
---------------------------------------------------------------------------
  Domain:     packt
  Created:    5:56 PM
  Gears:      7 (defaults to small)
  Git URL:    ssh://5383e2c8500446265e000271@scaledapp-packt.rhcloud.com/~/git/scaledapp.git/
  SSH:        5383e2c8500446265e000271@scaledapp-packt.rhcloud.com
  Deployment: auto (on git push)
  php-5.4 (PHP 5.4)
  -----------------
    Scaling: x6 (minimum: 1, maximum: available) on small gears
```

You can also view this information by looking at your application in the web console, as shown in the following screenshot:

[251]

Setting scaling limits

Often, there are times when you want to have your production application never fall below a certain threshold of gears that serve the application content. This would be true if you have a popular application where you know that in order to meet capacity, you always need at least two gears that serve the traffic. Fortunately, OpenShift supports this capability by allowing the developer to set a minimum number of gears using both the command line and the web console. To illustrate this, let's set the minimum number of gears for an application with the following command:

```
$ rhc scale-cartridge php-5.4 --min 2 --max -1 -a scaledapp
```

The preceding command will configure our application, which is `scaledapp`, to always have a minimum of two PHP-5.4 web gears associated with it. You might notice that we set the maximum to `-1`. The `-1` value configures the application to allow scale-up events until the maximum number of gears for the account has been reached. Once the command has been executed, you will see the following output on the terminal screen:

```
This operation will run until the application is at the minimum scale and
may take several minutes.
Setting scale range for php-5.4 ... done


php-5.4 (PHP 5.4)
-----------------
  Scaling: x2 (minimum: 2, maximum: available) on small gears
```

We can also set the minimum number of gears using the web console. Log in to the OpenShift website and browse the overview page for your application. For example, the `scaledapp` overview page looks like the following screenshot:

Chapter 12

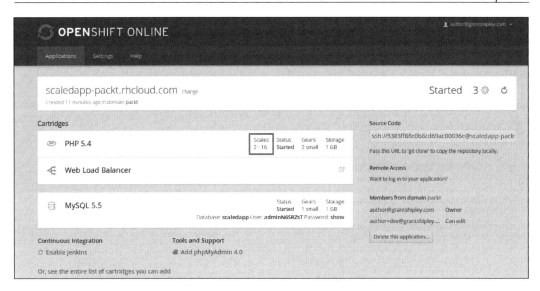

Once you are on the application's overview page, click on the link under the **Scales** tab that will allow us to configure the minimum and maximum number of gears for the application. Change the minimum number to **4** and press the **Save** button.

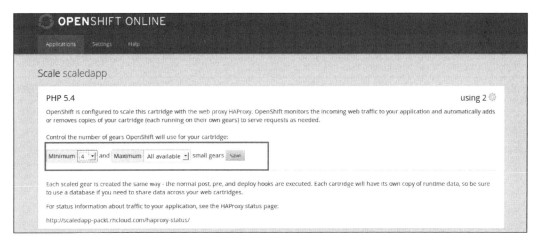

Scaling Applications

While having the ability to automatically or manually scale an application is a great feature, one must also consider the cost associated with an infrastructure that is scaled out. The OpenShift platform allows users to control the costs associated with scaling by configuring the maximum number of gears to scale to. For instance, let's pretend that we want our `scaledapp` application to have a minimum number of one gear but also only support the ability to scale up to two gears. This will enable us to control the costs associated with the application by never exceeding the two-gear limit for the PHP-5.4 runtime. To perform this action, we will enter the following command:

```
$ rhc scale-cartridge php-5.4 --min 1 --max 2 -a scaledapp
```

After entering the preceding command, you will see a confirmation message, as follows:

```
This operation will run until the application is at the minimum scale and
may take several minutes.
Setting scale range for php-5.4 ... done


php-5.4 (PHP 5.4)
-----------------
  Scaling: x2 (minimum: 1, maximum: 2) on small gears
```

This can also be performed on the web console using the same method that we discussed previously in this section by setting the values on the scaling dashboard, as shown in the following screenshot:

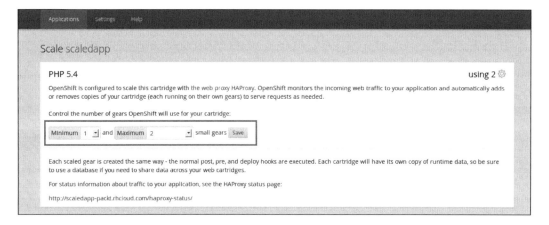

Viewing the load-balancer information

When scaling applications on the OpenShift platform, regardless of using manual or automatic scaling, a load balancer is used to pass requests to the appropriate gear. The load balancer that is implemented as part of the system is the popular HAProxy software load balancer.

> HAProxy is a software load balancer that is commonly used to improve the performance of web applications and services by balancing incoming requests over several servers. The load balancer is written in the C programming language and is used by some of the most popular websites on the Internet.

As part of the HAProxy installation on the OpenShift gears, a web dashboard is provided so that you can view the number of gears and traffic associated with an application. This dashboard is available at http://appname-domain.rhcloud.com/haproxy-status/.

For example, if our application was called scaledapp and our domain was called packt, the URL for the HAProxy dashboard will be http://scaledapp-packt.rhcloud.com/haproxy-status/.

Open your favorite web browser and point to the HAProxy dashboard URL of your application. The dashboard should look like the following screenshot:

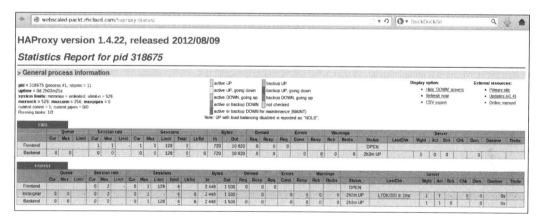

[255]

Scaling Applications

You can also access the HAProxy dashboard by clicking on the link next to the **Web Load Balancer** cartridge on the application's overview page on the web console:

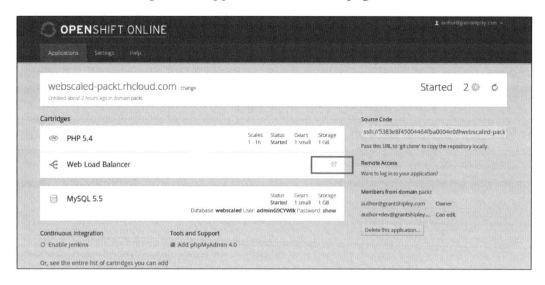

Customizing the scaling algorithm

Often, there are times when the default scaling algorithm that ships as part of your OpenShift gear is not meeting your needs. Perhaps you want to scale your application based on the memory usage instead of the number of concurrent users. Fortunately, there is an opportunity to modify this behavior by implementing your own algorithm that will be inside of the `action_hooks` directory that we learned about as part of *Chapter 11, Using the Marker and Action Hook System*.

 The default scaling control file is located on GitHub and is thoroughly documented. For a better understanding of how the default scaling action works, consider reading the source code located at https://github.com/openshift/origin-server/blob/master/cartridges/openshift-origin-cartridge-haproxy/usr/bin/haproxy_ctld.rb.

To illustrate how to write a custom scaling control file that will allow our application to be scaled based on memory, let's create a new application called `memscale` using the PHP-5.4 runtime:

```
$ rhc app create memscale php-5.4 -s
```

Once the application has been created, switch to the `.openshift/action_hooks` directory and perform the following command:

```
$ wget https://www.openshift.com/sites/default/files/haproxy_ctld.rb_.txt
```

This will download a sample control file that contains the necessary information to be scaled based on memory usage. We need to change the name of the file in order to remove the `_.txt` extension:

```
$ mv haproxy_ctld.rb_.txt haproxy_ctld.rb
```

Once you have the file downloaded and the correct filename applied, add the changes to your repository and then commit and push the file to your OpenShift gear:

```
$ git add .
$ git commit -am "Adding custom scaling"
$ git push
```

The interesting bits of code in the control file are as follows:

```
    # Scale up when any gear is using 400M or more memory.
            mem_scale_up = 419430400

            # Scale down when any gear is using 300M or less memory
            mem_scale_down = 314572800

            # min_gears - Once this number of gears is met, don't try to
    scale down any lower
            min_gears = 2

            gear_list['web'].each do |uuid, array|
              mem_usage = `ssh -i ~/.openshift_ssh/id_rsa
#{uuid}@#{array['dns']} 'oo-cgroup-read memory.memsw.usage_in_bytes'`.
    to_i
              if mem_usage >= mem_scale_up
                @log.error("memory usage (#{mem_usage}) on
#{array['dns']} is above threshold(#{mem_scale_up}), adding new gear")
                self.add_gear
              end
            end
```

In the preceding code sample, the application will automatically scale up when more than 400 MB of memory is used and will then scale down when any gear in the gear group consumes less that 300 MB of memory. The memory information is collected by establishing an SSH connection to each gear in the gear group, and then reading the memory information from the `oo-cgroup-read` command.

Summary

In this chapter, we learned how scaling works on the OpenShift platform. We started by learning how to use automatic scaling to ensure that your application can handle unexpected spikes in traffic. We then learned how to leverage manual scaling in order to proactively add capacity to your application when you know in advance that you will experience increased demand. After this, we learned how to control costs by configuring your application to support the maximum number of gears. Finally, we explored how to customize the scaling algorithm to scale based on memory usage instead of the number of concurrent HTTP requests.

In the next chapter, we are going to learn how to extend the OpenShift platform using the DIY cartridge. This cartridge will allow you to execute and run any binary on your OpenShift gear.

13
Using the Do-It-Yourself Cartridge

By default, OpenShift supports many of the most popular languages out of the box. This includes runtimes for PHP, Python, Perl, Node.js, Java, and Ruby. However, there might be times when you want to try out a new programming language or server that is not yet supported by the OpenShift platform with an official cartridge. In this chapter, we are going to learn how to use the DIY cartridge to create and deploy Version 8 of the popular Tomcat servlet container. OpenShift currently supports both Tomcat 6 and 7. However, at the time of writing this book, support for Version 8 of Tomcat as an official cartridge is not provided.

Understanding the DIY cartridge

The DIY cartridge creates an empty gear where users can run just about any program that can speak HTTP. OpenShift Online is essentially a secured **Red Hat Enterprise Linux (RHEL)** system. This means that any binary that will run on RHEL will run on the DIY cartridge.

The way that the OpenShift Online DIY runtime exposes your application to the outside world is by creating an HTTP proxy that is specified by the following environment variables:

- OPENSHIFT_DIY_IP
- OPENSHIFT_DIY_PORT

Using the Do-It-Yourself Cartridge

The application that you deploy only needs to listen for HTTP connections on the IP address and port that are specified in the preceding environment variables. The OpenShift proxy will then marshal requests from the outside world to your application.

In *Chapter 11, Using the Marker and Action Hook System*, we learned about the action hook and marker systems. The DIY application type takes advantage of these systems by using the .openshift/action_hooks/start script to control how the custom server is started. Likewise, the .openshift/action_hooks/stop script is used to control how the server is stopped.

> DIY applications are unsupported but are a great way for developers to try out unsupported languages, frameworks, or middleware that don't ship as official OpenShift Online cartridges. Furthermore, DIY-based applications are not able to scale using the default scaling algorithm.

Creating an application with the DIY cartridge

For the example in this chapter, we are going to create a DIY-based application that will house the Tomcat 8 servlet container. The first thing we need to do is create an application gear using the DIY cartridge. To perform this action, enter the following command:

```
$ rhc app create tomcat8 diy
```

After entering the preceding command, you will see the following information displayed on the screen:

```
Using diy-0.1 (Do-It-Yourself 0.1) for 'diy'


Application Options
-------------------
```

```
Domain:     packt
Cartridges: diy-0.1
Gear Size:  default
Scaling:    no

Creating application 'tomcat8' ... done

  Disclaimer: This is an experimental cartridge that provides a way to
try unsupported languages, frameworks, and middleware on OpenShift.

Waiting for your DNS name to be available ... done
Your application 'tomcat8' is now available.

  URL:        http://tomcat8-packt.rhcloud.com/
  SSH to:     53841746500446265e00075f@tomcat8-packt.rhcloud.com
  Git remote: ssh://53841746500446265e00075f@tomcat8-packt.rhcloud.com/~/
git/tomcat8.git/
  Cloned to:  /Users/gshipley/code/packt/tomcat8

Run 'rhc show-app tomcat8' for more details about your app.
```

As part of the output, you will notice that we created this application without scaling enabled. This is because the DIY cartridge does not support scaling. The reason for this is that scaling can be extremely complicated and is highly dependent on the runtime to handle operations such as session replication across a cluster of gears. Since the DIY cartridge allows you to execute any binary, the platform cannot determine how to handle the runtime in a scaled environment.

Using the Do-It-Yourself Cartridge

You can also create an application with the DIY cartridge using the web console, as shown in the following screenshot:

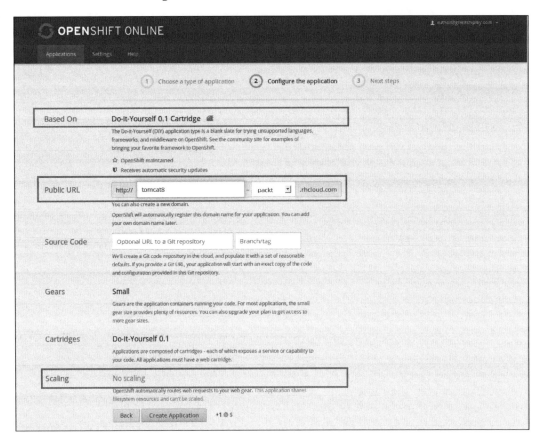

In the preceding screenshot, you will notice that the user is not given a choice to scale the application.

Now that we have our application created, visit `http://appname-domain.rhcloud.com` in your favorite web browser. For example, if our application was called `tomcat8` and our domain was called `packt`, the URL for the DIY-based application will be `http://tomcat8-packt.rhcloud.com`.

Once you have loaded the URL in your web browser, you will be presented with the following screenshot:

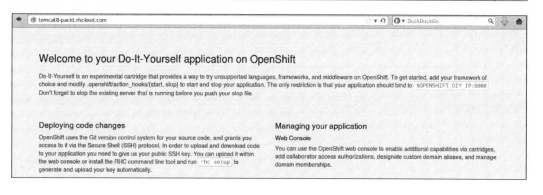

Stopping the default web server

Given the preceding screenshot, you are probably asking yourself how this is happening when we stated that the DIY application type allows you to run any binary. Knowing this information, you probably thought that you would be starting with a blank slate on the application gear. This is not actually the case as the platform ships a template for the DIY cartridge that includes a simple server written in the Ruby programming language.

Since we are going to be installing and using the Tomcat 8 servlet container, we want to stop the existing Ruby server that is running on our application gear. The Ruby service in question is started and stopped via the action hook system that we learned about in *Chapter 11*, *Using the Marker and Action Hook System*.

To view the start and stop script associated with the Ruby server, open your terminal window and go to the root directory of the `tomcat8` application. Once you are in this directory, execute the following command:

```
$ cat .openshift/action_hooks/start
```

This will display the source code that starts the server and should look like the following output:

```
#!/bin/bash
# The logic to start up your application should be put in this
# script. The application will work only if it binds to
# $OPENSHIFT_DIY_IP:8080
nohup $OPENSHIFT_REPO_DIR/diy/testrubyserver.rb $OPENSHIFT_DIY_IP $OPENSHIFT_REPO_DIR/diy |& /usr/bin/logshifter -tag diy &
```

Using the Do-It-Yourself Cartridge

In order to delete and clean up the unused Ruby server, we will need to delete several files, including the start and stop scripts. For this, perform the following commands:

```
$ git rm .openshift/action_hooks/start
$ git rm .openshift/action_hooks/stop
$ git rm diy/testrubyserver.rb
$ git commit -am "removing ruby server"
$ git push
```

Once the `push` command is executed, you will see the following output on the screen:

```
Counting objects: 9, done.
Delta compression using up to 8 threads.
Compressing objects: 100% (3/3), done.
Writing objects: 100% (5/5), 508 bytes | 0 bytes/s, done.
Total 5 (delta 0), reused 0 (delta 0)
remote: Stopping DIY cartridge
remote: Building git ref 'master', commit 5f8e295
remote: Preparing build for deployment
remote: Deployment id is e8469a7d
remote: Activating deployment
remote: Starting DIY cartridge
remote: -------------------------
remote: Git Post-Receive Result: success
remote: Activation status: success
remote: Deployment completed with status: success
To ssh://53841746500446265e00075f@tomcat8-packt.rhcloud.com/~/git/tomcat8.git/
   67e52aa..5f8e295  master -> master
```

Verify that the Ruby server has been stopped and deleted by visiting the URL for your application in a web browser. If the server was removed correctly, you should see the following error message, indicating that a server is not running on your gear:

Creating a Tomcat 8 server

At this point, we have an empty gear that does not have a server listening for HTTP connections. We now want to download the Tomcat application code on our remote gear. For this, we first need to SSH to our application gear with the following command:

```
$ rhc app ssh tomcat8
```

Once you have been authenticated to the gear, we want to change to the persistent data directory where we will place the Tomcat source code:

```
$ cd $OPENSHIFT_DATA_DIR
```

 The preceding command might look a bit odd if you are not familiar with the Linux operating system. What the command does is switch to the directory that is specified in the OPENSHIFT_DATA_DIR environment variable.

We now need to download the Tomcat 8 source code. For this, open a browser and go to the official project page for Tomcat, which is located at https://tomcat.apache.org/.

Once the project page loads, there is a link to download specific versions of the servlet container on the left-hand side. We are interested in Version 8 of the server, so click on that link as shown in the following screenshot:

You will then be presented with a list of downloads that are available for the requested version. Since we are on a Linux-based operating system, we want to download the `.tar.gz` binary distribution. Right-click on the link for the `.tar.gz` version and select to copy the link location, as shown in the following screenshot:

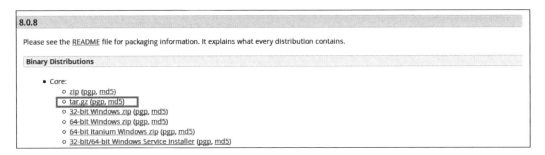

Now that we have a link that points to the binary distribution of the Tomcat 8 servlet container, we want to download it to our OpenShift gear. Open your terminal window again and ensure that you are connected to your remote gear and you are in the `$OPENSHIFT_DATA_DIR` directory. Once you have verified this, enter the following command, replacing the link in the example with the URL for the distribution that you have chosen to download:

```
$ wget http://mirrors.gigenet.com/apache/tomcat/tomcat-8/v8.0.8/bin/apache-tomcat-8.0.8.tar.gz
```

Once the download is complete, extract the contents using the `tar` command:

```
$ tar zxvf apache-tomcat-8.0.8.tar.gz
```

 If you no longer need the `.tar.gz` package, it is okay to remove it after you have extracted the contents.

This will create a new directory named `apache-tomcat-8.0.8` in the `$OPENSHIFT_DATA_DIR` directory.

At this point, we need to modify the configuration file for the Tomcat server to specify the port and IP address that we will be using for our gear. To find out the IP of your DIY gear, enter the following command on the remote gear:

```
$ env |grep DIY_IP
```

The output provided will contain the IP address for your gear.

Make a note of this information, as we will need it when we begin to modify the configuration file for Tomcat.

For example, the output returned for my gear is as follows:

OPENSHIFT_DIY_IP=127.11.60.1

The next thing that we need to do is modify the configuration that defines what IP address and ports the server uses. This configuration file is named `server.xml` and is in the `conf` directory of the server. To edit this file, enter the following command:

```
$ vi $OPENSHIFT_DATA_DIR/apache-tomcat-8.0.8/conf/server.xml
```

Once the file is opened, we will need to modify the `<Server port="8005" shutdown="SHUTDOWN">` line to `<Server port="18005" address="127.11.60.1" shutdown="SHUTDOWN">`.

 Ensure that in all the examples in this chapter, you replace the supplied IP address of 127.11.60.1 with the correct address for your gear.

Now, you need to make some changes to the following lines of code:

```
<Connector port="8080" protocol="HTTP/1.1"
   connectionTimeout="20000"
   redirectPort="8443" />
```

Change the preceding lines of code to the following lines of code:

```
<Connector port="8080" protocol="HTTP/1.1"
   connectionTimeout="20000"
   address="127.11.60.1"
   redirectPort="8443" />
```

We then need to change the ports and address for AJP from `<Connector port="18009" protocol="AJP/1.3" redirectPort="8443" />` to `<Connector port="18009" protocol="AJP/1.3" address="127.11.60.1" redirectPort="8443" />`.

We also need to change the hostname section to include the address of our gear:

```
<Host name="localhost"  appBase="webapps"
   unpackWARs="true" autoDeploy="true">
```

Using the Do-It-Yourself Cartridge

Change the preceding lines of code to the following lines of code:

```
<Host name="tomcat8-packt.rhcloud.com"  appBase="webapps"
  unpackWARs="true" autoDeploy="true">
```

Ensure that you provide the correct hostname for your gear and not the one provided.

Once you have made the changes to the configuration file, we can now start the server using the following command:

```
$ $OPENSHIFT_DATA_DIR/apache-tomcat-8.0.8/bin/startup.sh && tail -f $OPENSHIFT_DATA_DIR /apache-tomcat-8.0.8/logs/*
```

The preceding command will start the Tomcat 8 server and then tail the logfiles so that you can view any error messages that might be displayed during startup.

If you made the correct modifications to the `server.xml` configuration file, you should see the following indication in the logs:

```
 27-May-2014 01:34:01.140 INFO [main] org.apache.catalina.startup.Catalina.start Server startup in 5422 ms
```

To verify that the server was started correctly, open your web browser and point to the URL of your application gear. You will be greeted with the following page that lets you know that the server is up and running:

Chapter 13

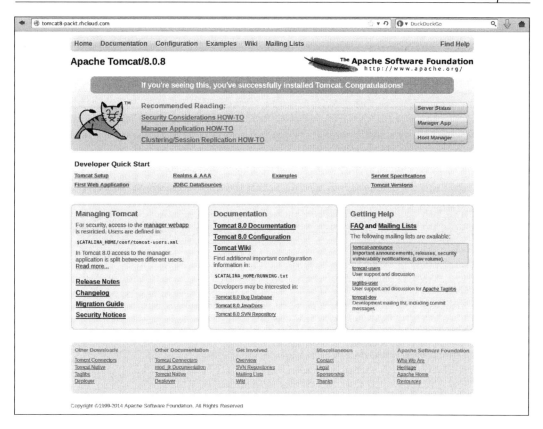

Pretty awesome, huh? We just created a new server using the Tomcat 8 binary distribution and got it up and running on OpenShift Online in a matter of minutes. I decided to use Tomcat for the example in this book because it is one of the most popular servers that people try to get running. With just a few modifications to the configuration, we were able to stand it up and have it start serving requests very quickly.

One last bit of information before we end this chapter. You might have wondered why we changed the port numbers, other than 8080, to something in the 18000 range. This is because OpenShift does not allow the binding of ports below 15000 for custom binaries except for a few exceptions, including 8080.

Summary

In this chapter, we learned how to use the DIY cartridge to create custom servers by utilizing any binary that is executable on the RHEL operating system. We started by creating an application, and then we removed the template Ruby server that ships with the cartridge. After we removed the Ruby server, we downloaded and configured the Tomcat 8 servlet container. Finally, we started the Tomcat 8 server using the `startup.sh` script and verified that it was working by loading the servlet container in our web browser.

Thank you for reading along through all the chapters in this book. Having progressed through the content, you now have the knowledge and skills to be successful with the OpenShift platform. You have learned the essential concepts that will enable you to create and deploy applications to the public cloud while also learning a few tricks that are not commonly known, such as changing the scaling algorithm, that will empower you to take your applications to the next level.

A
The RHC Command-line Reference

This appendix will serve as a reference for all of the available commands that a user can execute by utilizing the RHC command-line tools. I often find that browsing through an appendix such as this often exposes me to commands that I may not have known about just by using a system. Therefore, I decided to include it as part of this book so that you may stumble upon a feature that can save you time in your development efforts.

Top-level commands

The top-level commands are the first items that you would enter in after issuing the RHC command. These commands will allow you to control your OpenShift account as well as perform actions on applications.

Getting started

The commands listed in the following table will allow you to perform tasks such as setting up your account, creating applications, listing your applications, managing cartridges, and managing environment variables for your OpenShift gear:

Top-level commands	Description
`setup`	This will set up your local system in order to connect to the OpenShift servers. This includes creating and uploading an SSH key as well as creating authorization tokens.
`create-app`	This allows you to create an application that will be deployed to the OpenShift service

Top-level commands	Description
`apps`	Running this command will list all of the applications that you currently have deployed.
`cartridges`	This will list all the available cartridges that you can use for applications.
`add-cartridge`	This adds a cartridge to an existing application that you have deployed.
`set-env`	This allows you to create environment variables for a specific application.
`logout`	This will expire any authorization tokens that are active for your current session.

Working with applications

The commands in the following table provide a mechanism for managing applications that are actively deployed on the OpenShift platform:

Commands	Description
`tail`	This command opens up an SSH session and displays all the logfiles of your running application.
`port-forward`	This command forwards ports using SSH so that you can connect to remote services as if they were running locally on your machine.
`threaddump`	This command will allow you to view a thread dump of an application process.
`snapshot`	This command will allow you to create a backup of your application code and database that you can later use if you need to restore.
`git-clone`	This command will clone the remote Git repository to your local machine and create metadata that will allow you to perform context-aware RHC commands.

Management commands

The following table lists all the management commands along with their descriptions:

Command	Description
account	This command allows you to view information about your OpenShift account.
alias	This command allows you to create a custom domain name (vhost) for your application.
app	This command allows you to perform actions related to an application on the platform, such as creating, deleting, and modifying.
authorization	This command allows the management of authorization tokens for your account.
cartridge	This command allows you to manage cartridges that have been added to your application including the ability to stop, start, and delete add-on cartridges.
deployment	This command allows you to manage deployments for an application. This is typically used to roll back from the current deployment to a previous one.
domain	This command allows the management of domains for your OpenShift account including the ability to create new ones and delete the existing ones.
env	This command allows you to manage and view environment variables that have been set for your application.
member	This command allows you to manage membership items for a specific domain. This is commonly used in team environments where more than one developer needs access to deploy the application code.
scp	This command allows you to securely copy a file from your local machine to your remote OpenShift gear.
server	This command displays information about the remote OpenShift service, including any maintenance information.
ssh	This is a convenience command that will allow you to SSH to your remote OpenShift gear.
ssh-key	This command allows you to manage SSH keys that have been added to your account. This includes the ability to create new ones and delete old ones.
team	This command allows you manage teams that are associated with your account including the ability to create new ones and delete the existing teams.

B
Getting Involved with the Open Source Project

The open source project behind OpenShift, named OpenShift Origin, is a thriving and vibrant community that is ready and willing to accept contributions from new members. You might be wondering how you can get involved with the project. Good news; there are several ways to get involved even if you don't want to contribute at the source code level.

Now that you have decided that you want to contribute to the growing OpenShift Origin community, let's go over a few basics that will help get you started. The first thing you will want to look at is the official project website, which is located at `http://openshift.github.io`.

At this location, you can learn more about the project, and I suggest that you start by deploying your own OpenShift Origin environment in order to get familiar with the project. What does this mean? All of the examples that we have used in this book have been running on the publicly hosted version of OpenShift that is provided and managed by Red Hat. The great thing about open source software is that you are free to download the source code and compile it in order to run a PaaS that behaves almost identical to the publicly hosted OpenShift Online. Granted, one of the major benefits of PaaS, such as OpenShift Online, is that as a developer, you no longer have to worry about the system administration aspects of running and managing servers. However, if this is something you are interested in, you are welcome and encouraged to download and install your own version of OpenShift Origin. If you don't want to go through the hassle of installing and configuring the Origin code, the project provides prebuilt virtual machines that you can download and run and that should work out of the box. If you do decide that you want to install your own version instead of using a prebuilt virtual machine, a great tool to get started with is called *oo-install*. The information for this installation program can be found on `http:/install.openshift.com`.

Contributing to the project

First of all, why would you want to contribute to an open source project? There are many reasons why you would want to work on a FOSS project even though you will most likely not see any monetary reward for your efforts. Contributing to a project that you like to use can be a rewarding experience as it helps you become a more efficient and successful professional as well as gives you the benefit of helping other people out. On top of this, you also get to shape the future of the project and take part in developing a platform that is quickly becoming the next evolution of software development. This is also a very interesting and exciting experience in that you get to work on new technology that you might not get to use during the course of a normal workday. You will meet and collaborate with new people who might just end up being some of the smartest and passionate people that you have ever been able to work alongside. There are countless reasons why you could decide to contribute to a project, but the decision will have to be left to you. If you do decide to dip your toe in the water and contribute to one of the most innovative and game-changing projects that OpenShift Origin is, keep reading.

Let's start simple. The first step to contributing to OpenShift Origin could be to simply download and install the project. Once you have the project up and running, push it to the limits and try to find weird edge cases where the platform doesn't perform as expected. Once you find these cases, start creating bug reports and discussing the issue on the public mailing list. I can almost guarantee that you will be welcomed with open arms and greeted in a friendly manner.

Going just a little bit deeper, you can also start contributing documentation to the project. In my career, I have found that the pace at which open source projects move is mind blowing. Given that there is such a dedicated group of engineers who work on the code because it is a passion for them, the documentation often lags behind by one or many releases. The biggest win for you to gain early on in a community is by providing and helping out with documentation to explain new features to the consumer of the project.

Is documentation not your strong point? Consider creating and maintaining community-based cartridges and QuickStarts in order to allow users to run the latest and greatest version of a runtime or database.

Appendix B

Want to work on the core code base? Knock yourself out! Fork the project on GitHub and begin by fixing some of the bugs that have been logged against the project. Once you have shown that you understand the code base well enough to fix a few bugs, you can then explore adding new features to the project. Keep in mind that it is better to communicate all new features on the public mailing list before the implementation in order to ensure that others agree that the feature is a good idea. I would hate for you to spend hours upon hours coding a new feature only to get your pull request rejected because someone else is already working on it. Communicate early and communicate often!

Last but not least, join the community by signing up for the public mailing list and help users out on the official freenode IRC channel or on the StackOverflow OpenShift forums.

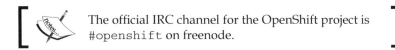

The official IRC channel for the OpenShift project is #openshift on freenode.

I hope this appendix has shown you multiple ways in which you can contribute to the project and has got you thinking that yes, you can provide valuable contributions if you decide to do so. Remember, for all the information you need to get started, simply head to the official project page and read the section on how to contribute. The community doesn't bite; I promise.

Index

Symbols

@ApplicationScoped annotation 104
-c teams command 100
-d $OPENSHIFT_APP_NAME
    command 100
/etc/passwd file
  viewing 58, 59
--file /tmp/mlbparks.json command 101
-h $OPENSHIFT_MONGODB_DB_HOST
    command 101
--jsonArray command 100
-p $OPENSHIFT_MONGODB_DB_
    PASSWORD command 101
--port $OPENSHIFT_MONGODB_DB_
    PORT command 101
--type json command 100
-u $OPENSHIFT_MONGODB_DB_
    USERNAME command 101

A

Abstract Window Toolkit (AWT) 94
access
  adding, SSH keys used 180, 181
account command, management
    commands 273
action hook
  build 230
  creating 231, 232
  deploy 230
  post_deploy 230
  pre_build 230
  system 229-231
  using 231, 232

add-cartridge command, top-level
    commands 272
add-on cartridges
  about 34, 35
  embedding 86, 87
Advanced Packaging Tool (APT) 14
alias command, management
    commands 273
app command
  about 273
  configure 30
  create 30
  delete 30
  deploy 30
  force-stop 30
  reload 30
  restart 30
  show 30
  start 30
  stop 30
  tidy 30
application
  and Secure shell 56-58
  backing up 53
  cartridges, adding 194-196
  cloning, URL adding for 200
  code 44, 45
  code anything area 185
  creating 183-185
  creating, with DIY cartridge 260-262
  custom domain name, adding 197-199
  databases, using with 38
  deleting 32, 90, 201, 202
  developing 42-44
  featured applications area 184

information, displaying 30, 31
instant applications area 184
instant applications, using 187-190
language-specific areas 184
logfiles, creating 51-53
logfiles, viewing 50, 51
managing 193
phpMyAdmin add-on cartridge,
    adding 38-42
restarting 196, 197
restoring 53
single logfile, viewing 53
snapshot, creating 54, 55
snapshot, restoring 55, 56
source code, modifying 191-193
SSL certificate, adding 197-199
starting 49, 50
stopping 49, 50
testing 120
application, creation process
  based on 189
  cartridges 189
  gears 189
  public URL 189
  scaling 189
  source code 189
application management, commands
  git-clone 272
  port-forward 272
  snapshot 272
  tail 272
  threaddump 272
apps command, top-level commands 272
apt command 14
authorization command, management
    commands 273
automatic scaling
  using 243, 244

B

beans.xml file
  creating 105
build
  triggering, manually 161, 162
  troubleshooting 160

C

cartridge command
  about 272, 273
  add 35
  list 35
  reload 35
  remove 35
  scale 35
  show 35
  start 35
  status 35
  stop 35
  storage 35
cartridges
  about 33
  adding 36, 37, 194-196
  add-on cartridges 34, 35
  using 35, 36
  web cartridges 33, 34
cgroup information
  viewing 59, 60
changes, OpenShift application
  deploying 80-85
CI. *See* continuous integration
clean build marker
  using 229
CNAME record
  URL 197
code
  between environments, promoting 176-178
  building, with Jenkins 158-160
  promoting 178, 179
CodeIgniter
  URL 188
command line
  new domain, adding with 166, 167
  scaled application, creating with 244-246
  used, for managing members 170
configuration, Spring application
  adding 131-134
Context Dependency Injection (CDI) 104
continuous integration 147-149
Control Groups (cgroups)
  about 19
  URL 20

create-app command, top-level
  commands 271
cron cartridge
  about 46
  adding 46, 47
  cron job, adding 47

D

database
  MLB stadiums, importing 99-101
  using, with application 38
database access class
  beans.xml file, creating 105
  creating 103, 104
database support, JBoss EAP application
  adding 98
  adding, to Java application 102
debugging
  logfiles, using for 219-222
default web server
  stopping 263, 264
deploy, action hook
  about 230
  creating 232-235
  testing 236-239
deployment command, management
  commands 273
deployment process 148
details, OpenShift application
  viewing 89
development staff 178
dir command 21
DIY cartridge
  about 259
  application, creating with 260-262
domain
  member, deleting from 172
  members, adding 169
  members role, modifying 171
  new domain, adding with
    command line 166, 167
  new domain, adding with
    web console 167-169

domain command, management
  commands 273
domain model
  adding 134
  creating 105, 106
domain name, application
  adding 197-199

E

easy way 121
Eclipse
  downloading 68-71
  installing 68-71
  URL 68
  using, for Java debugging 208-214
enable_jpda marker 226
Enterprise JavaBeans (EJB) 94
env command, management commands 273
environment variables
  about 61, 62
  setting 64-66
  viewing 88, 89

F

findParksWithin() method 136
force_clean_build marker 226

G

getAllParks() method 136
git-clone command, application
  management commands 272
Git
  for OS X installation, URL 13
  for Windows, URL 12
GitHub
  URL 126

H

horizontal scaling 242, 243
hot_deploy marker
  about 225, 226
  using 228

I

IDE
 about 67
 advantages 68
 OpenShift application, integrating with 91
information
 for application, displaying 30, 31
integrated development environments. *See* IDE
IntelliJ
 using, for Java debugging 214-219

J

java7 marker 227
Java API for RESTful Web Services (JAX-RS) API 106
Java application
 database support, adding 102
Java debugging
 Eclipse, using for 208-214
 IntelliJ, using for 214-219
Java EE
 history 93
Java Platform Debugger Architecture (JPDA) socket 226
JBoss
 URL 72
JBoss Enterprise Application Platform (JBoss EAP application)
 about 93
 creating 96, 97
 database support, adding 98
 database support, adding to Java application 102
 MLB stadiums, importing into database 99-101
JBoss Tools
 URL 73
Jenkins
 build, manually triggering 161, 162
 build, troubleshooting 160
 code, building with 158-160

Jenkins server
 embedding, into existing application 152-154
 status, verifying 151, 152
 support, adding for 149, 150
Jenkins web console
 using 154-157
JPDA
 URL 209

L

Leaflet
 used, for creating map 112-116
Linux
 RHC command-line tools, installing 14
load-balancer information
 setting 255
Logentries 220, 223
logfiles, application
 creating 51-53
 single logfile, viewing 53
 using, for debugging 219-222
 viewing 50, 51, 60, 85, 86
logout command, top-level commands 272
ls command 21

M

management commands
 account 273
 alias 273
 app 273
 authorization 273
 cartridge 273
 deployment 273
 domain 273
 env 273
 member 273
 scp 273
 server 273
 ssh 273
 ssh-key 273
 team 273
manual scaling 249-251

map
  automatic updation 120
  creating, Leaflet used 112-116
  creating, OpenStreetMap used 112-116
  deployment, verifying 117, 118
  response, verifying 117, 118
  stadiums, adding 119, 120

marker
  clean build marker, using 229
  creating 227
  enable_jpda marker 226
  force_clean_build marker 226
  hot_deploy marker 225, 226
  hot_deploy marker, using 228
  java7 227
  JBoss specific 226, 227
  skip_maven_build marker 226
  system 225
  using 227

member command, management commands 273

members
  adding, to domain 169
  deleting 176
  deleting, from domain 172
  domain role, modifying 171
  managing, command line used 170
  managing, web console used 172-175
  role, modifying 176

Microsoft Windows
  RHC command-line tools, installing 10, 11

MLB stadiums, JBoss EAP application
  importing, into database 99-101

MongoDB
  connecting to 205-208
  URL 98

MongoDB NoSQL database, Spring application
  adding 128-130

mongoimport command 100

multiple domains
  setting up 166

N

Nintendo Entertainment System (NES) 33

O

oo-install
  URL 275

OpenShift application
  add-on cartridges, embedding 86, 87
  changes, deploying 80-85
  creating 77-80
  deleting 90
  details, viewing 89
  environment variables, viewing 88, 89
  existing OpenShift application, importing 74-77
  integrating, with other IDEs 91
  logfiles, viewing 85, 86
  managing 79, 80
  open source project 275
  Tomcat gear, creating 127, 128
  URL 183, 275

OpenShift Online application
  about 7
  account, creating 7-9, 19
  configuring 20
  creating 16, 18
  gear placement 19
  Git repository, cloning 20
  source code, adding 21-23
  URL 8
  web console, using 23-28

OpenShift Online platform
  cartridges 33

OpenShift Partner page
  URL 223

OpenShift plugin
  downloading 72, 73
  installing 72, 73

open source project
  about 275
  contributing to 276, 277

OpenStreetMap
  used, for creating map 112-116

OS X
  RHC command-line tools, installing 13

P

phpMyAdmin add-on cartridge
  adding 38-42
Pivotal 124
Plain Old Java Object (POJO) 94
Platform as a Service (PaaS) 241
port-forward command, application
      management commands 272
port forwarding
  using 203, 204
post_deploy, action hook 230
pre_build, action hook 230
production staff 178

Q

QA staff 178

R

Red Hat Cloud command-line tools
  about 9
  configuring 15, 16
  installing, for Linux 14
  installing, for Microsoft Windows 10-12
  installing, for OS X 13
Red Hat Enterprise Linux (RHEL)
    system 259
REST endpoint, Spring application
  adding 136
REST services
  creating 106-110
  REST web services, verifying 110, 111
  stadiums, getting from 119
REST web services
  verifying 110
RHC command, action arguments
  about 29, 30, 271
  app 36
  create 36
  lampstack 36
  php-5.4 36
  rhc 36
Ruby language runtime
  installing 10
  URL 10

S

sample application 95, 96
scaled application
  creating, with command line 244-246
  creating, with web console 246-249
scaling
  algorithm, customizing 256, 257
  automatic scaling 243, 244
  horizontal 242, 243
  limits, setting 252-254
  manually 249-251
  matters 241, 242
  scaled application, creating with
      command line 244-246
  scaled application, creating with
      web console 246-249
  vertical 242, 243
scp command, management commands 273
Secure shell
  and application 56-58
Security Enhanced Linux (SELinux)
  about 19
  URL 20
server command, management
    commands 273
set-env command, top-level commands 272
setup command, top-level commands 271
skip_maven_build marker 226
snapshot
  creating 54, 55
  restoring 55, 56
snapshot command, application
      management commands 272
source code
  adding, to OpenShift Online
      application 21, 23
  modifying 191-193
Spring application
  configuration, adding 131-134
  creating 125, 126
  deploying 137, 138
  domain model, adding 134
  easy way 126, 127
  MongoDB NoSQL database,
      adding 128-130
  REST endpoint, adding 136

Spring support, adding 130, 131
Tomcat gear, creating on
    OpenShift 127, 128
Spring Framework
  about 123-125
  core modules 125
  URL 125
  versions 124
ssh command, management commands 273
**ssh-key command, management
    commands** 273
SSH keys
  used, for adding access 180, 181
SSL certificate, application
  adding 197-199
stadiums
  adding, to map 119, 120
  getting, from REST services 119
Standard Widget Toolkit 94
support, continuous integration
  adding, for Jenkins server 149, 150

T

**tail command, application management
    commands** 272
**team command, management
    commands** 273
**threaddump command, application
    management commands** 272
timeout parameter
  setting 60
Tomcat 8 server
  creating 265-269
Tomcat gear, Spring application
  creating, on OpenShift 127, 128
top-level commands
  about 271
  add-cartridge 272
  applications, working with 272
  apps 272
  cartridges 272
  create-app 271
  logout 272
  management commands 273
  set-env 272
  setup 271

U

UMongo
  URL 206
URL, application
  creating, for application cloning 200
user interface
  creating 111
  map, automatic updation 120
  map creating, Leaflet used 112-116
  map creating, OpenStreetMap
      used 112-116
  map deployment, verifying 117
  map response, verifying 117, 118
  stadiums, adding to map 119, 120
  stadiums, getting from REST services 119

V

vertical scaling 242, 243

W

web cartridges 33, 34
web console
  about 183
  new domain, adding with 167-169
  scaled application, creating with 246-249
  used, for managing members 172-175
  using 23-28
web frontend
  adding 138-142
web UI 143, 144

Thank you for buying
Learning OpenShift

About Packt Publishing

Packt, pronounced 'packed', published its first book "*Mastering phpMyAdmin for Effective MySQL Management*" in April 2004 and subsequently continued to specialize in publishing highly focused books on specific technologies and solutions.

Our books and publications share the experiences of your fellow IT professionals in adapting and customizing today's systems, applications, and frameworks. Our solution based books give you the knowledge and power to customize the software and technologies you're using to get the job done. Packt books are more specific and less general than the IT books you have seen in the past. Our unique business model allows us to bring you more focused information, giving you more of what you need to know, and less of what you don't.

Packt is a modern, yet unique publishing company, which focuses on producing quality, cutting-edge books for communities of developers, administrators, and newbies alike. For more information, please visit our website: www.packtpub.com.

About Packt Open Source

In 2010, Packt launched two new brands, Packt Open Source and Packt Enterprise, in order to continue its focus on specialization. This book is part of the Packt Open Source brand, home to books published on software built around Open Source licenses, and offering information to anybody from advanced developers to budding web designers. The Open Source brand also runs Packt's Open Source Royalty Scheme, by which Packt gives a royalty to each Open Source project about whose software a book is sold.

Writing for Packt

We welcome all inquiries from people who are interested in authoring. Book proposals should be sent to author@packtpub.com. If your book idea is still at an early stage and you would like to discuss it first before writing a formal book proposal, contact us; one of our commissioning editors will get in touch with you.

We're not just looking for published authors; if you have strong technical skills but no writing experience, our experienced editors can help you develop a writing career, or simply get some additional reward for your expertise.

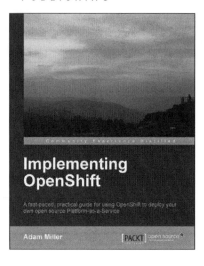

Implementing OpenShift

ISBN: 978-1-78216-472-2   Paperback: 116 pages

A fast-paced, practical guide for using OpenShift to deploy your own open source Platform-as-a-Service

1. Discover what the cloud is, tear through the marketing jargon, and go right to the tech.
2. Understand what makes an open source Platform-as-a-Service work by learning the OpenShift architecture.
3. Deploy your own OpenShift Platform-as-a-Service cloud using DevOps orchestration and configuration management.

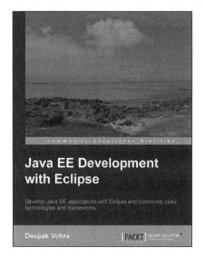

Java EE Development with Eclipse

ISBN: 978-1-78216-096-0   Paperback: 426 pages

Develop Java EE applications with Eclipse and commonly used technologies and frameworks

1. Each chapter includes an end-to-end sample application.
2. Develop applications with some of the commonly used technologies using the project facets in Eclipse 3.7.
3. Clear explanations enriched with the necessary screenshots.

Please check www.PacktPub.com for information on our titles

Java EE 7 First Look

ISBN: 978-1-84969-923-5　　　　Paperback: 188 pages

Discover the new features of Java EE 7 and learn to put them together to build a large-scale application

1. Explore changes brought in by the Java EE 7 platform.

2. Master the new specifications that have been added in Java EE to develop applications without any hassle.

3. A quick guide on the new features introduced in Java EE 7.

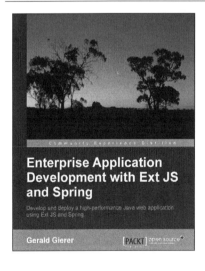

Enterprise Application Development with Ext JS and Spring

ISBN: 978-1-78328-545-7　　　　Paperback: 446 pages

Develop and deploy a high-performance Java web application using Ext JS and Spring

1. Embark on the exciting journey through the entire enterprise web application development life cycle.

2. Leverage key Spring Framework concepts to deliver comprehensive and concise Java code.

3. Build a real-world Ext JS web application that interacts with dynamic database driven data.

Please check **www.PacktPub.com** for information on our titles

Printed in Great Britain
by Amazon